HIPPOCREN

FARSI-ENGLISH
ENGLISH-FARSI
(PERSIAN)

HIPPOCRENE CONCISE
DICTIONARIES

HIPPOCRENE CONCISE DICTIONARY

FARSI-ENGLISH
ENGLISH-FARSI
(PERSIAN)

A. M. Miandji

WITHDRAWN

HIPPOCRENE BOOKS, INC.
New York

For information, address:
HIPPOCRENE BOOKS, INC.
171 Madison Avenue
New York, NY 10016
www.hippocrenebooks.com

Library of Congress Cataloging-in-Publication Data

Miandji, Anooshirvan M. (Anooshirvan Mohammadzadeh) 1971-
    Farsi-English/English-Farsi (Persian) / A. M. Miandji.
        p.   cm. -- (Hippocrene concise dictionary)
    ISBN-10: 0-7818-0860-X
    ISBN-13: 978-0-7818-0860-6
        1. Persian language--Dictionaries--English. 2. English
language--Dictionaries--Persian. I. Title. II. Series.

    PK6379.M53 2003
    491'.55321--dc21

                                                        2002191333

Printed in the United States of America.

Contents

Acknowledgments

I wish to express my deep gratitude to my parents, Pari and Ibrahim, as well as my brother Daryush and my sister Parvaneh, whom I love very much. Editors Caroline Gates and Anne Kemper indicated the changes they wanted to see in the book, made many suggestions as to the general treatment, and read the final text. Thanks to Prof. Dr. B. Azabdaftari, who both motivated me in my first work and advised me from his rich experience; Dr. Naser Azarpuya and Taghi Gheisari, for their comments and help on my first work; and my dear friend Saeed Naserolfoghara, for his valuable aid in providing references. I'm also indebted to Alireza Muhammadi and Hamid Ardam, who always help me kindly. Thanks to typists Kevser and Hikmet Karatosun for their patient and hard work. I'm most grateful to all those who have helped me in this work: Prof. Dr. M. F. Sahin, Prof. Dr. Okan Atay, Dr. Pinar Bulut, Dr. Erden Banoglu, Jemal Akkaya, Oguz Ertug, and Mojtaba Farokhnezhad. I also would like to recognize Prof. Dr. Ningur Noyanalpan and Hasan Petekkaya for their encouragement.

Also, I would like to express my thanks to Dr. Ziya Selcuk for his help, understanding, and encouragement.

In particular, I should like to take this opportunity to thank Hippocrene Books for patiently managing the technical procedures and supporting all stages of the work.

Anooshirvan Mohammadzadeh Miandji
September 2003, Ankara

Introduction

Iran is a multilingual and culturally diverse society, and the majority of the population is extremely young. Nearly one-half of the people speak Farsi, and another one-fourth speak some other Indo-European language or dialect.

Farsi is a Persian language and a member of the Iranian branch of the Indo-Iranian language family; it is the official language of Iran. It is most closely related to Persian, former language of the region of Fars (Persia) in southwestern Iran. Modern Persian is thus called Farsi by native speakers.

Farsi is written with the Farsi alphabet from right to left, in the opposite direction from English. This dictionary is in two parts: English-Farsi and Farsi-English. The English-Farsi part includes the English word, its English pronunciation, its part of speech, and its equivalent in Farsi with pronunciation as well. In the Farsi-English part of the book, the Farsi entries are introduced on the right side. These strictly follow the order of the Farsi alphabet. Each entry includes its pronunciation and its equivalent in English with pronunciation.

The text has been specially formatted in order to make the layout more practical and the entries clearer and easier to read. The pronunciation guide should ensure that the reader encounters no problem in using the book.

Remember, when English-speakers understand the language and people of Iran, it can only lead to better interactions and to a brighter future for all.

Key to the English Pronunciation

a	as	*a*	in	h<u>a</u>t
â	as	*u*	in	c<u>u</u>p
e	as	*e*	in	p<u>e</u>n
o	as	*o*	in	h<u>o</u>me
u	as	*u*	in	p<u>u</u>t
oo	as	*oo*	in	t<u>oo</u>
ao	as	*ow*	in	n<u>ow</u>
I	as	*i*	in	s<u>i</u>t
ii	as	*ee*	in	s<u>ee</u>
ch	as	*ch*	in	<u>ch</u>in
th	as	*th*	in	<u>th</u>an
sh	as	*sh*	in	<u>sh</u>e
zh	as	*s*	in	mea<u>s</u>ure
kh	as	*ch*	in	lo<u>ch</u>
b	as	*b*	in	<u>b</u>ook
d	as	*d*	in	<u>d</u>o
f	as	*f*	in	<u>f</u>at
g	as	*g*	in	<u>g</u>o
h	as	*h*	in	<u>h</u>and
j	as	*j*	in	<u>j</u>oke
k	as	*c*	in	<u>c</u>at
l	as	*l*	in	<u>l</u>eg
m	as	*m*	in	<u>m</u>e
n	as	*n*	in	<u>n</u>o
p	as	*p*	in	<u>p</u>en
r	as	*r*	in	<u>r</u>ed
s	as	*s*	in	<u>s</u>o
t	as	*t*	in	<u>t</u>en
v	as	*v*	in	<u>v</u>oice
w	as	*w*	in	<u>w</u>et
y	as	*y*	in	<u>y</u>es
z	as	*z*	in	<u>z</u>oo

Key to the Farsi alphabet, names and pronunciation

آ	/alef/	as	a	in	b<u>a</u>r
ا	/alef/	as	a	in	b<u>a</u>r
ب	/be/	as	b	in	<u>b</u>ook
پ	/pe/	as	p	in	<u>p</u>en
ت	/te/	as	t	in	<u>t</u>en
ث	/se/	as	s	in	<u>s</u>o
ج	/je/	as	j	in	<u>j</u>oke
چ	/che/	as	ch	in	<u>ch</u>in
ح	/he/	as	h	in	<u>h</u>and
خ	/khe/	as	kh	in	lo<u>ch</u>
د	/dâl/	as	d	in	<u>d</u>o
ذ	/zâl/	as	z	in	<u>z</u>oo
ر	/re/	as	r	in	<u>r</u>ed
ز	/ze/	as	z	in	<u>z</u>oo
ژ	/zhe/	as	s	in	mea<u>s</u>ure
س	/sin/	as	s	in	<u>s</u>o
ش	/shin/	as	sh	in	<u>sh</u>e
ص	/sâd/	as	s	in	<u>s</u>o
ض	/zâd/	as	z	in	<u>z</u>oo
ط	/tâ/	as	t	in	<u>t</u>en
ظ	/zâ/	as	z	in	<u>z</u>oo

ع /ayin/ is pronounced in the same way as the glottal stop but more strongly. Generally the glottal stop is represented in transliteration by an apostrophe ('). In modern spoken Farsi, however, there is a tendency to pronounce it like an vowel, so that it is pronounced like some vowels depending on position.

غ /ghain/ This letter has a harsh guttural sound and is pronounced *q* but voiced.

ف ف /fâ/ as *f* in *f*at

ق /ghâf/ This letter is pronounced as غ

ك /kâf/ as *c* in *c*at

گ /gâf/ This letter is pronounced as hard *g* in *g*o

ل	/lâm/	as	*l*	in	*l*eg
م	/mim/	as	*m*	in	*m*e
ن	/nun/	as	*n*	in	*n*o

و /vâv/ This letter is pronounced as *oo* in t*oo* and as *v* in *v*oice

ه /he/ This letter is pronounced as *h* in *h*and and as *i* in s*i*t

ى /yâ/ is pronounced as *y* in *y*es, *ee* in s*ee*, and as ع in some positions.

Abbreviations

adj	adjective
adv	adverb
conj	conjunction
indef	indefinite
intj	interjection
n	noun
prep	preposition
pron	pronoun
vi	intransitive verb
vt	transitive verb

FARSI-ENGLISH

DICTIONARY

آب / âb / **water** / woter /
آب (میوه) / âb (e mive) / **juice** / joos /
آب شیرین / âbe shirin / **freshwater** / freshwoter /
آب کردن / âb kardan / **melt** / melt /
آب وهوا / âbohavâ / **climate** / klâymit /
ابتکار / ebtekâr / **initiative** / inishiyetiv /
ابتلاء / ebtelâ / **infection** / infekshen /
آبتنی کردن / âbtani kardan / **bathe** / beydh /
آبجو / âbjo / **beer** / biyer /
آبدار / âbdâr / **juicy** / joosii /
ابدیت / abadiyat / **eternity** / iternitii /
ابدی / abadi / **perpetual** / perpechuwâl /
ابر / abr / **cloud** / klaod /
ابراز / ebrâz / **manifestation** / manifesteyshen /
آبراه / âbrâh / **canal** / kanal /
ابرو / abru / **eyebrow** / âybrov /
ابریشم / abrisham / **silk** / silk /
ابری / abri / **cloudy** / klaodii /
ابزار / abzâr / **tackle** / takel /

ابزار / abzâr / **tool** / tool /

آبستن / âbestan / **pregnant** / pregnent /

آبگوشت / âbgusht / **broth** / bros /

آبنبات / âbnabât / **candy** / kandii /

آبی / âbi / **aquatic** / ekwatik /

آبی / âbi / **blue** / bloo /

آپارتمان / âpârtemân / **apartment** / epârtment /

اپرا / operâ / **opera** / âperâ /

اتاق / otâgh / **room** / room /

اتاق انتظار / otaghe entezâr / **waiting room** / weyting-rum /

اتاق خواب / otag hekhâb / **bedroom** / bedrum /

اتحاد / ettehâd / **solidarity** / sâlidaritii /

اتحاد / ettehad / **union** / yooniyen /

اتحاد اروپا / ettehâde urupâ / **European Union** / yuropien yooniyen /

اتحادیه / ettehâdeyeh / **confederacy** / kânfederasii /

آتش / âtash / **bonfire** / bânfâyer /

آتش / âtash / **fire** / fâyer /

اتصال / ettesâl / **junction** / jânkshen /

اتفاق / ettefâgh / **coincidence** / koinsidens /

اتفاق افتادن / ettefâgh oftâdan / **happen** / hapen /

اتفاق افتادن / ettefagh oftâdan / **occur** / âker /

/ kazhuwâl / **casual** / ettefâghi / اتفاقی

/ weyst / **waste** / etlâf / اتلاف

/ atem / **atom** / atom / اتم

/ chârj / **charge** / ettehâm / اتهام

/ hich-hâyking / **hitchhiking** / otostâp / اتواستاپ

/ hâyway / **highway** / otobân / اتوبان

/ bâs / **bus** / otobus / اتوبوس

/ kâr / **car** / otomobil / اتومبیل

/ afemeyshn / **affirmation** / esbât / اثبات

/ lfekt / **effect** / asar / اثر

/ impres / **impress** / asar gozâshtan / اثرگذاشتن

/ rent / **rent** / ejâre / اجاره

/ permishen / **permission** / ejâze / اجازه

/ to elao / **to allow** / ejâzedâden / اجازه دادن

/ to let / **to let** / ejâze dâdan / اجازه دادن

/ to permit / **to permit** / ejâze dâdan / اجازه دادن

/ kuker / **cooker** / ojâgh / اجاق

/ stov / **stove** / ojâgh / اجاق

/ kâmpâlseri / **compulsory** / ejbâri / اجباری

/ kâmyooniti / **community** / ejtemââ / اجتماع

/ soshâl / **social** / ejtemâii / اجتماعی

/ forfâdherz / **forefathers** / ajdâd / اجداد

/ brik / **brick** / âjor / آجر

5

اجرا / ejrâ / **performance** / performens /

اجرا کردن / ejrâ kardan / **to execute** / to eksikyoot /

اجرایی / ejrâyi / **executive** / igzekyutiv /

احاطه کردن / ehâte kardan / **surround** / sâraond /

احترام / ehterâm / **respect** / rispekt /

احترام کردن / ehterâm kardan / **venerate** / venereyt /

احتمالاً / ehtemâlan / **probably** / prâbebli /

احتمالی / ehtemâli / **probable** / prâbebl /

احساس / ehsâs / **sensation** / senseyshen /

احساساتی / ehsâsâti / **demonstrative** / dimânstrativ /

احساساتی / ehsâsâti / **passionate** / pashenit /

احضار کردن / ehzâr kardan / **recall** / rikol /

احمق / ahmagh / **idiot** / idiyet /

احمق / ahmagh / **silly** / sili /

احمقانه / ahmaghâne / **idiotic** / idiyâtik /

اختراع / ekhterâ / **invention** / invenshen /

اختراع کردن / ekhterââ kardan / **invent** / invent /

اختلاف / ekhtelâf / **disagreement** / disagriiment /

اختیار / ekhtiyâr / **adoption** / edâpshn /

اختیار / ekhtyâr / **option** / âpshn /

آخر / âkhar / **last** / last /

اخراج / ekhrâj / **sack** / sak /

آخرین / âkharin / **latest** / leytist /

اخطار / ekhtâr / **warning** / worning /

اخلاق / akhlâgh / **conduct** / kândâkt /

اخلاقى / akhlâghi / **ethical** / eticl /

اخلاقى / akhlâghi / **moral** / morâl /

اخیر / akhir / **recent** / riisent /

اخیراً / akhiran / **lately** / leytli /

اخیراً / akhiran / **recently** / riisently /

اداره / edâre / **administration** / edministreshen /

اداره کردن / edâre kardan / **to administer** / to edminister /

اداره کردن / edâre kardan / **to manage** / to manij /

ادارى / edâri / **administrative** / edministreytiv /

ادامه / edâme / **last** / last /

ادامه دادن / edâme dâdan / **to continue** / to kântinyoo /

ادعا / eddeââ / **claim** / kleym /

ادعا / eddeâ / **pretension** / pritenshes /

آدم / âdam / **human** / heuman /

آدم دزدیدن / âdam dozdidan / **kidnap** / kidnap /

آدم احمق / âdame ahmagh / **fool** / fool /

آدم بدبین / âdame badbin / **pessimist** / pesimist /

آدم برفى / âdam barfi / **snowman** / snoman /

آدم جاه طلب / âdame jâhtalab / **go-getter** / go-geter /

آدم خبیث / âdame khabis / **devil** / devil /

آدم شوخ طبع / âdame shukhtab / **humorist** / hyoomerist /

آدم نا‌موفق / âdame nâmovaffagh / **failure** / feyliyer /

آدمخوار / âdamkhâr / **cannibal** / kanibâl /

اذیت / aziyat / **harm** / hârm /

ارائه کردن / erâee kardan / **to present** / to prizent /

اراده / erâde / **will** / will /

آراستگی / ârâstegi / **elegance** / eligans /

آراسته / ârâste / **elegant** / eligent /

آرام / ârâm / **calm** / kâm /

آرام / ârâm / **mild** / mâyld /

آرایش / ârâyesh / **decorate** / dekereyt /

ارتباط / ertebât / **communication** / kâmyoonikeyshen /

ارتباط / ertebât / **connection** / kânekshen /

ارتباط داشتن / ertebât dâshtan / **connect** / kânekt /

ارتش / artesh / **army** / ârmi /

ارتفاع / ertefâ / **height** / hâyt /

اردك / ordak / **duck** / dâk /

اردو / ordu / **camp** / kamp /

ارزان / arzân / **cheap** / chiip /

ارزش / arzesh / **value** / valyoo /

ارزش / arzesh / **worth** / werth /

ارزش داشتن / arzesh dâshtan / **to merit** / to merit /

ارزشمند / arzeshmand / **priceless** / prâyslis /

ارزنده / arzande / **valuable** / valyu-ebel /

8

آرزو / ârezu / **desire** / dizâyer /

آرزو کردن / ârezu kardan / **wish** / wish /

ارزیابی کردن / arzyâbi kardan / **to evaluate** / to ivalyuweyt /

ارضا کردن / erzâ kardan / **to satisfy** / to satisfây /

ارغوانی / arghavâni / **purple** / perpel /

آرنج / âranj / **elbow** / elbo /

آره / âre / **yeah** / ye /

آرواره / ârvâre / **jaw** / jâv /

اروپا / urupâ / **Europe** / yurop /

اروپایی / urupâyi / **European** / yuropiyen /

از / az / **from** / frâm /

از / az / **of** / âv /

از / az / **than** / than /

از سر گرفتن / az sargereftan / **to resume** / to rizyoom /

از نظر فنی / aznazare fanni / **technologically** / teknolâjikli /

از نفس افتاده / az nafas oftade / **breathless** / brethlis /

از نو ساختن / az no sâkhtan / **to rebuild** / to riibild /

از هم پاشیده / az ham pâshide / **broken** / broken /

از هنگامی که / az hengâmi ke / **since** / sins /

آزاد / âzâd / **free** / frii /

آزاد / âzâd / **loose** / loos /

آزاد کردن / âzâd kardan / **emancipate** / imânsipeyt /

آزادی / âzâdi / **freedom** / friidum /

آزادی / âzâdi / **liberty** / liberti /

آزارنده / âzârande / **offensive** / âfensive /

ازدست دادن / azdast dâdan / **miss** / mis /

ازدواج / ezdevâj / **marriage** / marij /

ازدواج کردن / ezdevâch kardan / **marry** / mari /

آزردن / âzordan / **annoy** / enoi /

ازعقب / azaghab / **behind** / bihâynd /

آزمایش / âzmâyesh / **experiment** / iksperiment /

آزمایش کردن / âzemâyesh kardan / **to experiment** /
to iksperiment /

آزمایشی / âzemâyeshi / **experimental** / iksperimentâl /

ازمدافتاده / azmodoftâde / **old-fashioned** / oldfashend /

آزمون / âzmun / **test** / test /

آزمون کوتاه / âzmune kutâh / **quiz** / kwiz /

آژیر / âzhir / **alarm** / elâm /

اساس / asâs / **basis** / beysis /

اساس قرار دادن / asâsgharâr dadan / **base** / beys /

اساسی / asâsi / **basic** / beysik /

اساسی / asâsi / **fundamental** / fândementl /

آسان / âsân / **easy** / iizi /

آسانسور / âsânsor / **elevator** / eliveyter /

10

آسایش / comfort / kâmfort /

اسب / horse / hors /

اسب آبی / hippopotamus / hipopâtemes /

اسباب / appliance / epplayens /

اسباب بازی / toy / asbâbbâzi /

آسپرین / aspirin / asprin /

است / is / iz /

استثنا / exception / iksepshen /

استثنایی / extraordinary / ikstrordineri /

استخدام / employment / imployment /

استخدام کردن / to employ / estekhdâm kardan /
to imploy /

استخدام کردن / to engage / estekhtam kardan / to ingeyj /

استخر / pool / pool /

استخر / swimming pool / swiming pool /

استخوان / bone / bon /

استراحت / rest / rest /

استرالیا / Australia / âstreyliyâ /

استرالیایی / Australian / âstreyliyen /

استعداد / aptitude / aptitud /

استعداد / facility / fasiliti /

استعداد / talent / talent /

استعفا / resignation / rizigneyshen /

استعفا کردن / esteefâ kardan / **to resign** / to rizâyn /

استعماری / esteemâri / **colonial** / koloniyâl /

استفاده / estefade / **use** / yoos /

استقلال / esteghlâl / **independence** / indipendens /

استوار / ostovâr / **stable** / steybel /

استوانه ای / ostovâneii / **cylindrical** / silindrikâl /

استودیو / estodiyo / **studio** / stoodiyo /

إستیك / esteyk / **steak** / steyk /

آستین / âstin / **sleeve** / sliiv /

اسطوره / osture / **myth** / mit /

اسفالت / âsfâlt / **asphalt** / asfolt /

اسفنج / esfanj / **sponge** / spânj /

اسکلت / eskelet / **skeleton** / skeliten /

اسکناس / eskenâs / **bill** / bil /

اسکی / eski / **ski** / skii /

اسلام / eslâm / **Islam** / izlâm /

اسلامی / eslâmi / **Islamic** / izlâmik /

اسم / esm / **name** / neym /

اسم / esm / **noun** / nâun /

اسم عبور / esme ubur / **password** / paswed /

آسمان / âsemân / **sky** / skây /

آسه / âse / **axis** / aksis /

آسوده کردن / âsude kardan / **to relieve** / to riliiv /

آسیایی / eyshen / **Asian** / âsiyâyi /

آسیب / injeri / **injury** / âsib /

اسکناس / banknot / **banknote** / eskenâs /

اشاره کردن / poynt / **point** / eshâre kardan /

اشاره کردن به / rifer / **refer** / eshâre kardan be /

آشامیدن / drink / **drink** / âshâmidan /

آشامیدنی / beverij / **beverage** / âshâmidani /

آشپز خانه / kichin / **kitchen** / âshpazi khane /

آشپزی کردن / kuk / **cook** / âshpazi kardan /

آشپزی / kuking / **cooking** / âshpazi /

اشتباه / erer / **error** / eshtebâh /

اشتباه / misteyk / **mistake** / eshtebâh /

اشتباه / râng / **wrong** / eshtebâh /

اشتباه کردن / **to confound** / eshtebâh kardan /
/ to kânfaond

اشتغال / akyupây / **occupy** / eshteghâl /

اشتها / appetayt / **appetite** / eshtehâ /

اشتیاق / inthyooziyazem / **enthusiasm** / eshtiâgh /

اشراف / aristâkrasi / **aristocracy** / ashrâf /

اشراف زاده / aristokrat / **aristocrat** / ashrâf zâde /

اشراف زاده / lord / **Lord** / ashrâfzâde /

اشرافی / nobel / **noble** / ashrafi /

اشرافی / aristokratik / **aristocratic** / ashrâfi /

13

اشعه ایکس / **X-ray** / ashaeye iks / eksrey /

آشفته / **confused** / âshofte / kânfiyoozd /

اشك / **tear** / ashk / tiyer /

آشکار / **apparent** / âshekâr / eparent /

آشکار / **obvious** / âshekâr / âbviyes /

آشکار شدن / **to appear** / âshekâr shodan / to epiyer /

آشنا / **familiar** / âshenâ / familiyâr /

آشکارا / **openly** / âshekârâ / openly /

اصراركردن / **to insist** / esrâr kardan / to insist /

اصطبل / **stable** / establ / steybel /

اصطلاح / **idiom** / estelâh / idiem /

اصلاح / **reform** / eslâh / rifâm /

اصلی / **cardinal** / asli / kârdinâl /

اصیل / **full blooded** / asil / fol beloded /

اضافی / **extra** / ezâfi / ekstrâ /

اضافی / **spare** / ezâfi / sper /

اضطراب / **anxiety** / ezterâb / angzâyeti /

اطاعت کردن / **to obey** / etâat kardan / to obey /

اطلاعات / **information** / ettelâât / informeyshen /

اطمینان دادن / **to reassure** / etminân kardan / to riieshor /

اظهار / **statement** / ezhâr / steytment /

اظهار تعجب / **exclamation** / ezhâre taajjob / ekslmeyshen /

14

اظهار داشتن / ezhâr dâshtan / **to remark** / to rimârk /

اظهار نظر / ezhâr nazar / **remark** / rimârk /

اعتراض / eeterâz / **objection** / âbjekshen /

اعتراض / eeterâz / **protest** / protest /

اعتراض کردن / eeterâz kardan / **to object** / to âbjekt /

اعتصاب / eetesâb / **strike** / strâyk /

اعتقاد / eeteghâd / **belief** / biliif /

اعتقاد / eeteghâd / **faith** / feyth /

اعتماد / eetemâd / **confidence** / kânfidens /

اعتماد کردن / eetemâd kardan / **to trust** / to trâst /

اعتماد کردن / eetemâd kardan / **to confide** / to kânfayd /

اعتنا نکردن / eetenâ nakardan / **to ignore** / to ignor /

اعلام / eelâm / **declaration** / deklereyshen /

اعلام کردن / eelâmkardan / **to announce** / to anaons /

اعلام کردن / eelâm kardan / **to declare** / to dikler /

اعلام کردن / eelâm kardan / **to proclaim** / to prokleym /

اعلان / eelân / **proclamation** / prâklameyshen /

اغلب / aghlab / **often** / âfen /

آفتاب / âftab / **sunshine** / sânshâyn /

آفتابی / âftabi / **sunny** / sâni /

افتادن / oftâdan / **fall** / fol /

افتخار / eftekhâr / **glory** / glori /

افتخار / eftekhâr / **honor** / âner /

15

Farsi-English

افتخار / eftekhâr / **pride** / prâyd /

آفریدن / âfaridan / **create** / kriyeyt /

افریقا / âfrikâ / **Africa** / afrikâ /

افریقایی / âfrighâii / **African** / afriken /

آفرینش / âfarinesh / **creation** / kriyeyshen /

آفریننده / âfarinande / **creator** / kriyeyter /

آفزارمند / afzarmand / **artisan** / ârtizn /

افزایش / afzâyesh / **to increase** / to inkriis /

افزایش / afzâyesh / **rise** / râyz /

افزایش دادن / afzâyesh dâdan / **to increase** / to inkriis /

افسر / afsar / **officer** / âfiser /

افسردگی / afsordegi / **depression** / dipreshen /

افق / ofogh / **horizon** / herâyzn /

آقا / âghâ / **gentleman** / jentelman /

آقا / âghâ / **master** / mâster /

آقا / âghâ / **sir** / ser /

آقای / aghâye / **Mr.** / mister /

اقتدار / eghtedâr / **authority** / othâriti /

اقتصاد / eghtesâd / **economy** / ikânami /

اقتصاددان / eghtesâddân / **economist** / ikânemist /

اقتصادی / eghtesâdi / **economic** / iikânâmik /

اقلیت / aghaliyyat / **minority** / mâynâriti /

اقیانوس / oghyânus / **ocean** / oshen /

اكتبر / October / oktobr / âktober /

اكثريت / majority / aksariyyat / majâriti /

اكسيژن / oxygen / oksizhen / âksijen /

آگهى / advertisement / âgahi / advertâyzment /

اگر / if / agar / if / oldho /

اگرچه / although / agarche / oldho /

آگهى / advertisement / âgahi / advertisment /

آگهى / notice / âgahi / notis /

آگهى دادن / to advertise / âgahi dâdan / to advetâyz /

آگهى دهنده / advertiser / âgahi dahande / advertâyzer /

آلرژى / allergy / âlerzi / alerji /

الفبا / alphabet / alefbâ / alfabet /

الگو / pattern / olgu / patern /

الماس / diamond / almâs / dâyemend /

آلمان / Germany / âlmân / jermani /

آلمانى / German / âlmâni / jemen /

آلودگى / pollution / âludegi / polooshen /

آلوده كردن / to infect / âlude kardan / to infekt /

آلوده كردن / to pollute / âlude kardan / to poloot /

آلوده كننده / polluter / âlude konande / polooter /

آلومينيوم / aluminium / âlominyum / alyuminiem /

الک / sieve / alak / siv /

آلى / organic / âli / organik /

17

اما / ammâ / **but** / bât /

آماتور / âmâtor / **amateur** / amater /

آمادگی / âmâdegi / **preparation** / prepareyshen /

آماده / âmâde / **equipped** / ikwipt /

آماده کردن / âmâde kardan / **to prepare** / to priper /

آمار / âmâr / **statistics** / statistiks /

آمبولانس / âmbulâns / **ambulance** / ambyulens /

امپراتوری / emprâturi / **empire** / empâyr /

امتحان / emtehân / **exam** / igzam /

امتحان / emtehân / **examination** / igzajereyshen /

امتحان کردن / emtehân kardan / **to examine** / to igzamin /

امتیاز / emtiyâz / **advantage** / advântij /

امتیاز / emtiyâz / **privilege** / privilij /

امتیاز / emtiyâz / **score** / skor /

آمدن / âmadan / **come** / kâm /

امروز / emruz / **today** / tudey /

امروزه / emruze / **nowadays** / nao-edeyz /

امریکا / âmerikâ / **America** / emerikâ /

آمریکایی / amrikayi / **Yankee** / yanki /

امریکایی / âmrikâyi / **American** / emeriken /

امشب / emshab / **tonight** / tunâyt /

امضا / emzâ / **signature** / signicher /

امضا / emzâ / **autograph** / otogrâf /

/ pâsibiliti / **possibility** / emkân / امکان

/ ineybel / **enable** / emkân dâdanm be / امکان دادن به

/ âmlit / **omelette** / omlet / املت

/ emonie / **ammonia** / âmonyâk / آمونیاک

/ sikyuriti / **security** / amniyyat / امنیت

/ rootiin / **routine** / emure ruzmerre / امور روزمره

/ ejukeyshen / **education** / âmuzesh / آموزش

/ instrâkshen / **instruction** / âmuzesh / آموزش

/ to ejukeyt / **to educate** / âmuzesh dâdan / آموزش دادن

/ hopful / **hopeful** / omid / امید

/ it / **it** / ân / آن

/ dhat / **that** / ân / آن

/ biyând / **beyond** / ân tarafe / آن طرفِ

/ pâynapel / **pineapple** / ânânâs / آناناس

/ chays / **choice** / entekhâb / انتخاب

/ silekshen / **selection** / entekhâb / انتخاب

/ to chooz / **to choose** / entekhâb kardan / انتخاب کردن

/ to ilekt / **to elect** / entekhab kardan / انتخاب کردن

/ to pik / **to pick** / entekhâb kardan / انتخاب کردن

/ ilekshen / **election** / entekhâbât / انتخابات

/ internet / **internet** / internet / انترنت

/ pâblikeyshen / **publication** / enteshâr / انتشار

/ ekspekteyshen / **expectation** / entezâr / انتظار

انتظار داشتن / entezâr dâshtan / **to expect** / to iksept /

انتقاد / enteghâd / **criticism** / kritisizem /

انتقاد کردن / enteghâd kardan / **criticize** / kritisâyz /

انتقال / enteghâl / **transfer** / transfer /

انتقال دادن / enteghâl dâdan / **to transfer** / to transfer /

انتقام / enteghâm / **revenge** / rivenj /

آنجا / ânjâ / **there** / dher /

انجام / anjâm / **achievement** / echivment /

انجام دادن / anjâm dâdan / **to achieve** / to echiv /

انجام دادن / anjâm dadan / **to perform** / to perform /

انداختن / andâkhtan / **to throw** / to thro /

اندازه / andâze / **dimension** / dimenshn /

اندازه / andâze / **size** / sâyz /

اندازه گرفتن / andâze gereftan / **to measure** / to mezher /

اندازه گیری / andâzegiri / **measurement** / mezherment /

اندام / andâm / **organ** / organ /

انسان / ensân / **human** / hyooman /

انضباط / enzebât / **discipline** / disiplin /

انعام / anââm / **tip** / tip /

انعکاس / eneekâs / **reflection** / riflekshen /

انفجار / enfejâr / **explosion** / iksplozhen /

آنفلوانزا / ânfulânzâ / **flu** / floo /

انگشت / angosht / **finger** / finger /

انگلستان / engelestân / **England** / ingland /

انگور / angur / **grape** / greyp /

انگلیسی / engilisi / **English** / inglish /

آنها / ânhâ / **their** / dher /

آنها / ânhâ / **they** / dhey /

آنها را / ânhârâ / **them** / dhem /

انکار کردن / enkâr kardan / **deny** / dinây /

آهای! / âhây / **hey** / hey /

اهدا / ehdâ / **dedication** / dedikeyshn /

اهدا کردن / ehdâ kardan / **dedicate** / dedikeyt /

آهسته / âheste / **silently** / sâylently /

آهسته / âheste / **slow** / slo /

آهسته / âheste / **slowly** / sloli /

اهل تصوف / ahle tasavvof / **mystic** / mistik /

اهل مریخ / ahle merrikh / **martian** / marshen /

اهمیت / ahammiyyat / **importance** / importens /

اهمیت دادن / ahammiyyet dâdan / **care** / ker /

آهن / âhan / **iron** / âyern /

آهنگ / âhang / **tone** / ton /

آهنگ / âhang / **tune** / tyoon /

آهنگساز / âhangsâz / **composer** / kâmpozer /

او / u / **he** / hii /

او / u / **she** / shii /

او را / u râ / her / **her** /

آواز / âvâz / song / **sâng** /

آواشناسی / âvâshenâsi / phonetics / **fenetiks** /

اوت / out / August / **ogest** /

اوج / oj / climax / **klaymaks** /

اورا / urâ / him / **him** /

آوردن / âvardan / to bring / **to bring** /

آوریل / âvril / April / **eypril** /

اوستا / avestâ / Avesta / **âvestâ** /

اول / avval / beginning / **bigining** /

اولین / avvalin / first / **ferst** /

اونس / ons / ounce / **aons** /

آویختن / âvikhtan / to hang / **to hang** /

آیا / âyâ / whether / **wedher** /

ایالات متحده / ayâlâte motahede / United States / **yoonâytidsteyts** /

ایتالیا / itâliyâ / Italy / **itali** /

ایتالیایی / itâliyâyi / Italian / **italiyen** /

اکیداً / akidan / strictly / **striktli** /

ایدز / eydz / AIDS / **eydz** /

ایران / irân / Iran / **irân** /

ایران / irân / Persia / **Pershâ** /

ایرانی / irâni / Iranian / **ireynien** /

ایرانی / irâni / **Persian** / perzhn /

ایرلند / irland / **Ireland** / âyerland /

ایرلندی / irlandi / **Irish** / âyerish /

ایست / ist / **stop** / stâp /

ایستادن / istâdan / **to stand** / to stand /

ایستگاه اتوبوس / istgâh otobos / **bus stop** / bâsstâp /

ایستگاه / istgâh / **Station** / steyshen /

ایمنی / imeni / **safety** / seyfti /

این / in / **this** / dhis /

اینچ / inch / **inch** / inch /

آینده / âyande / **future** / fyoocher /

ایوان / eyvân / **porch** / porch /

آیینه / âyine / **mirror** / mirer /

با / bâ / **with** / widh /

با احتیاط / bâ ehtiyât / **carefully** / kerfuli /

با اندوه / bâ anduh / **sadly** / sadli /

با بیرحمی / bâ birahmi / **harshly** / hârsli /

با تأنی / bâ taanni / **leisurely** / lezherli /

با تجربه / bâ tajrobe / **experienced** / ikspriyenst /

با خشم / bâ Khashm / **angrily** / angrili /

با دقت / bâ deghghat / **nicely** / nâysli /

با زمانده / bâzmânde / **survivor** / servâyver /

با سردی / bâ sardi / **coldly** / koldli /

با شادمانی / bâ shâdemâni / **joyously** / joyesli /

با ضعف / bâ zaaf / **feebly** / fiibli /

با معنی / bâ maani / **meaningful** / miniingful /

با ملاحظه / bâ molâheze / **thoughtfully** / thotfuli /

با ملایمت / bâ molâyemat / **softly** / sâftli /

با موفقیت / bâ movaffaghiyyat / **successfully** / sâksesfuli /

با هیجان / bâ heyejân / **excitedly** / iksâytdli /

بابا / bâbâ / **daddy** / dadi /

باتری / bâtri / **battery** / bateri /

باجه تلفن / bâjeye telefon / **callbox** / kolbâks /

باجه فروش بليت / bajeye furushe belit / **booking office** /
buking-âfis /

باخبر / bâkhaber / **aware** / ewer /

باخستگی / bâkhastegi / **wearily** / wiyerili /

باد / bâd / **wind** / wind /

بادبان / bâdbân / **sail** / seyl /

بادكنك / badkonak / **balloon** / balloon /

بار / bâr / **baggage** / bagij /

بار / bâr / **load** / lod /

بار / bâr / **pub** / pâb /

باران / bârân / **rain** / reyn /

بارانداز / bâr andâz / **dock** / dâk /

بارانی / bârani / **raincoat** / reynkot /

بارانی / bârani / **rainy** / reyni /

باربر / bârbar / **porter** / porter /

باروت / bârut / **gunpowder** / gânpaoder /

باریك / bârik / **narrow** / naro /

باریک / bârik / **slim** / slim /

باز / bâz / **open** / open /

باز كردن / bâz kardan / **to detach** / to ditach /

بازار / bâzâr / **market** / mârkit /

بازآفرینی / bâzâfarini / **recreation** / riikriyeyshen /

25

بازدید کننده / bâzdid konande / **visitor** / viziter /

بازرگان / bâzargân / **trader** / treyder /

بازرس / bâzras / **inspector** / inspekter /

بازرسی / bâzrasi / **check** / chek /

بازرگان / bâzargân / **businessman** / biznisman /

بازرگانی / bâzargâni / **commercial** / kâmershâl /

بازرگانی / bâzargâni / **commerce** / kâmers /

بازسازی / bâzsâzi / **reconstruction** / riikânstrâkshen /

بازنده / bâzande / **underdog** / ânderdâg /

بازی / bâzi / **game** / geym /

بازی / bâzi / **play** / pley /

بازی کردن / bâzi kardan / **to play** / to pley /

بازیکن / bâzi kon / **player** / pleyer /

باستان شناسی / bâstân shenâni / **archaeology** / akioleji /

باستانی / bâstâni / **ancient** / eynshent /

باشگاه / bâshgâh / **club** / klâb /

باشه / bâshe / **okay** / okey /

باشکوه / bâ shokuh / **splendid** / splendid /

باصرفه / bâsarfe / **economical** / iikânamikal /

باعظمت / bâazamat / **impressive** / impresiv /

باغ / bâgh / **garden** / gârden /

باغ وحش / bâghvahsh / **zoo** / zoo /

باغبان / bâghbân / **gardener** / gârdner /

باغبانى / bâghbâni / **gardening** / gârdning /

باغچه / baghche / **flowerbed** / flaowerbed /

بافت / bâft / **tissue** / tishu /

بافت بردارى / bâft bardâri / **biopsy** / bayopsi /

بافتن / bâftan / **weave** / wiiv /

باقى / bâghi / **remains** / rimeynz /

باكترى / bâkteri / **bacteria** / baktierie /

باكره / bâkere / **virgin** / vejin /

بال / bâl / **whale** / weyl /

بال / bâl / **wing** / wing /

بالا / bâlâ / **above** / ebâv /

بالا / bâlâ / **up** / âp /

بالا رفتن / bâlâ raftan / **ascend** / esend /

بالا رفتن / bâlâ raftan / **ascent** / esent /

بالارفتن / bâlâraftan / **climb** / klâym /

بالارونده / bâlâ ravande / **climber** / klâymer /

بالاى شهر / bâlâye shahr / **uptown** / âptaon /

بالايى / bâlâyi / **upper** / âper /

بالاى / bâlaye / **over** / over /

بالش / bâlesh / **pillow** / pilo /

بالغ / bâlegh / **adolescent** / adelesnt /

باله / bâle / **ballet** / baley /

بالكن / bâlkon / **balcony** / balkoni /

27

بامزه / bâmaze / **humorous** / hyoomeres /

باند / bând / **bandage** / bandij /

باند / bând / **gang** / gang /

بانك / bânk / **bank** / bank /

بانوان / bânovan / **Ladies** / leydiz /

باهم / bâham / **together** / tugedher /

باهوش / bâhush / **clever** / klever /

باهوش / bâhush / **intelligent** / intelijent /

باور کردن / bâvar kardan / **to believe** / to biliiv /

باور نکردنی / bâvar nakardani / **unbelievable** /
ânbiliivebel /

باوفا / bâvafâ / **faithful** / feythful /

باید / bâyad / **must** / mâst /

باید / bâyad / **need** / niid /

باید / bâyad / **ought** / ât /

باید / bâyad / **should** / shud /

ببخشید / bebakhshid / **sorry** / sâri /

ببر / babr / **tiger** / tâyger /

بتون / beton / **concrete** / kânkriit /

بجز / bejoz / **except** / iksept /

بچگی / bachchegi / **childhood** / châyl-hud /

بچه / bachche / **child** / châyld /

بچه / bachche / **kid** / kid /

/ dibeyt / **debate** / bahs / بحث

/ diskâshen / **discussion** / bahs / بحث

/ dispyoot / **dispute** / bahs / بحث

/ to diskâs / **to discuss** / bahs kardan / بحث کردن

/ krâysis / **crisis** / bohrân / بحران

/ kritikâl / **critical** / bohrâni / بحرانی

/ to stiim / **to steam** / bokhâr kardan / بخار کردن

/ forchoon / **fortune** / bakht / بخت

/ ikskyooz / **excuse** / bakhshidan / بخشیدن

/ forgiv / **forgive** / bakhshidan / بخشیدن

/ pardon / **pardon** / bakhshesh / بخشش

/ bad / **bad** / bad / بد

/ iivel / **evil** / bad / بد

/ faol / **foul** / bad / بد

/ nâsti / **nasty** / bad / بد

/ mizrebel / **miserable** / badbakht / بدبخت

/ smeli / **smelly** / badbu / بدبو

/ pesimistik / **pessimistic** / badbinâne / بدبینانه

/ pesimizem / **pessimisim** / bad bini / بدبینی

/ werst / **worst** / badtarin / بدترین

/ badli / **badly** / badjuri / بدجوری

/ ânforchunit / **unfortunate** / badshâns / بدشانس

/ ânlâki / **unlucky** / bad shâns / بدشانس

بدهكار بودن / bedehkâr budan / **to owe** / to o /

بدون / bedune / **without** / widhaot /

بدين ترتيب / bedin tartib / **thus** / dhâs /

بر خورد / bar khord / **clash** / klash /

بر كنار كردن / bar kenâr kardan / **to oust** / to aost /

برابر / barâbar / **equal** / iikwâl /

برابرى / barâbari / **equality** / ikwâliti /

برادر / barâdar / **brother** / brâdher /

براى / barâye / **for** / for /

بريتانيا / beritâniyâ / **Britain** / briten /

بريتانيايى / beritâniyâyi / **British** / british /

برتر / bartar / **superior** / soopiriyer /

برج / borj / **tower** / tao-er /

برخورد / barkhord / **conflict** / kânflikt /

برداشتن / bardâshtan / **to remove** / to rimoov /

بردبارى / bordbâri / **bearing** / bering /

بردگى / bardegi / **servitude** / servityood /

بردگى / bardegi / **slavery** / sleyveri /

بردن / bordan / **win** / win /

برده / barde / **slave** / sleyv /

برزيل / berezil / **Brazil** / brezil /

برزيلى / berezili / **Brazilian** / breziliyen /

بُرس / bores / **brush** / brâsh /

برش / boresh / **slice** / slâys /

برف / barf / **snow** / sno /

برق / bargh / **electricity** / ilektrisiti /

برق / bargh / **lightning** / lâytning /

برق کار / bargh kar / **electrician** / ilektrishen /

برقی / barghi / **electrical** / ilektrikâl /

برقی / barghi / **electric** / ilektric /

برگ / barg / **leaf** / liif /

برگ / barg / **sheet** / shiit /

برگرداندن / bargardândan / **to upset** / to âpset /

برگشت / bargasht / **return** / ritern /

برگشتن / bargashtan / **back** / bak /

برگشتن / bargashtan / **to bounce** / to baons /

برنامه / barnâme / **broadcast** / brodkâst /

برنامه / barnâme / **program** / program /

برنامه / barnâme / **schedule** / skejul /

برنامه ریزی کردن / barnâmerizi kardan / **project** / projekt /

برنج / berenj / **brass** / brâs /

برنج / berenj / **rice** / rays /

برنده / barande / **winner** / winer /

بره / barre / **lamb** / lam /

برونشیت / bronshit / **bronchitis** / brânkâytis /

بریدن / boridan / **cut** / kât /

بزرگ / bozorg / **big** / big /

بزرگ / bozorg / **enormous** / inormes /

بزرگ / bozorg / **great** / greyt /

بزرگ / bozorg / **grown-up** / gronâp /

بزرگ / bozorg / **large** / lârj /

بزرگ / bozorg / **major** / meyjer /

بزرگتر / bozorgtar / **elder** / elder /

بزرگتر / bozorghtar / **senior** / siniyer /

بزرگترین / bozorgtarin / **eldest** / eldist /

بزرگسال / bozorgsâl / **adult** / adâlt /

بستن / bastan / **to bind** / to bâynd /

بستن / bastan / **to block** / to blâk /

بستن / bastan / **to fasten** / to fâsen /

بستن / bastan / **to pack** / to pak /

بستن / bastan / **to shut** / to shât /

بستن / bastan / **to tie** / to tây /

بستنی / bastani / **ice cream** / âyskriim /

بسته / baste / **parcel** / pârsel /

بسته بندی / bastebandi / **packing** / paking /

بسکتبال / basketbâl / **basketball** / baskitbol /

بسیار سرد / besiyâr sard / **frosty** / frâsti /

بشقاب / boshghâb / **plate** / pleyt /

بصری / basari / **visual** / vizhel /

32

بطری / **bottle** / bâtel /

بعد / baad / **after** / âfter /

بعد / baad / **following** / fâlo-ing /

بعد / baad / **next** / nekst /

بعد / baad / **then** / dhen /

بعد ازظهر / baad azzohr / **afternoon** / âfternoon /

بعداً / baadan / **afterwards** / âfterwordz /

بعداز ظهر / baad azzohr / **p.m.** / piiem /

بعلاوه / baalâve / **plus** / plâs /

بغل کردن / baghal kardan / **to embrace** / to imbreys /

بقاء / baghâ / **survival** / servâyvel /

بقال / baghghâl / **grocer** / groster /

بلژیک / belzhiki / **Belgium** / beljem /

بلژیکی / belzhiki / **Belgian** / beljen /

بلند / boland / **high** / hây /

بلند / boland / **loud** / laod /

بلند / boland / **loudly** / laodli /

بلند / boland / **tall** / tol /

بلند کردن / boland kardan / **to lift** / to lift /

بلند کردن / boland kardan / **to raise** / to reyz /

بلند کردن / boland kardan / **to elevate** / to eliveyt /

بلندگو / bolandgu / **loudspeaker** / laod spiiker /

بلندی / bolandi / **altitude** / altitud /

33

بله / bale / **yes** / yes /

بلور / buluz / **crystal** / blur / kristl /

بلوز / buluz / **blouse** / blaoz /

بلیت / belit / **ticket** / tikit /

بمب / bomb / **bomb** / bâm /

بمب افکن / bomb afkan / **bomber** / bâmer /

بمباران / bombârân / **bombing** / bâming /

بنابراین / banâbarin / **therefore** / dherfor /

بنای یادبود / benâye yâdbud / **monument** / mânyumentn /

بند / band / **paragraph** / paragrâf /

بندر / bandar / **port** / port /

بندرگاه / bandargâh / **harbor** / hârber /

بنزین / benzin / **gas** / gas /

بنزین / benzin / **gasoline** / gasolin /

بنزین / benzin / **petrol** / petrol /

بنفشه / banafshe / **violet** / vâyolit /

بنیاد / bonyâd / **foundation** / faondeyshen /

به آرامی / beârâmi / **gently** / jentlii /

به آرامی / be ârâmi / **quietly** / kwâyetlii /

به آسانی / beâsâni / **easily** / iizilii /

به تازگی / be tâzegi / **newly** / nyoolii /

به تدریج / betadrij / **gradually** / grajulii /

به تدریج / be tadrij / **progressively** / progresivlii /

به ترتیب / be tertib / **ascending** / ascending /

به دست آوردن / bedast âvardan / **acquire** / ekvayer /

به دست آوردن / be dast âvardan / **obtain** / âbteyn /

به روشنی / be roshani / **brightly** / brâytlii /

به زودی / be zudi / **soon** / soon /

به زور وارد شدن / bezur vâred shodan / **break-in** /
breyk-in /

به ساحل / be sâhel / **ashore** / eshor /

به سختی / be sakhti / **hardly** / hârdlii /

به سرعت / besoraat / **swiftly** / swiftlii /

به سلامتی! / besalâmati / **cheers!** / chiyerz /

به شوخی / beshukhi / **in jest** / injest /

به طرف / betarafe / **toward(s)** / tuword(z) /

به طرف پایین / betarafe pâyin / **downward(s)** /
daonword(z) /

به طور اختصار / be tore ekhtesâr / **briefly** / briiflii /

به طور جزئی / be tore jozii / **partially** / pârshâlii /

به طور دردناکی / be tore dardnâki / **painfully** / peynfullii /

به طور متوالی / be tore motavâli / **successively** /
sâksesivlii /

به کار انداختن / bekâr andakhtan / **operate** / âpereyt /

به کار بردن / bekâr bordan / **use** / yooz /

به کار بردن / bekâr bordan / **utilize** / yootilâyz /

به کلی / **altogether** / be kolli / oltegeter /

به ندرت / **rarely** / be nodrat / rerlii /

به ندرت / **seldom** / be nodrat / seldem /

به نظر / **sound** / be nazar / saond /

به نظر رسیدن / **seem** / benazar residan / siim /

به هرحال / **anyway** / beharhâl / eniwey /

به هم زدن / **cancel** / beham zadan / kansel /

به هیجان آوردن / **excite** / be heyejân âvardan / iksâyt /

به یاد آوردن / **to evoke** / be yâd âvardan / to ivok /

به یاد آوردن / **to remember** / beyâd âvardan /
to rimember /

به یک اندازه / **equally** / be yek andâze / iikwâlii /

بهار / **spring** / bahâr / spring /

بهبود / **improvement** / behbud / improovment /

بهبود یافتن / **to heal** / behbud yâftan / to hiil /

بهبود یافتن / **to recover** / behbud yâftan / to rikâver /

بهتر / **better** / behtar / beter /

بهترکردن / **to improve** / behtar kardan / to improov /

بهترین / **best** / behtarin / best /

بهشت / **heaven** / behesht / heven /

بهشت / **paradise** / behesht / paredâys /

بودن / **to be** / budan / to bii /

بوسه / **kiss** / buse / kis /

بوفالو / bufâlo / **buffalo** / bâfâlo /

بوقلمون / bughalamun / **turkey** / torki /

بوکس / boks / **boxing** / bâksing /

بوم شناسی / bumshenâsi / **ecology** / iikâloji /

بومی / bumi / **indigenous** / indigines /

بوی خوش / buye khosh / **aroma** / erome /

بویایی / buyâyl / **smell** / smel /

بی خوابی / bi khâbi / **insomnia** / insâmnie /

بی سیم / bisim / **wireless** / wâyelis /

بیابان / biyâbân / **desert** / dezert /

بی‌ادب / biadab / **impolite** / impolâyt /

بیان / bayân / **expression** / ikspreshen /

بیان کردن / bayân kardan / **to express** / to ikspres /

بی‌تاب / bitâb / **impatient** / impeyshent /

بی‌حرکت / biharkat / **immobile** / imobâyl /

بی‌حرکتی / biharkati / **immobility** / imobiliti /

بیدار / bidâr / **awake** / eweyk /

بیدار شدن / bidâr shodan / **to awake** / to eweyk /

بیدار کردن / bidâr Kardan / **awaken** / eweyken /

بیدارشدن / bidâr shodan / **to wake** / to weyk /

بیرحم / birahm / **bloodthirsty** / blâd-thersti /

بیرحمی / birahmi / **cruelty** / kroo-elti /

بیرون / birun / **out** / aot /

37

بيرون / birun / **outdoor** / aotdor /

بيرون / birun / **outside** / aotsâyd /

بيرون آمدن / birun âmadan / **to come out** / to kâm ât /

بيرونى / biruni / **external** / ikstenl /

بيرونى / biruni / **outer** / aoter /

بيزار بودن / bizâr budan / **to hate** / to heyt /

بيس بال / beysbâl / **baseball** / beysbol /

بيست / bist / **twenty** / twenti /

بيستم / bistom / **twentieth** / twentiyeth /

بيسكويت / biskuvit / **biscuit** / biskit /

بيشتر / bishtar / **longer** / lânger /

بيشتر / bishtar / **more** / mor /

بيشترين / bishtarin / **most** / most /

بيضى / beyzi / **oval** / ovl /

بى‌كفايت / bikefâyat / **inefficient** / inifishent /

بيگانه / bigâne / **alien** / eylien /

بيگانه پرست / bigâneparast / **xenophile** / zeneufayl /

بيمار / bimâr / **patient** / peyshent /

بيمار / bimâr / **sick** / sik /

بيمارستان / bimârestân / **hospital** / hâspitâl /

بيمارى / bimâri / **disease** / diziiz /

بيمارى / bimâri / **illness** / ilnis /

بيمارى قند / bimâriye ghand / **diabetes** / dâyebitiz /

بیمه / bime / **assurance** / ashurens /

بیمه / bime / **insurance** / inshurens /

بیمه کردن / bime kardan / **to insure** / to inshur /

بین / beyne / **between** / bitwiin /

بین المللی / beynalmelali / **international** / internashnâl /

بینایی / binâyi / **sight** / sâyt /

بینی / bini / **nose** / noz /

بیکار / bikâr / **unemployed** / ânimployd /

بیکاری / bikâri / **unemployment** / ânimplyment /

بی احتیاط / bi ehtiyât / **careless** / kerlis /

بی پایان / bi pâyân / **endless** / endlis /

بی پول / bi pul / **broke** / brok /

بی ثمر / bi samar / **futile** / Fyootâyl /

بی جان / bi jân / **lifeless** / lâyffis /

بی خبری / bi khâbari / **ignorance** / ignorens /

بی شک / bi shak / **doubtless** / daotlis /

بی صبرانه / bi sabrâne / **impatiently** / impeyshentli /

بی ضرر / bi zarar / **harmless** / hârmlis /

بی طبقه / bi tabaghe / **classless** / klaslis /

بی طرف / bi taraf / **neutral** / nyootrâl /

بی عدالتی / bi adâleti / **injustice** / injâstis /

بی قرار / bigharâr / **restless** / restlis /

بی گناه / bi gonâh / **innocent** / inosent /

39

بی مزه / bi maze / **tasteless** / teystlis /

بی معنی / bi maani / **meaningless** / miiningful /

بی میل / bimeyl / **unwilling** / ânwiling /

بی نظمی / bi nazmi / **disorder** / **disorder** / disorder /

پا / pâ / **foot** / fut /
پا / pâ / **leg** / leg /
پادشاه / pâdeshâh / **king** / king /
پارچه / pârche / **cloth** / klos /
پارس کردن / pars kardan / **bark** / bârk /
پارکینگ / pârking / **garage** / garaj /
پاره کردن / pare kardan / **to tear** / to ter /
پاسبان / pâsbân / **cop** / kâp /
پاسخ / pasokh / **response** / rispâns /
پاسخ گفتن / pasokh koftan / **to respond** / to rispând /
پاشیدگی / pâshidegi / **mess** / mes /
پافشاری کردن / pâfeshâri kardan / **to persist** / to pesist /
پاك کردن / pâk kardan / **to wipe** / to wâyp /
پاكت (نامه) / pâkat (nâme) / **envelop** / envelop /
پالایش / pâlâyesh / **refinement** / rif âynment /
پالتو / pâlto / **coat** / kot /
پانزده / pânzdah / **fifteen** / fiftiin /
پانسیون / pânsiyon / **boardinghouse** / boring haos /
پای / pây / **pie** / pây /

/ kânkloozhen / **conclusion** / pâyân / پایان

/ end / **end** / pâyân / پایان

/ kapitâl / **capital** / pâytakht / پایتخت

/ beys / **base** / pâygâh / پایگاه

/ pâynt / **pint** / pâynt / پاینت

/ otem / **autumn** / pâyiz / پاییز

/ daon / **down** / pâyin / پایین

/ ireyser / **eraser** / pâkkon / پاک کن

/ blankit / **blanket** / patu / پتو

/ beyk / **bake** / pokhtan / پختن

/ pedel / **pedal** / pedâl / پدال

/ fâdher / **father** / pedar / پدر

/ grandfâdher / **grandfather** / pedar bozorg / پدر بزرگ

/ finâminen / **phenomenon** / padide / پدیده

/ to entertain / pazirâii kardan / پذیرایی کردن
/ to enterteyn

/ risepshen / **reception** / paziresh / پذیرش

/ to aksept / **to accept** / paziroftan / پذیرفتن

/ to edmit / **to admit** / paziroftan / پذیرفتن

/ to aproov / **to approve** / paziroftan / پذیرفتن

/ to kemplây / **to comply** / paziroftan / پذیرفتن

/ ful / **full** / por / پر

/ overkraodid / **overcrowded** / por jamiyat / پر جمعیت

پر کردن / por kardan / **to fill** / to fil /
پرتاب کردن / partâb kardan / **to bowl** / to bol /
پرتقال / portaghâl / **orange** / ârinj /
پرتو / partov / **ray** / rey /
پرجمعیت / porjamiyet / **crowded** / kraodid /
پرچم / parcham / **flag** / flag /
پرداخت / pardâkht / **settlement** / setelment /
پرداخت کردن / pardâkht kardan / **to pay** / to pey /
پرده / parde / **curtain** / kerten /
پرده / parde / **screen** / skriin /
پرده‌کرکره / parde ker kere / **blind** / blâynd /
پرستار / parastâr / **nurse** / ners /
پرستیدن / parastidan / **to adore** / to edor /
پرستیدن / parastidan / **to worship** / to wership /
پرسش / porsesh / **inquiry** / inkwâyri /
پرسش / porsesh / **question** / kweschen /
پرسشنامه / porsechnâme / **questionnaire** / kweschener /
پرسیدن / porsidan / **ask** / âsk /
پرسیدن / porsidan / **to inquire** / to inkwayr /
پرشور / porshur / **vehement** / viyement /
پرماجرا / por mâjarâ / **eventful** / iventful /
پرنده / parande / **bird** / berd /
پرواز / parvâz / **flight** / flâyt /

پرواز کردن / parvâz kardan / **fly** / flây /

پروانه / parvâne / **butterfly** / bâterflây /

پروانه / parvane / **license** / lâysens /

پروتستان / protestân / **Protestant** / prâtistent /

پریدن / paridan / **to bound** / to baons /

پریدن / paridan / **to jump** / to jâmp /

پریدن / paridan / **to leap** / to liip /

پز دادن / poz dâdan / **to boast** / to bost /

پزدادن / poz dâdan / **to brag** / to brag /

پزشك / pezeshk / **physician** / fizishen /

پزشکی / pezeshki / **medical** / medikâl /

پژمرده شدن / pazhmorde shodan / **to fade** / to feyd /

پژواك / pezhvâk / **echo** / eko /

پس انداز / pasandâz / **savings** / seyver /

پست / post / **mail** / meyl /

پست / post / **post** / post /

پست الكترونیکی / poste elektroniki / **e-mail** / i-meyl /

پستاندار / pestândâr / **mammal** / maml /

پسر / pesar / **boy** / boy /

پسر / pesar / **son** / sân /

پسندیده / pasandide / **admirable** / admerebl /

پشت / posht / **back** / bak /

پشم / pashm / **wool** / wul /

44

/ wulen / **woolen** / pashmi / پشمی
/ bridge / **bridge** / pol / پل
/ plastik / **plastic** / pelâstiki / پلاستیکی
/ sterz / **stairs** / pellekân / پلکان
/ leperd / **leopard** / palang / پلنگ
/ pulover / **pullover** / plover / پلوور
/ poliis / **police** / polis / پلیس
/ âylid / **eyelid** / pelke cheshm / پلک چشم
/ shelter / **shelter** / panâh / پناه
/ feryujii / **refugee** / panâhande / پناهنده
/ fifti / **fifty** / panjâh / پنجاه
/ windo / **window** / panjare / پنجره
/ therzdi / **Thursday** / panjshanbe / پنجشنبه
/ fifth / **fifth** / panjomi / پنجمی
/ chiiz / **cheese** / panir / پنیر
/ brod / **broad** / pahn / پهن
/ wâyd / **wide** / pahn / پهن
/ spred / **spread** / pahn kardan / پهن کردن
/ widith / **width** / pahnâ / پهنا
/ klodhing / **clothing** / pushâk / پوشاک
/ pudding / **pudding** / puding / پودینگ
/ epoleji / **apology** / puzesh / پوزش
/ epâlojâyz / **apologize** / puzesh khâstan / پوزش خواستن

پوست / pust / **skin** / skin /

پوستر / poster / **poster** / poster /

پوسته / puste / **sheel** / shel /

پوسیدن / pusidan / **molder** / molder /

پوشش / pushesh / **cover** / kâver /

پوشه / pushe / **folder** / folder /

پوشیدن / pushidan / **to wear** / to wer /

پوشک / pushâk / **diaper** / d dikteyt yper /

پول / pul / **currency** / kârensi /

پول / pul / **money** / mâni /

پول نقد / pulenaghd / **case** / kash /

پوند / pond / **pound** / paond /

پویایی / puyâyi / **dynamism** / dâynamizem /

پی بردن / peybordan / **realize** / riyalâyz /

پیاده رو / piyâdero / **pavement** / peyvment /

پیاز / piyâz / **onion** / ânyen /

پیازی / piyâzi / **bulbous** / bâlbes /

پیانو / piyâno / **piano** / piyano /

پیاه رو / piyâdero / **sidewalk** / sâydwok /

پیپت / pipet / **pipette** / pipet /

پنج / pich / **five** / fâyv /

پیچ / pich / **bend** / bend /

پیچ / pich / **turn** / tern /

پیچیدن / pichidan / **to curve** / to kerv /

پیچیدن / pichidan / **envelop** / invelop /

پیچیدن / pichidan / **to wrap** / to rap /

پیچیده تر کردن / pichidetar kardan / **to complicate** / to kâmplikeyt /

پیدا کردن / peydâ kardan / **to find** / to fâynd /

پیر / pir / **old** / old /

پیراهن / pirâhan / **shirt** / shert /

پیروز / piruz / **exultant** / igzâltant /

پیروز شدن / piruz shodan / **overcome** / overkâm /

پیروزی / piruzi / **triumph** / trâyâmf /

پیروزی / piruzi / **victory** / viktri /

پیژامه / pizhâme / **pajamas** / pejâmâz /

پیش / pish / **ago** / ego /

پیش / pish / **ahead** / ehed /

پیش از ظهر / pish az zohr / **a.m.** / eyem /

پیش آمدن / pish âmadan / **arise** / erâyz /

پیش بینی / pish bini / **anticipation** / antisipeyshen /

پیش بینی / bishbini / **prediction** / pridikshen /

پیش بینی کردن / pish bini kardan / **to anticipate** / to antisipeyt /

پیش بینی کردن / bishbini kardan / **to predict** / to pridikt /

پیش رفتن / pishraftan / **to proceed** / to prosiid /

پیش گیر / pishgir / **bib** / bib /
پیشبند / pishband / **apron** / eypren /
پیشبینی / pishbini / **forecast** / forkâst /
پیشخدمت / pishkhedmat / **waiter** / weyter /
پیشخدمت زن / pishkhedmate zan / **waitress** / weytris /
پیشخوان / pishkhân / **counter** / kaonter /
پیشداوری / pishdâvari / **prejudice** / prejudis /
پیشرفت / pishraft / **progress** / progres /
پیشرفت کردن / pishraft kardan / **advance** / advâns /
پیشگام / pishgâm / **pioneer** / pâyoniyer /
پیشگویی / pishguyi / **prophecy** / prâfisi /
پیشنهاد / pishnehâd / **proposal** / prepozl /
پیشنهاد / pishnahâd / **suggestion** / sâjeschen /
پیشنهاد کردن / pishnehâd kardan / **to suggest** / to sâjest /
پیشنهاد کردن / bishnahâd kardan / **to offer** / to âfer /
پیشنهاد کردن / pishnehâd kardan / **to propose** / to propoz /
پیشه / pishe / **craft** / kraft /
پیغام / peyghâm / **message** / mesij /
پیکنیک / piknik / **picnic** / piknik /
پیمان / peymân / **contract** / kontrakt /
پیمان / peymân / **league** / liig /
پیمان / peyman / **treaty** / triiti /
پیوستگی / peyvastegi / **continuity** / kântinyoowiti /

48

پیوسته / peyvaste / **continuous** / kântinyuwes /

پیوند دادن / peyvand dâdan / **to associate** /

to asoshiyeyt /

ت

تا / tâ / **till** / til /
تا / tâ / **to** / too /
تا / tâ / **until** / ântil /
تا کردن / tâ kardan / **to fold** / to fold /
تاب خوردن / tâb khordan / **to swing** / to swing /
تابستان / tâbestan / **summer** / sâmer /
تابع / tâbee / **citizen** / sitizn /
تابوت / tâbut / **coffin** / kâfin /
تأثیر / taasir / **impression** / impreshen /
تأثیر گذاشتن / tasir gozâshtan / **to affect** / to afekt /
تاج / tâj / **crown** / krâvn /
تاحالا / tâhâlâ / **already** / alredi /
تاحدی / tahaddi / **partly** / pârtli /
تاحدی / tahaddi / **somewhat** / sâmwât /
تأخیر / taakhir / **delay** / diley /
تاریخ / târikh / **date** / deyt /
تاریخ / târikh / **history** / histri /
تاریخی / târikhi / **historical** / histârikâl /
تاریک / târik / **dark** / dârk /

تاریکی / târiki / **darkness** / dârknis /

تازه / tâze / **fresh** / fresh /

تأسف / taassof / **sorrow** / sâro /

تأسف آور / taassof âvar / **regrettable** / rigretebel /

تأسیس کردن / tasis kardan / **establish** / istablish /

تاکسی / tâksi / **cab** / kab /

تامین کردن / tamin kardan / **to provide** / to provâyd /

تأمین کردن / taamin kardan / **to supply** / to sâplây /

تایپ کردن / tayp kardan / **to type** / to tâyp /

تایر / tâyer / **tire** / tâyer /

تأیید / taiid / **confirmation** / kânfermeyshen /

تأیید / taaiid / **affirmation** / afermeyshen /

تأیید کردن / tayid kardan / **to affirm** / to eferm /

تأیید کردن / taayid kardan / **to confirm** / to kenferm /

تب / tab / **fever** / fiiver /

تبدیل کردن / tabdil kardan / **to convert** / to kânvert /

تبر / tabar / **ax** / aks /

تبر / tabar / **axe** / aks /

تبریک / tabrik / **congratulation** / kângrachuleyshen /

تبعید کردن / tabiid kardan / **to deport** / to diport /

تبهکار / tabahkâr / **gangster** / gangster /

تپانچه / tapânche / **pistol** / pistel /

تپانچه / tapânche / **revolver** / rivâlver /

تپه / hil / **hill** / tape /

تجارت کردن / to treyd / **to trade** / tejârat kardan /

تجاوز / egreshen / **aggression** / tajâvoz /

تجاوز کردن / to inveyd / **to invade** / tajâvoz kardan /

تجربه / ikspiriyens / **experience** / tajrobe /

تجزیه / enalisis / **analysis** / tajziye /

تجزیه کردن / to analâyz / **to analyze** / tajziye kardan /

تجمل / lâksheri / **luxury** / tajammol /

تجهیز / ikwipment / **equipment** / tajhiz /

تحریک / prâvokeyshen / **provocation** / tahrik /

تحریک کردن / to provok / **to provoke** / tahrik kardan /

تحرک / mobiliti / **mobility** / taharrok /

تحسین / admireyshen / **admiration** / tahsin /

تحسین کردن / to ekleym / **to acclaim** / tahsin kardan /

تحسین کردن / to preyz / **to praise** / tahsin kardan /

تحقیق / investigeyshen / **investigation** / tahghigh /

تحقیق / riserch / **research** / tahghigh /

تحقیق کردن / **to investigate** / tahghigh kardan /
/ to investigeyt

تحمل / tâlerens / **tolerance** / tahammol /

تحمل کردن / to indyur / **to endure** / tahammol kardan /

تحمل کردن / to tâlereyt / **to tolerate** / tahammol kardan /

تحمیل کردن / to impoz / **to impose** / tahmil kardan /

52

تحول / tahavvol / **revolution** / revolooshen /

تحویل / tahvil / **delivery** / diliveri /

تختخواب / takhtekhâb / **bed** / bed /

تخته / takhte / **board** / bord /

تخته(سیاه) / takhte (siyah) / **blackboard** / blâkbord /

تخفیف / takhfif / **discount** / diskaont /

تخلیه کردن / takhliye kardan / **to evacuate** /
to ivakyuweyt /

تخم چشم / tokhme cheshm / **eyeball** / âybol /

تخم مرغ / tokhmemorgh / **egg** / eg /

تخیل / takhayyol / **imagination** / imajineyshen /

تخیلی / takhayyoli / **imaginative** / imajinetiv /

تخیلی / ta khauyoil / **unreal** / ânriyel /

تدریجی / tadriji / **gradual** / grajuwal /

ترابری / tarâbari / **transportation** / transporteyshen /

ترازو / tarâzu / **balance** / balens /

ترافیک / terafik / **traffic** / trafik /

تراموا / tramvâ / **tram** / tram /

تربیت / tarbiyat / **training** / treyning /

ترتیب / tartib / **order** / order /

ترجمه / tarjome / **translation** / transleyshen /

ترجمه کردن / tarjome kardan / **to interpret** / to interprit /

ترجمه کردن / tarjome kardan / **to translate** / to transleyt /

ترجیح دادن / tarjih dâdan / **to prefer** / to prifer /

ترجیح دادن / tarjih dâdan / **rather** / râdher /

ترجیحاً / tarjihan / **preferably** / prefebli /

تردید / tardid / **hesitation** / heziteyshen /

تردید کردن / tardid kardan / **to hesitate** / to heziteyt /

ترس / tars / **fear** / fiyer /

ترس / tars / **fright** / frâyt /

ترساندن / tarsândan / **to scare** / to sker /

ترساندن / tarsândan / **to terrify** / to terifây /

ترسناک / tarsnâk / **dreadful** / dredfol /

ترسیدن / tarsidan / **afraid** / efreyd /

ترسیدن از / tarsidan az / **dread** / dred /

ترش / torsh / **acid** / asid /

ترشی / torshi / **acidity** / esideti /

ترک کردن / tark kardan / **to quit** / to kwit /

ترکی / torki / **Turkish** / terkish /

ترکیب / tarkib / **combination** / kombineyshn /

ترکیب کردن / tarkib kardan / **to combine** / to kâmbâyn /

ترکیدن / tarakidan / **to burst** / to berst /

ترکیه / torkiye / **Turkey** / terki /

ترمز / tormoz / **brake** / breyk /

ترمینال / terminâl / **terminal** / terminâl /

ترکیب / tarkib / **composition** / kâmpozishen /

تریلر / **trailer** / treyler / treyler /

ترک / **Turk** / tork / terk /

تزریق / **injection** / tazrigh / injekshen /

تزریق کردن / **to inject** / tazrigh kardna / to injekt /

تزیین / **decoration** / taziin / dekoreyshen /

تزیین / **ornament** / tazyin / ornament /

تسکین / **relief** / taskin / riliif /

تسلط / **control** / tasallot / kântrol /

تسلی دادن / **to console** / tasalli dâdan / to kensol /

تسلیم شدن / **surrender** / taslim shodan / sârender /

تسهیل کردن / **facilitate** / tashil kardan / fasiliteyt /

تسهیلات / **facilities** / tas-hilât / fasilitiz /

تشنگی / **thirst** / teshnegi / therst /

تشنه / **thirsty** / teshne / thersti /

تشویق / **encouragement** / tashvigh / inkârijment /

تشویق کردن / **to encourage** / tashvigh kardan / to encourage /
to inkârij /

تشکیل دادن / **to compose** / tashkil dâdan / to kâmpoz /

تشک / **mattress** / toshak / matris /

تصادف / **accident** / tasâdof / aksident /

تصادف / **crash** / tasâdof / krash /

تصادفاً / **casually** / tasâdofan / kazhuwali /

تصفیه کردن / **to refine** / tasfiye kardan / to rifâyn /

55

تصمیم / decision / disizhen /

تصمیم گرفتن / tasmim gereftan / to decide / to disâyd /

تصور کردن / tasavvor kardan / fancy / fansi /

تصور کردن / tasavvor kardan / to imagine / to imajin /

تصورکردن / tasavvor kardan / to conceive / to kânsiiv /

تصویر / tasvir / image / imij /

تطبیق کردن / tatbigh kardan / to correspond / to kârispând /

تظاهر / tazâhor / affectation / afecteyshen /

تظاهر کردن / tazâhor kardan / to pretend / to pritend /

تعبیر / taabir / interpretation / interpriteyshen /

تعجّب / taajjob / surprise / serprâyz /

تعطیل / taatil / holiday / hâlidey /

تعطیلات / taatilât / vacation / vakeyshen /

تعطیلات آخرهفته / taatilâte âkharehafte / weekend / wiikend /

تعقیب / taaghib / chase / cheys /

تعقیب / taaghib / pursuit / persyoot /

تعلق داشتن / taallogh dâshtan / to belong / to bilâng /

تعمیر کردن / taamir kardan / to mend / to mend /

تعمیر کردن / taamir kardan / to repair / to riper /

تعمیرگاه / taamirgâh / garage / garâzh /

تعیین / taayin / determination / ditermineyshn /

تغذیه کردن / taghziye kardan / **to feed** / to fiid /

تغییر / taghyir / **alteration** / altereyshn /

تغییر دادن / taghiir dâdan / **to alter** / to alter /

تغییر کردن / taghiir kardan / **to vary** / to veri /

تفاوت / tafâvot / **difference** / difrens /

تفاوت / tafâvot / **distinction** / distinkshen /

تفریح / tafrih / **entertainment** / enterteynment /

تفریح / tafrih / **fun** / fân /

تفریحگاه / tafrihgâh / **playground** / pleygraound /

تفسیر / tafsir / **commentary** / kâmentri /

تفنگ / tofang / **rifle** / râyfel /

تقاضا / taghâzâ / **petition** / pitishen /

تقاضا / taghâzâ / **requisition** / rekwizition /

تقاضا کردن / taghâzâ kardan / **apply** / eplây /

تقاضا کردن / taghâzâ kardan / **plead** / pliid /

تقاطع / taghâto / **crossing** / krâsing /

تقاطع / taghâto / **crossroads** / krâsrodz /

تقریباً / taghriban / **almost** / olmost /

تقریباً / taghriban / **nearly** / niyerli /

تقریباً / taghriban / **approximately** / âproksimtley /

تقسیم / taghsim / **division** / divizhen /

تقطیع کردن / taghtii kardan / **to scan** / to skan /

تقلا کردن / taghallâ kardan / **to struggle** / to estrugel /

57

تقليد / taghlid / **imitation** / imiteyshen /
تقليد كردن / taghlid kardan / **to imitate** / to imiteyt /
تقويم / taghvim / **calendar** / kalinder /
تكامل / takâmol / **evolution** / iivolooshen /
تكان / tekân / **shock** / shâk /
تكرار / tekrâr / **repetition** / repitishen /
تكرار كردن / tekrâr kardan / **to repeat** / to ripiit /
تكليف / taklif / **homework** / homwerk /
تكه / tekke / **bit** / bit /
تكه / tekke / **piece** / piis /
تكه چوب / tekke chub / **stick** / stik /
تكيه گاه / tekiyegâh / **prop** / prâp /
تلخ / talkh / **bitter** / biter /
تلف كردن / talaf kardan / **to waste** / to weyst /
تلفظ / talaffoz / **pronunciation** / pronânsiyeshen /
تلفظ كردن / talaffoz kardan / **to pronounce** / to pronaons /
تلفن / telefon / **phone** / fon /
تلفن / telefon / **telephone** / telifon /
تلگراف / telgerâf / **telegraph** / teligrâf /
تلگرام / telgerâm / **telegram** / teligram /
تله پاتى / telepâti / **telepathic** / telipathik /
تلويزيون / televiziyon / **television** / telivizhen /
تماس / tamâs / **contact** / kontakt /

تماشا / tamâshâ / **watch** / wâch /

تماشاچی / tamâshâchi / **spectator** / spekteyter /

تمام / tamam / **entire** / intâyr /

تمام کردن / tamâm kardan / **to finish** / to finish /

تمایل / tamâyol / **bent** / bent /

تمبر / tamr / **stamp** / stamp /

تمدن / tamaddon / **civilization** / sivilâyzeyshen /

تمرین / tamrin / **exercise** / eksersâyz /

تمیز / tamiz / **clean** / kliin /

تمیز کردن / tamiz Kardan / **to brush up** / to brâsh âp /

تن / tan / **body** / bâdi /

تُن / ton / **ton** / tân /

تناسب داشتن / tanâsob dâshtan / **to fit** / to fit /

تنبل / tanbal / **lazy** / leyzi /

تنبیه / tanbih / **punishment** / pânishment /

تنبیه کردن / tanbih kardan / **punish** / pânish /

تند / tond / **fast** / fâst /

تند / tond / **quick** / kwik /

تند / tond / **quickly** / kwikli /

تند / tond / **rapid** / rapid /

تند / tond / **rapidly** / rapidli /

تند / tond / **vehemently** / viyementli /

تندتر / tondtar / **outrun** / aotrân /

تنش / tanesh / **tension** / tenshen /

تنظیم / tanzim / **regulation** / regyuleyshen /

تنفر / tanaffor / **dislike** / disleyk /

تنگه / tange / **channel** / chanel /

تنگی نفس / tangiye nafas / **asthma** / azme /

تنه / tane / **trunk** / trânk /

تنها / tanhâ / **alone** / elon /

تنها / tanhâ / **lonely** / lonli /

تنها / tanhâ / **only** / onli /

تنها / tanhâ / **solitary** / sâliteri /

تنوع / tanavvoo / **variation** / veriyeyshen /

تنوع / tanavvoo / **variety** / verâyeti /

تنیس / tenis / **tennis** / tenis /

ته / tah / **bottom** / bâtem /

تهدید / tahdid / **menace** / menis /

تهدید کردن / tahdid kardan / **threaten** / threten /

تو / tu / **into** / intoo /

تو / tu / **through** / throo /

توفانی / tufâni / **windy** / windi /

توافق / tavâfog / **agreement** / egriiment /

توالت / tuvâlet / **lavatory** / lavatri /

توالت / tuvâlet / **toilet** / toylit /

توانستن / tavânestan / **afford** / eford /

60

توانستن / tavânestan / **can** / kan /

توپ / tup / **ball** / bol /

توپ / tup / **roll** / rol /

توپ زن / tupzan / **batter** / bater /

توپخانه / tupkhâne / **artillery** / ârtileri /

توت فرنگی / tutfarangi / **strawberry** / stroberi /

توتون / tutun / **tobacco** / tobako /

توجه / tavajjoh / **attention** / atenshen /

توجه / tavajjoh / **regard** / rigârd /

توجه کردن / tavajjoh kardan / **to attend** / to atend /

توجه کردن / tavvajjoh kardan / **to note** / to not /

توجیه / tojih / **justification** / jâstifikeyshen /

توجیه کردن / tojih kardan / **justify** / jâstifây /

توده / tude / **heap** / hiip /

توده / tude / **mass** / mas /

تور / tur / **tour** / tur /

توزیع کردن / tozii kardan / **to distribute** / to distribyoot /

توسعه / tosee / **extension** / ikstenshen /

توسعه دادن / tosee dâdan / **extend** / ikstend /

توصیف / tosif / **description** / diskripshen /

توصیه / tosiye / **recommendation** / rekâmendeyshen /

توصیه کردن / tosiye kardan / **advise** / advâyz /

توصیه کردن / tosiye kardan / **recommend** / rekâmend /

61

توضیح / eksplaneyshen / **explanation** / tozih /

توضیح دادن / ikspleyn / **explain** / tozih dâdan /

توطئه / plât / **plot** / totee /

توطئه چیدن / to intriigu / **to intrigue** / totee chidan /

توفان / geyl / **gale** / tufân /

توفان / storm / **storm** / tufan /

توفان تندری / **thunderstorm** / tufan tondari /
/ thânderstorm

تولد / berth / **birth** / tavallod /

تولید / jenereyshen / **generation** / tolid /

تولید / prodâkshen / **production** / tolid /

تولید انبوه / **mass production** / tolide anbuh /
/ mas prodâkshen

تولید مثل / riiprodâkshen / **reproduction** / tolide mesl /

تولید مثل کردن / to briid / **to breed** / tolide nesl kardan /

تولید مثل کردن / **to reproduce** / tolide mesl kardan /
/ to riiprodyoos

تولیدی / prodâktiv / **productive** / tolidi /

تونل / tânel / **tunnel** / tunel /

تیر / aro / **arrow** / tir /

تیر / biim / **beam** / tir /

تیر / dârt / **dart** / tir /

تیر / pol / **pole** / tir /

62

تیر چراغ / tire cherâgh / **lamppost** / lamp post /
تیره / tire / **dull** / dâl /
تیز / tiz / **acute** / ekyut /
تیز / tiz / **keen** / kiin /
تیز / tiz / **sharp** / shârp /
تیغ / tigh / **razor** / reyzer /
تیلیک / tilik / **click** / klik /
تکیه دادن به / tekiye dâdan be / **to lean** / to liin /
تکامل یافتن / takâmol yâftan / **to evolve** / to ivâlv /
تکان خوردن / tekân khordan / **to stir** / to ster /
تکان دادن / tekân dâdan / **to rock** / to râk /
تکان دهنده / tekân dahande / **shocking** / shâking /
تکی / taki / **single** / singel /

ثابت / sâbet / **constant** / kânstant /
ثابت / sâbet / **permanent** / permanent /
ثابت / sâbet / **set** / set /
ثابت کردن / sâbet kardan / **to prove** / to proov /
ثابت کردن / sâbet kardan / **to demonstrate** /
to demonstreyt /
ثانوی / sânavi / **secondary** / sekendri /
ثبات / sobet / **permanence** / permanens /
ثبت / sabt / **register** / rejister /
ثروت / servat / **affluence** / afluwens /
ثروت / servat / **affluent** / afluwent /
ثروت / servat / **wealth** / welth /
ثروتمند / servatmand / **rich** / rich /

ج

جا / jâ / **place** / pleys /

جادار / jâdâr / **spacious** / speyhes /

جاده / jâdde / **road** / rod /

جادو / jâdu / **magic** / majik /

جادوگر / jâdugar / **magician** / majishen /

جاذبه / jâzebe / **fascination** / fasineyshen /

جاذبه / jâzebe / **gravity** / graviti /

جارو کردن / jâru kardan / **sweep** / swiip /

جاری / jâri / **current** / kârent /

جاری شدن / jâri shodan / **flow** / flo /

جاز / jâz / **jazz** / jaz /

جاسوس / jâsus / **spy** / spây /

جالب / jâleb / **fascinating** / fasineyting /

جالب / jâleb / **interesting** / intristing /

جامایکا / jâmâykâ / **Jamaica** / jemeykâ /

جامد / jâmed / **solid** / sâlid /

جامعه / jâmee / **society** / sosâyeti /

جانور / jânevar / **animal** / animâl /

جانور خانگی / jânevare khânegi / **pet** / pet /

جانورشناسی / jânevar shenâsi / **zoology** / zoâleji /

جاودانه / jâvedâne / **immortal** / imortâl /

جای دیگر / jâyedigar / **elsewhere** / elswer /

جایزه / jâyeze / **prize** / prâyz /

جایزه / jâyeze / **trophy** / trofi /

جایگزین کردن / jâygozin kardan / **to replace** / to ripleyz /

جایی / jâyi / **anywhere** / eniwer /

جایی / jâyii / **somewhere** / sâmwer /

جای پرت / jâye part / **outback** / aotbak /

جد / jad / **ancestor** / ansester /

جدا / jodâ / **separate** / seprit /

جداً / jeddan / **earnestly** / ernestli /

جدا از هم / joda az ham / **apart** / epârt /

جدا کردن / jodâ kardan / **to isolate** / to âysoleyt /

جداگانه / jodâgâne / **separately** / sepritli /

جدایی / jodâii / **segregation** / segrigeyshen /

جدّی / jeddi / **serious** / siriyes /

جدید / jadid / **modern** / mâdern /

جدید / jadid / **new** / nyoo /

جدی / jeddi / **austere** / ostriyer /

جدی / jeddi / **severe** / siviyer /

جذاب / jazb / **attractive** / atraktiv /

جذابیت / jazzâbiyat / **attraction** / atrakshen /

جذب کردن / jazb kardan / **attract** / atrakt /

جذب کردن / jazb kardan / **absorb** / absorb /

جرأت کردن / joraat kardan / **to dare** / to der /

جرّاح / jarrâh / **surgeon** / serjen /

جرّاحی / jarrâhi / **surgery** / serjeri /

جرم / jorm / **crime** / krâym /

جروبحث / jarrobahs / **argument** / ârgyument /

جروبحث کردن / jarrobahs kardan / **to argue** / to ârgyoo /

جریمه / jarime / **fine** / fâyn /

جریمه / jarime / **penalty** / penâlti /

جزئ / jozii / **partial** / pârshâl /

جزئ / jozii / **slight** / slâyt /

جزئ / jozii / **minor** / mâyner /

جزئیات / joziyyât / **detail** / diiteyl /

جزر و مد / jazromad / **tide** / tâyd /

جزیره / jazire / **island** / âyland /

جسارت / jesârat / **boldness** / bâldnes /

جستجو کردن / jostejv kardan / **to seek** / to siik /

جسور / jasur / **aggressive** / agresiv /

جشن / jashn / **celebration** / selibreyshen /

جشن / jashn / **festival** / festivâl /

جشن گرفتن / jashn gereftan / **to celebrate** / to celibreyt /

جعبه / jaabe / **box** / bâks /

جعبه / jaabe / **case** / keys /

67

جغرافیا / **geography** / joghrâfiyâ / jiyâgrafi /

جفت / **couple** / joft / kâpel /

جفت / **pair** / joft / per /

جلد / **volume** / jeld / vâlyum /

جلسه / **meeting** / jalase / miiting /

جلگه / **plain** / jolge / pleyn /

جلو / **forward(s)** / jelo / forworld(z) /

جلو / **front** / jelo / frânt /

جلو رفتن / **to lead** / jelo raftan / to liid /

جلوگیری کردن / **prevent** / jelogiri kardan / privent /

جلیقه نجات / **life jacket** / jaligheye nejât / lâyf jakit /

جمجمه / **skull** / jomjome / skâl /

جمع / **addition** / jam / edishen /

جمع / **plural** / jam / pluerel /

جمع آوری / **collection** / jamâvari / kâlekshen /

جمع شدن / **to assemble** / jam shodan / to asembel /

جمع شدن / **to gather** / jam shodan / to gadher /

جمع کردن / **to add** / jam kardan / to ad /

جمع کردن / **to collect** / jam kardan / to kâlekt /

جمعه / **Friday** / jomee / frâydi /

جمعیت / **crowd** / jamiyyat / kraod /

جمعیت / **population** / jamiiyat / pâpyuleyshen /

جمله / **sentence** / jomle / sentens /

جمهورى / jemhuri / **republic** / ripâblik /

جنگ / jang / **fight** / fâyt /

جناغى / jenâghi / **zigzag** / zigzag /

جنباندن / jonbândan / **shake** / sheyk /

جنبش / jonbesh / **motion** / moshn /

جنبه / janbe / **aspect** / aspekt /

جنبیدن / jonbidan / **to wave** / to weyv /

جنس / jens / **sex** / seks /

جنسى / jensi / **sexual** / sekshuwâl /

جنگ / jang / **war** / wor /

جنگجو / jangju / **fighter** / fâyter /

جنگل / jangal / **forest** / fârist /

جنوب / junub / **south** / saoth /

جنوبى / jonub / **southern** / sâdhern /

جهان / jahân / **universe** / yoonivers /

جهانگرد / jahângard / **explorer** / iksplorer /

جهانگرد / jahângard / **tourist** / turist /

جهانى / jahâni / **global** / globl /

جهانى / jahâni / **worldwide** / weldwâyd /

جهنم / jahannam / **hell** / hel /

جو / jo / **barley** / bâli /

جواب / javâb / **answer** / ânser /

جواب دادن / javâp dâdan / **to answer** / to ânser /

جواب رد دادن / javâbe rad dâdan / **to refuse** / to rifyooz /

جوان / javân / **young** / yâng /

جوان / javân / **youthful** / yoothful /

جوانه / javâne / **bud** / bâd /

جوانی / javani / **youth** / yooth /

جواهر / javâher / **jewel** / juwel /

جواهرات / javâherât / **jewelery** / juwelri /

جوجه / juje / **chicken** / chikin /

جور / jur / **sort** / sort /

جوراب / jurab / **sock** / sâk /

جوراب ساقه بلند زنانه / jurâbe sâghebolande zanâne /
stocking / stâking /

جوراب نایلون / jurâbe naylon / **nylons** / nâylânz /

جوش دادن / jush dâdan / **to weld** / to weld /

جوش صورت / jushe surat / **acne** / akn /

جوشیدن / jushidan / **to boil** / to boyl /

جَوّ / javv / **atmosphere** / atmosfiyer /

جویبار / juybâr / **stream** / striim /

جویدن / javidan / **to chew** / to choo /

جیب / jib / **pocket** / pâkit /

جیب بُر / jibbor / **pickpocket** / pikpâkit /

جیره / jire / **ration** / rashn /

جیغ زدن / jigh zadan / **to scream** / to skriim /

چ

چابك / swift / **swift** / châbok /

چابک / ajâyl / **agile** / châbok /

چابکی / ejiliti / **agility** / châboki /

چاپ / idishen / **edition** / châp /

چاپ کردن / to print / **to print** / châp kardan /

چاخان / lây / **lie** / châkhân /

چادر / tent / **tent** / châdor /

چاق / fat / **fat** / châgh /

چاقو زدن / to stab / **to stab** / châghu zadan /

چانه / chin / **chin** / châne /

چای / tii / **tea** / chay /

چاک / slash / **slash** / châk /

چپ / left / **left** / chap /

چتر / âmbrelâ / **umbrella** / chatr /

چرا / wây / **why** / cherâ /

چراغ / hedlyâyt / **headlight** / cherâgh /

چراغ / lamp / **lamp** / cherâgh /

چراغ قوه / torch / **torch** / cherâghe ghovve /

چرخ خیاطی / **sewing machine** / charkhe khayyati
/ so-ing mashiin /

چرخ وفلك / **merry-go-round** / charkhofalak / merigoraond

چرک / pârk / **park** / pârk

چرم / charm / **leather** / ledher

چرند / charand / **nonsense** / nânsens

چسب / chasb / **gum** / gâm

چسباندن / chasbândan / **to attach** / to etach

چسباندن / chasbândan / **to paste** / to peyst

چسبنده / chasbande / **adhesive** / edhisiv

چسبیدن / chasbidan / **adhere** / edhier

چشایی / cheshâyi / **taste** / teyst

چشم / cheshm / **eye** / ây

چشمگیر / cheshmgir / **remarkable** / rimârkebel

چشمک زدن / chesmak zadan / **to blink** / to blink

چطور / chetor / **how** / hao

چك / chak / **check** / chek

چکش / chakkosh / **hammer** / hamer

چکمه / chakme / **boot** / boot

چمدان / chamadân / **luggage** / lâgij

چمن / chaman / **lawn** / lon

چند / chand / **several** / severâl

چنگال / changâl / **fork** / fork

چنین / chenin / **such** / sâch

72

چه / che / **what** / wât /
چه کسی / che kasi / **whom** / hoom /
چه وقت / che vaght / **when** / wen /
چهار / châhâr / **four** / for /
چهارپا / châhârpâ / **beast** / biist /
چهارده / châhârdah / **fourteen** / fortiin /
چهارشانه / châhârshâne / **broad-shouldered** /
brod-sholderd /
چهارشنبه / châhârshanbe / **Wednesday** / wenzdi /
چهارنعل رفتن / châhârnaal raftan / **to gallop** / to galop /
چهل / chehel / **forty** / forti /
چوب / chub / **bat** / bat /
چوب / chub / **wood** / wud /
چوب زیربغل / chube zirbaghal / **crutch** / krâch /
چوپان / chupân / **shepherd** / sheped /
چون / chon / **for** / for /
چونکه / chonke / **because** / bikâz /
چیپس / chips / **chips** / chips /
چیدن / chidan / **mow** / mo /
چیز / chiz / **thing** / thing /
چیزی / chizi / **anything** / enithing /
چیزی / chizi / **something** / sâmthing /
چین / chin / **China** / châyne /

ح

حادثه / hâdese / **episode** / episod /
حادثه / hâdese / **event** / ivent /
حادثه / hâdese / **incident** / insident /
حاشیه / hâshiye / **margin** / mârjin /
حاصلخیز / hâselkhiz / **fertile** / fertâyl /
حاضر / hâzer / **present** / prezent /
حاضر / hâzer / **ready** / redi /
حافظه / hâfeze / **memory** / memori /
حاکم / hâkem / **ruler** / rooler /
حال / hâl / **mood** / mood /
حالا / hâlâ / **now** / nao /
حالت جنون / hâlate jenun / **frenzy** / frenzi /
حامی / hâmi / **supporter** / sâporter /
حاوی بودن / hâvi budan / **to contain** / to kânteyn /
حباب / hobâb / **bubble** / bâbl /
حتمی / hatmi / **certain** / serten /
حتی / hattâ / **even** / iiven /
حداقل / haddeaghal / **minimum** / minimem /
حداکثر / hadde aksar / **maximum** / mâksimen /

74

حدس / hads / **guess** / ges /

حدمرز / hadomarz / **limit** / limit /

حذف کردن / hazf kardan / **eliminate** / ilimineyt /

حرارت / harârat / **heat** / hiit /

حرف اضافه / harfe ezâfe / **preposition** / prepezishn /

حرف زدن / harf zadan / **to speak** / to spiik /

حرفه / herfe / **profession** / profeshen /

حرفه ای / herfeii / **professional** / profeshenâl /

حرکت / harekat / **departure** / dipârcher /

حرکت / harakat / **movement** / moovment /

حرکت دادن / harakat dâdan / **to move** / to moov /

حرکت کردن / harakat kardan / **to depart** / to dipart /

حزب / hezb / **party** / pârti /

حس / hes / **feel** / fiil /

حس / hes / **feeling** / fiiling /

حس / hes / **sense** / sens /

حساب / hesab / **arithmetic** / arithmetik /

حساب کردن / hesâb kardan / **to calculate** / to kalkyuleyt /

حساب کردن / hesab kardan / **to compute** / to kâmpyoot /

حسادت / hesâdat / **envy** / envi /

حسادت / hasâdat / **jealousy** / jelesi /

حسن / hosn / **virtue** / verchoo /

حسود / hasud / **envious** / enviyes /

حسود / hasud / **jealous** / jeles /

حشره / hashare / **insect** / insekt /

حفاظت / hefâzat / **conservation** / kânserveyshen /

حفظ کردن / hefz kardan / **to maintain** / to meynteyn /

حفظ کردن / hefz kardan / **to conserve** / to kânserv /

حق / hagh / **behalf** / bihaf /

حقوق / hughugh / **salary** / saleri /

حقیقت / haghighat / **truth** / trooth /

حکم / hokm / **judgment** / jâyment /

حل کردن / hal kardan / **to solve** / to sâlv /

حلقه / halghe / **loop** / loop /

حلقه / halghe / **ring** / ring /

حلقه زنجیر / halgheye zanjir / **link** / link /

حمام / hamâm / **bath** / bâth /

حمام / hamâm / **bathhouse** / bashâus /

حمایت کردن / hemâyat kardan / **to support** / to sâport /

حمل / haml / **transport** / transport /

حمل کردن / haml kardan / **to carry** / to kari /

حمل کردن / haml kardan / **to bear** / to ber /

حمله / hamle / **assault** / esolt /

حمله / hamle / **attack** / etak /

حمله / hamle / **invasion** / inveyzhen /

حمله / hamle / **raid** / reyd /

حوله / tao-el / **towel** / hole /

حومه / sâberb / **suburb** / home /

حومه / sâberben / **suburban** / home /

حيات / lâyf / **life** / hayât /

حياتى / vâytl / **vital** / hayâti /

حياط / yârd / **yard** / hayât /

حيرت انگيز / mârves / **marvelous** / heyrat angiz /

حيوان دورگه / hâybrid / **hybrid** / heyvane dorage /

حكومت كردن / to gâvern / **to govern** / hukumat kardan /

خ

خارجی / khâreji / **alien** / eylien /

خارجی / khâreji / **foreign** / fârin /

خارجی / khâreji / **foreigner** / fârner /

خارق العاده / khâregholâdde / **unearthly** / ânerthli /

خاص / khâs / **particular** / pârtikyuler /

خاص / khâs / **peculiar** / pikyooliyer /

خاطر / khâter / **sake** / seyk /

خاك / khâk / **soil** / soyl /

خاكستر / khâkestar / **ash** / ash /

خاكسترى / khâkestari / **gray** / grey /

خاكى / khâki / **khaki** / kâki /

خال / khâl / **spot** / spât /

خالص / khâles / **pure** / pyur /

خاله / khâle / **aunt** / ânt /

خالى / khâli / **empty** / empti /

خالى / khâli / **vacant** / veykent /

خام / khâm / **raw** / ro /

خامه / khâme / **cream** / kriim /

خاموش / khâmush / **extinct** / ikstinkt /

خانگی / kânegi / **homemade** / hommeyd /
خانگی / khânegi / **indoor** / indor /
خانم / khânom / **lady** / leydi /
خانم / khânom / **madam** / madem /
خانم / khânom / **Mrs.** / misiz /
خانم / khânom / **wife** / wâyf /
خانم خانه / khânome khâne / **housewife** / haoswâyf /
خانم معلّم / khânome moallem / **mistress** / mistris /
خانه / khâne / **home** / hom /
خانه / khâne / **house** / haos /
خانواده / khânevâde / **family** / famili /
خاور / khâvar / **east** / iist /
خبر / khâbâr / **news** / nyooz /
خبرنگار / khabarnegâr / **correspondent** / kârispândent /
خبرنگار / khabarnegâr / **reporter** / riporter /
خجالت / khejâlat / **shame** / sheym /
خجالتی / khejâlati / **shy** / shây /
خدا / khoda / **God** / gâd /
خدا حافظ / khodâhâfez / **bye-bye** / bâybây /
خدمت / khedmat / **service** / servis /
خدمتکار / khedmatkâr / **servant** / servent /
خدمه / khadame / **crew** / kroo /
خراب کردن / kharâb kardan / **to destroy** / to distory /

خرابی / kharâbi / **ruin** / roo-in /

خرابی / kharâbi / **breakdown** / breykdaon /

خرابی / kharâbi / **destruction** / distrâkshen /

خرج کردن / kharj kardan / **to spend** / to spend /

خردمند / kheradmand / **wise** / wâyz /

خرس / khers / **bear** / ber /

خرگوش / khargush / **rabbit** / rabit /

خرناس / khornâs / **snore** / sner /

خروج / khuruj / **exit** / eksit /

خروس / khurus / **cock** / kâk /

خرید / kharid / **purchase** / perchis /

خریدار / kharidâr / **buyer** / bâyer /

خریدن / kharidan / **to buy** / to bây /

خزنده / khazande / **reptile** / reptâyl /

خزیدن / khazidan / **creep** / kriip /

خسارت / khesârat / **damage** / damij /

خستگی / khastegi / **fatigue** / fatiig /

خسته / khaste / **bored** / bord /

خسته / khaste / **tired** / tâyerd /

خسته / khaste / **weary** / wiyeri /

خسته کردن / khaste kardan / **bore** / bor /

خسته کننده / khaste konande / **boring** / boring /

خسته کننده / khaste konande / **tiring** / tâyering /

خشایارشا / khashâyârshâ / **Xerxes** / zeksiiz /

خشك / khoshk / **dry** / drây /

خشم / khashm / **anger** / anger /

خشم / khashm / **rage** / reyj /

خشمگین / khashmgin / **angry** / angri /

خشن / khashen / **violent** / vâyolent /

خشنودی / khoshnudi / **satisfaction** / satisfakshen /

خشونت / khushunat / **violence** / vâyolens /

خصمانه / khasmâne / **hostile** / hâstâyl /

خط / khat / **line** / lâyn /

خط تیره / khatte tire / **dash** / dash /

خط لوله / khatte lule / **pipeline** / pâyp-lâyn /

خط هوایی / khatte havâii / **airway** / erwey /

خطر / khatar / **danger** / deynjer /

خطر / khatar / **risk** / risk /

خطرناك / khatarnâk / **dangerous** / deynjeres /

خلأ / khalaa / **vaccuum** / vakyuem /

خلاصه / kholâse / **digest** / dâyjest /

خلافت / khalâfate / **contrary** / kântreri /

خلاق / khallâgh / **creative** / kriyeytiv /

خلاق / khallâgh / **inventive** / inventiv /

خلبان / khalabân / **pilot** / pâylet /

خُلق / kholgh / **temper** / temper /

81

خلوص / khulus / **purity** / pyuriti /

خليج / khalij / **bay** / bey /

خم كردن / kham kardan / **bend** / bend /

خمير / khamir / **paste** / peyst /

خمير دندان / khamir dandân / **toothpaste** / toothpeyst /

خنک / khonak / **dumb** / dâm /

خنده / khande / **grin** / grin /

خنده / khande / **laughter** / lâfter /

خنده دار / khandedâr / **comic** / kâmik /

خنده دار / khandedâr / **funny** / fâni /

خنده دار / khandedâr / **ridiculous** / ridikyules /

خنديدن / khandidan / **to laugh** / to lâf /

خنک / khonak / **cool** / kool /

خواب / khâb / **sleep** / sliip /

خواب آلود / khâbâlud / **sleepy** / sliipi /

خوابيده / khâbide / **asleep** / esliip /

خواستن / khâstan / **to intend** / to intend /

خواستن / khâstan / **to like** / to lâyk /

خواستن / khâstan / **to pray** / to prey /

خواستن / khâstan / **to require** / to rikwâyr /

خواستن / khâstan / **to want** / to wânt /

خواندن / khândan / **to read** / to riid /

خواندن / khândan / **reading** / riiding /

خواندن / khândan / **to sing** / to sing /
خواننده / khânande / **reader** / riider /
خواننده / khânande / **singer** / singer /
خواهر / khâhar / **sister** / sister /
خواهش / khâhesh / **request** / rikwest /
خوب / khub / **fine** / fâyn /
خوب / khub / **good** / gud /
خوب / khub / **grand** / grand /
خوب / khub / **nice** / nâys /
خوب / khub / **well** / wel /
خود / khod / **oneself** / wânselif /
خود / khod / **own** / on /
خود / khod / **self** / self /
خودت را / khodat râ / **yourself** / yorself /
خودتان را / khodetân râ / **yourselves** / yorselvz /
خودخواه / khodkhâh / **selfish** / selfish /
خودداری / khoddari / **refusal** / rifyoozâz /
خودداری کردن / khoddâri kardan / **to avoid** / to evoyd /
خودش را / khodoshrâ / **himself** / himself /
خودش را / khodashrâ / **itself** / itself /
خودشان را / khodeshân râ / **themselves** / dhemselvz /
خودشرا / khodashrâ / **herself** / herself /
خودکار / khodkâr / **automatic** / otomatik /

خودم / **myself** / mâyself /

خودمانرا / **ourselves** / khodemânrâ / aorselvz /

خودمختاری / **autonomy** / khodmokhtâri / otânemi /

خوردن / **to eat** / khordan / to iit /

خوردن به / **bump** / khordan be / bâmp /

خورشید / **sun** / khorshid / sân /

خورشیدی / **solar** / khorshidi / solâr /

خوش / **happy** / khosh / hapi /

خوش آمد / **welcome** / khoshâmad / welkâm /

خوشایند / **pleasing** / khoshâyand / pliizing /

خوشبخت / **lucky** / khoshbakht / lâky /

خوشبختانه / **fortunately** / khoshbakhtâne / forchunitli /

خوشبو / **aromatic** / khoshbu / arematic /

خوشبینانه / **optimistic** / khoshbinâne / âptimistik /

خوشبینی / **optimisim** / khoshbini / âptimizem /

خوشحال / **glad** / khoshhâl / glad /

خوشحال بودن / **cheer up** / khoshhal budan / chiyer âp /

خوشگل / **bonny** / khoshgel / bâni /

خوشمزه / **delicious** / khoshmaze / dilishes /

خوشی / **happiness** / khoshi / hapinis /

خوشی / **pleasure** / khoshi / plezher /

خوك / **pig** / khuk / pig /

خون آمدن / **to bleed** / khun âmadan / to bliid /

خونین / khunin / **bloody** / blâdi /
خیابان / khiyâbân / **avenue** / avenyoo /
خیابان / khiyâbân / **street** / striit /
خیار / khiyar / **cucumber** / kyookâmber /
خیاط / khayyat / **tailor** / teyler /
خیالی / khiyâli / **imaginary** / imajineri /
خیانت / khiyânat / **treason** / triizen /
خیره کننده / khire konande / **breathtaking** / bretheyking /
خیس / khis / **wet** / wet /
خیلی / kheyli / **very** / veri /
خیلی خیلی / kheyli kheyli / **awfully** / ofuli /

داد / dâd / **shout** / shât /
دادگاه / dâdgâh / **court** / kort /
دادن / dâdan / **give** / giv /
دارایی / dârâyi / **property** / prâperti /
دارو / dâru / **drug** / drâg /
دارو / dâru / **medicine** / medsin /
داروخانه / dârukhâne / **drugstore** / drâgstor /
داروخانه / dârukhâne / **pharmacy** / fâmesi /
داروساز / dârusâz / **pharmacist** / fârmâsist /
دارچین / dârchin / **cinnamon** / sinemen /
داستان / dâstân / **fiction** / fikshen /
داستان / dâstan / **narrative** / narativ /
داستان / dâstân / **story** / stori /
داستان بلند / dâstâne boland / **novel** / nâvel /
داستان علمی‌تخیلی / dâstane elmitakhayyali /
sci-fi / sâyfây /
داشتن / dâshtan / **to have** / to hav /
داغ / dâgh / **hot** / hât /
دام / dâm / **trap** / trap /

دامن / dâman / **skirt** / skert /
دانستن / dânestan / **know** / no /
دانش / dânesh / **knowledge** / nâlij /
دانش آموز / dâneshâmuz / **student** / student /
دانشگاه / dâneshgâh / **university** / yooniversiti /
دانشمند / dâneshman / **scientist** / sâyentist /
دانشکده / dâneshkade / **college** / kalij /
دانه / dâne / **berry** / beri /
دانه / dâne / **seed** / siid /
داوطلب / dâvtalab / **volunteer** / vâlentiyer /
دایره / dâyere / **circle** / serkel /
دایی / dâyi / **uncle** / ânkel /
دبستان / dabestân / **primary school** / perâimaryskool /
دختر / dokhtar / **daughter** / doter /
دختر / dokhtar / **girl** / gerl /
در / dar / **at** / at /
در / dar / **door** / dor /
در / dar / **doorway** / dorwey /
در / dar / **in** / in /
در / dar / **within** / widhin /
دراز / derâz / **length** / length /
دراز / derâz / **long** / lâng /
دراز کشیدن / derâz keshidan / **to lie** / to lay /

دراصل / darasl / **originally** / orijinâli /

درام / drâm / **drama** / drâme /

درآمد / darâmad / **income** / inkâm /

درآمد داشتن / darâmed dâshtan / **to earn** / to ern /

دراين فاصله / darin fâsele / **meanwhile** / miinwâyl /

دراينجا / darinjâ / **here** / hiyer /

درجه / daraje / **degree** / digrii /

درجه / daraje / **grade** / greyd /

درحدودِ / darhudude / **about** / ebaot /

درخانه / dar khâne / **in** / in /

درخت / derakht / **tree** / trii /

درخشان / drakhshân / **brilliant** / brilyent /

درخشش / drakhshesh / **flash** / flash /

درخشيدن / derakhshidan / **to shine** / to shâyn /

درخواست / darkhâsh / **application** / aplikeyshen /

درخواست / darkhâst / **demand** / dimând /

درخواست کردن / darkhâst kardan / **to claim** / to kleym /

درد / dard / **discomfort** / diskâmfort /

درد / dard / **pain** / peyn /

درد داشتن / dard dâshtan / **to suffer** / to sâfer /

درد کردن / dard kardan / **to ache** / to eyk /

درد کردن / dard kardan / **to hurt** / to hert /

دردسترس / dardastras / **available** / eveylebel /

دردناك / **painful** / peynful /

درّه / **valley** / darre / vali /

درست / **correct** / dorost / kârekt /

درست / **honest** / dorost / ânist /

درست / **just** / dorost / jâst /

درست / **precisely** / dorost / prisâysli /

درست / **right** / dorost / râyt /

درشکه / **carriage** / doroshke / karij /

درصد / **percent** / darsad / persent /

درصد / **percentage** / darsad / persentij /

درطول / **during** / dartule / dyuring /

درعوض / **instead** / daravaz / insted /

درکنار / **beside** / darkenâre / bisâyd /

درمان / **remedy** / darmân / remidi /

درمان / **therapy** / darmân / terepi /

درمانگاه / **clinic** / darmângâh / klinik /

درمانی / **therapeutic** / darmâni / terepyutik /

درنظر گرفتن / **to consider** / darnazar gereftan /
to kânsider /

درنگ زدگی / **jet lag** / derang zadegi / zhet lag /

درهرصورت / **anyhow** / darharsurat / enihao /

دروازه / **gate** / darvâze / geyt /

درواقع / **actually** / darvâghe / akchuwâlii /

دروغ گفتن / durugh goftan / **to lie** / to lây /

دروغی / durughi / **false** / fols /

درون / darun / **inside** / insâyd /

درونی / daruni / **internal** / internl /

دریا / daryâ / **sea** / sii /

دریاچه / daryâche / **lake** / leyk /

دریازده / daryâzade / **seasick** / siisik /

دریاسالار / daryâsâlâr / **admiral** / admiral /

دریافت / daryâft / **receipt** / risiit /

دریافت کردن / daryâft kardan / **to receive** / to risiiv /

درگیر شدن / dargir shodan / **to clash** / to klash /

درک / dark / **understanding** / ânderstanding /

دزد / dozd / **burglar** / bergler /

دزد / dozd / **robber** / râber /

دزد / dozd / **thief** / thiif /

دزد مسلح / dozde mosallah / **bandit** / bandit /

دزدیدن / dozdidan / **to steal** / to stiil /

دژ / dezh / **fort** / fort /

دسامبر / desâmr / **December** / disember /

دست / dast / **arm** / ârm /

دست / dast / **hand** / hand /

دست لباس / dastlebâs / **suit** / soot /

دستبرد زدن / dastbord zadan / **to rob** / to râb /

دستکش / **glove** / glâv /
دستگاه / **apparatus** / dastgâh / apareytes /
دستگیر کردن / **to arrest** / dastgir kardan / to erest /
دستگیره / **knob** / dastgire / nâb /
دستمال / **handkerchief** / dastmâl / hangkerchif /
دستمزد / **fee** / dastmozd / fii /
دسته / **handle** / daste / handel /
دسته / **pile** / daste / pâyl /
دستور / **command** / dastur / kâmand /
دستور دادن / **to order** / dastur dâdan / to order /
دستورزبان / **grammar** / dasturezabân / gramer /
دستوری / **grammatical** / dasturi / gramatikâl /
دستیار / **assistant** / dastyâr / esistent /
دشمن / **adversary** / doshman / adverserii /
دشمن / **enemy** / doshman / enemii /
دشمنی / **antagonism** / doshmani / antagonizem /
دعا / **prayer** / doa / preyer /
دعوا / **quarrel** / daavâ / kwârel /
دعوا کردن / **to fight** / daavâ kardan / to fâyt /
دعوت / **invitation** / daavat / inviteyshen /
دعوت کردن / **to invite** / daavat kardan / to invâyt /
دفاع / **defense** / defâ / difens /
دفاع / **defend** / defââ / difend /

دفتر / daftar / **office** / âfis /

دفتر راهنما / daftare râhnemâ / **directory** / directeri /

دفتر یادداشت / daftare yâddâsht / **notebook** / notbuk /

دفن کردن / dafn kardan / **to bury** / to berii /

دقت / deghghat / **concentration** / kânsentreyshen /

دقت / deghghat / **precision** / prisizhen /

دقیق / daghigh / **exact** / ikzakt /

دقیق / daghigh / **precise** / prisâys /

دقیقاً / daghighan / **exactly** / igzaktlii /

دقیقه / daghighe / **minute** / minit /

دکتر / doktor / **doctor** / dâkter /

دکمه / dokme / **button** / bâten /

دکه / dakke / **kiosk** / kiâsk /

دلار / dolâr / **dollar** / dâler /

دلال / dallâl / **broker** / broker /

دلپذیر / delpazir / **pleasant** / plezent /

دلخواه / delkhâh / **ideal** / âydiyel /

دلربا / delrobâ / **glamorous** / glameres /

دلسرد کردن / delsard kardan / **to discourage** /
to diskârij /

دلسردی / delsardi / **disappointment** / disapoyntment /

دُلفین / dolfin / **dolphin** / dâlfin /

دلقک / dalghak / **zany** / zeyni /

92

دلیر / **bold** / dalir /
دلیل / **proof** / dalil /
دلیل / **reason** / riizen /
دُم / **tail** / dom / teyl /
دما / **temperature** / temprecher /
دماغه / **cape** / keyp /
دنبال (کسی) دویدن / donbâle (kasi) dovidan /
to chase / to cheys /
دنبال کردن / **to follow** / donbâl kardan / to fâlo /
دندان / **tooth** / dandân / tooth /
دندان درد / **toothache** / dandân dard / tootheyk /
دندانپزشك / **dentist** / dandânpezeshk / dentist /
دنده / **gear** / dande / giyer /
دنیا / **world** / donya / werld /
ده / **ten** / dah / ten /
ده / **village** / deh / vilij /
دهان / **mouth** / dahân / maoth /
دو / **run** / do / rân /
دو / **two** / do / too /
دوازده / **twelve** / davâzdah / twelv /
دوازدهم / **twelfth** / davâzdahom / twelfth /
دوام / **endurance** / davâm / indurans /
دوبار / **twice** / dobâr / twâys /

دوباره / dobâre / **again** / egen /

دوبرابر / dobarâbar / **double** / dâbel /

دوجین / dujin / **dozen** / dâzen /

دوچرخه / docharkhe / **bicycle** / bâysikel /

دوچرخه / docharkhe / **bike** / bâyk /

دوچرخه / docharkhe / **cycle** / sâykel /

دوچرخه سوار / docharkhesavâr / **biker** / bâyker /

دوختن / dukhtan / **to sew** / to so /

دود / dud / **smoke** / smok /

دودکش / dudkesh / **chimney** / chimny /

دور / dur / **away** / ewey /

دور / dur / **distant** / distant /

دور / dur / **far** / fâr /

دور / dur / **off** / âf /

دوران باستان / dorâne bâstan / **antiquity** / antikwiti /

دوربین / durbin / **camera** / kamerâ /

دورتر / durtar / **farther** / fârdher /

دورتر / durtar / **further** / ferdher /

دورترین / durtarin / **furthest** / ferdhist /

دوردست / durdast / **far away** / fârewey /

دوره / dore / **period** / piriyed /

دوره / dore / **term** / term /

دوره‌ٔ نو جوانی / doreye nojavâni / **teens** / tiinz /

دورهای / periodical / piriyâdikâl /

دوزبانه / bilingual / bâylinguel /

دوزیست / amphibian / amfibien /

دوست / friend / frend /

دوست پسر / boyfriend / boyfrend /

دوست داشتن / to love / to lâv /

دوست داشتنی / lovable / lâvebel /

دوستانه / friendly / frendli /

دوست نداشتن / to dislike / to dislâyk /

دوستی / friendship / frendship /

دوش / shower / shao-er /

دوشنبه / Monday / mândi /

دوشیزه / Miss / mis /

دوقلو / twin / twin /

دولت / government / gâverment /

دوم / second / seekend /

دونده / runner / râner /

دوهفته / fortnight / fornâyt /

دوک / duke / dyook /

دیپلم / diploma / diplomâ /

دید / view / vyoo /

دیدن / to see / to sii /

دیدن / to visit / to vizit /

ديده ور / didevar / **scout** / skaot /

ديروز / diruz / **yesterday** / yesterdi /

ديروقت / dirvaght / **late** / leyt /

ديسكو / disko / **disco** / disko /

ديگ / dig / **boiler** / boiler /

ديگر / digar / **another** / enâdher /

ديگر / digar / **anymore** / enimor /

ديگر / digar / **else** / els /

ديگر / digar / **other** / âdher /

دين / din / **religion** / rilijen /

ديندار / dindâr / **devout** / divot /

دينى / dini / **religious** / rilijes /

ديوار / divâr / **wall** / wol /

ديوانه / divâne / **crazy** / kreyzi /

ديوانه / divâne / **mad** / mad /

ديكتاتور / diktâtor / **dictator** / dikteyter /

ديكته گفتن / dikte goftan / **to dictate** / to dikteyt /

دكل / dakal / **mast** / mâst /

ذاتاً / zâtan / **naturally** / nachrâli /

ذخیره / zakhire / **store** / stor /

ذخیره کردن / zakhire kardan / **to reserve** / to rizerv /

ذهن / zehn / **mind** / mâynd /

ذهنی / zehni / **mental** / mentâl /

ذکر کردن / zekr kardan / **to mention** / to menshen /

ر

رؤیا / royâ / **dream** / driim /

رابطه / râbete / **relationship** / rileyshenship /

راحت / râhat / **comfortable** / kâmftebel /

راحتی / râhati / **comfortably** / kâmftebli /

راحتی / râhati / **convenience** / kânviiniyens /

رادار / râdâr / **radar** / reydâr /

رادیاتور / râdiyâtor / **radiator** / reydiyeyter /

رادیو / râdio / **radio** / reydiyo /

راز / râz / **mystery** / mistri /

راز / râz / **secret** / siikrit /

راست / râst / **straight** / streyt /

راست / râst / **true** / troo /

راستی / râsti / **indeed** / indiid /

راضی کردن / râzi kardan / **to please** / to pliiz /

راضی / râzi / **content** / kântent /

راغب / râgheb / **willing** / wiling /

راگبی / râgbi / **rugby** / râgbi /

رام / râm / **tame** / teym /

رانندگی / rânandegi / **drive** / drâyv /

98

راننده اتوبوس / **bus driver** / rânandeye otobus /
bâs drâyver /

راه / **lane** / râh / leyn /

راه / **path** / râh / path /

راه / **route** / râh / root /

راه / **way** / râh / wey /

راه آهن / **railway** / râhâhan / reylwey /

راه حل / **solution** / râhehal / solooshen /

راهرو / **passageway** / rahro / pasijwey /

راهنما / **guide** / râhnamâ / gâyd /

راهنمایی / **lead** / râhnamâyi / liid /

رای دادن / **to poll** / ray dâdan / to pol /

رایانه / **computer** / râyâne / kâmpyooter /

رایج / **standard** / rayej / standerd /

راکت / **racket** / râket / rakit /

رای / **vote** / ray / vot /

ربودن / **hijack** / rebudan / hâyjak /

رجحان / **preference** / rejhân / preferens /

رحم / **pity** / rahm / piti /

رخت کن / **cloakroom** / rakht kan / klokrum /

رد / **track** / rad / trak /

رد / **trail** / rad / treyl /

رد شدن / **to fail** / radshodan / to feyl /

رد کردن / rad kardan / **to reject** / to rijekt /

پرداخت / pardâkht / **payment** / peyment /

ردیف / radif / **rank** / rank /

ردیف / radif / **row** / ro /

رزم آرایی / razm ârâyi / **strategy** / stratiji /

رزمناو / razmnâv / **warship** / worship /

رساندن / resândan / **deliver** / diliver /

رسانه های گروهی / rasânehâye guruhi / **mass media** /
masmiidiya /

رستوران / resturân / **restaurant** / restrânt /

رسم / rasm / **custom** / kâstem /

رسم کردن / rasm kardan / **draw** / dro /

رسمی / rasmi / **formal** / formâl /

رسمی / rasmi / **official** / âfishâl /

رسیدن / residan / **arrival** / erâyvâl /

رسیدن / residan / **to arrive** / to erâyv /

رسیدن / residan / **to reach** / to riich /

رسیده / reside / **ripe** / râyp /

رشته / reshte / **range** / reynj /

رشد / roshd / **development** / divelopment /

رشد کردن / roshd kardan / **to develop** / to divelop /

رشد کردن / roshd kardan / **to grow** / to gro /

رضایت / rezâyat / **approval** / aproovâl /

رضایت بخش / rezâyet bakhsh / **satisfactory** /
satisfakteri /

رعد / raad / **thunder** / thânder /

رفاه / refâh / **prosperity** / prâsperiti /

رفتار / raftâr / **behavior** / biheyviyer /

رفتار کردن / raftâr kardan / **to behave** / to biheyv /

رفتن / raftan / **to go** / to go /

رفتن / raftan / **to leave** / to liiv /

رفوکردن / refu kardan / **to darn** / to dân /

رفیق / rafigh / **pal** / pal /

رقابت / reghâbat / **competition** / kâmpitishen /

رقابت / reghâbat / **contest** / kântest /

رقابت کردن / reghâbat kardan / **to compete** / to kâmpiit /

رقابتی / reghâbati / **competitive** / kâmpetitiv /

رقت خون / reghghate khun / **hemophilia** / himefilie /

رقص / raghs / **dance** / dans /

رقم / ragham / **figure** / figer /

رقیب / raghib / **rival** / râyvâl /

رکود / rekud / **recession** / riseshen /

رگ / rag / **vein** / veyn /

رمز شخصی / ramze shakhsi / **PIN** / pin /

رنگ / rang / **color** / kâler /

رنگ / rang / **paint** / peynt /

101

رنگ پریده / rang paride / **pale** / peyl /

رنگ کردن / rang kardan / **to dye** / to dây /

رنگارنگ / rangârang / **multicolored** / mâltikâlerd /

رنگی / rangi / **colored** / kâlerd /

رهبر / rahbar / **conductor** / kândâkter /

رهبر / rahbar / **leader** / liider /

روادید / ruvadid / **visa** / viizâ /

روان شناسی / ravânshenâsi / **psychology** / sâykâleji /

روباز / rubâz / **exposed** / egzpozed /

روباه / rubâh / **fox** / fâks /

روح / ruh / **ghost** / gost /

روح / ruh / **soul** / sol /

روح / ruh / **spirit** / spirit /

روحانی / ruhâni / **clergyman** / klejimen /

روحانیون / ruhâniyyun / **clergy** / kleji /

روحی / ruhi / **spiritual** / sprichuwâl /

رود / rud / **river** / river /

روز / ruz / **day** / dey /

روز / ruz / **daylight** / deylâyt /

روز / ruz / **weekday** / wiikdey /

روزانه / ruzâne / **daily** / deyli /

روزتولد / ruzetavallod / **birthday** / berth-dey /

روزنامه / ruznâme / **newspaper** / nyoozpeyper /

روزنامه نگار / ruzhâme negâr / **journalist** / jernâlist /

روستایی / rustâii / **countryman** / kântriman /

روستایی / rustâyi / **villager** / vilijer /

روسری / rusari / **scarf** / skârf /

روش / ravesh / **fashion** / fashen /

روش / ravesh / **method** / methed /

روشن / roshan / **bright** / brâyt /

روشن / roshan / **clearly** / kliyerli /

روشن / roshan / **vivid** / vivid /

روشن ساختن / roshan sâkhtan / **to illustrate** / to ilâstreyt /

روشن کردن / roshan sahodan / **to light** / to lâyt /

روشنفکر / roshanfekr / **broad-minded** / brod-mâyndid /

روغن / roghan / **grease** / griis /

روغن / roghan / **oil** / oyl /

روی / ruye / **on** / ân /

روی / roy / **zinc** / zink /

روی / ruye / **upon** / âpân /

رویداد / ruydâd / **happening** / hapening /

رویداد جالب / ruydâde jâleb / **highlight** / hâylâyt /

ریاضیات / riyâziyât / **mathematics** / mathimatiks /

ریتم / ritm / **rhythm** / ridhem /

ریختن / rikhtan / **pour** / por /

ریش / **beard** / rish / biyerd /

ریش زدن / **to shave** / rish zadan / to sheyv /

ریشه / **root** / rishe / rut /

ریشه کن کردن / **to exterminate** / rishekan kardan /
to ikstermineyt /

ریل / **rail** / reyl / reyl /

رییس / **chief** / raais / chiif /

رییس / **principal** / rais / prinsipâl /

رییس / **boss** / rais / bâs /

رییس جمهور / **president** / raisjemhur / prezident /

ز

زائر / zâeer / **pilgrim** / pilgrim /
زانو / zânu / **knee** / nii /
زانو زدن / zânu zadan / **to kneel** / to niil /
زاویه / zâviye / **angle** / angel /
زبان / zabân / **language** / langwij /
زبان / zabân / **tongue** / tâng /
زبان لاتین / zabâne lâtin / **Latin** / latin /
زبانی / zabâni / **linguistic** / lingwistik /
زحمت / zahmat / **toil** / toyl /
زحمت / zahmat / **trouble** / trâbel /
زخم / zakhm / **wound** / woond /
زخمی / zakhmi / **wounded** / woondid /
زدن / zadan / **to hit** / to hit /
زدن / zadan / **to knock** / to nâk /
زدن / zadan / **to strike** / to strâyk /
زرتشت / zartosht / **Zoroaster** / zoroaster /
زرتشتی / zartoshti / **Zoroastrian** / zoroastrien /
زرد / zard / **yellow** / yelo /
زردآلو / zardâlu / **apricot** / eyprikât /
زرنگ / zerang / **smart** / smârt /

زشت / **hateful** / heytful /

زشت / **ugly** / âgli /

زغال / **charcoal** / zoghâl / chârkol /

زغال سنگ / **coal** / zoghâlesang / kol /

زلزله / **earthquake** / zelzele / ertkveyk /

زمان / **tense** / zamân / tens /

زمان / **time** / zamân / tâym /

زمانی / **sometimes** / zamâni / sâmtâymz /

زمستان / **winter** / zemestân / winter /

زمین / **earth** / zamin / erth /

زمین / **ground** / zamin / graond /

زمین / **land** / zamin / land /

زن / **woman** / zan / wuman /

زنانه / **effeminate** / zanâne / ifeminit /

زنانه / **female** / zanâne / feminin /

زنانه / **feminine** / zanâne / feminin /

زنبورعسل / **bee** / zanbureasal / bii /

زنجیر / **chain** / zanjir / cheyn /

زندان / **jail** / zendân / jeyl /

زندان / **prison** / zendân / prizen /

زندگی / **living** / zendegi / living /

زندگی نامه شخصی / zendeginâmeye shâkhsi /
autobiography / otobâyâgrafi /

زنده / zende / **alive** / elâyv /
زنده / zende / **lively** / lâyvli /
زنده بودن / zende budan / **live** / liv /
زنگ / zang / **bell** / bel /
زود / zud / **early** / erli /
زور / zur / **force** / fors /
زوزه / zuze / **howl** / haol /
زیاد / ziyâd / **frequently** / friikwentli /
زیاد / ziyâd / **lot** / lât /
زیاد / ziyâd / **many** / meni /
زیاد / ziyâd / **much** / mâch /
زیاد / ziyâd / **numerous** / nyoomeres /
زیاد / ziyad / **so** / so /
زیاد کار کردن / ziyâd kâr kardan / **to overwork** /
to overwerk /
زیبا / zibâ / **beautiful** / byootiful /
زیبا / zibâ / **lovely** / lâvli /
زیبایی / zibâyi / **beauty** / byooti /
زیبایی / zibâyi / **charm** / chârm /
زیبایی / zibâii / **grace** / greys /
زیر / zir / **below** / bilo /
زیر / zir / **under** / ânder /
زیر زمینی / zirzamini / **underground** / ândergraound /

زیرآبی / **underwater** / zirâbi / ânderwoter /

زیراکس / **xerox** / zirâks / zierâks /

زیرزمین / **basement** / zirzamin / beysment /

زیرزمین / **cellar** / zirzamin / celâr /

زیرسیگاری / **ashtray** / zirsigâri / ashtrey /

زیست شناسی / **biology** / zistshenâsi / bâyâlâji /

ژ

ژاپن zhâpon / **Japan** / japan /

ژاپنی zhâponi / **Japanese** / japaniiz /

ژاکت zhâket / **sweater** / sweter /

ژامبون zhâmbon / **bacon** / beyken /

ژامبون zhâmbon / **ham** / ham /

ژانویه zhânviye / **January** / janyuweri /

ژاکت zhâket / **cardigan** / kârdigen /

ژست zhest / **gesture** / jescher /

ژوئن zhoan / **June** / joon /

ژوئیه zhuiye / **July** / joolây /

سابقه / sâbeghe / **background** / bakgraond /

سابقه / sâbeghe / **precedent** / president /

ساحل / sâhel / **coast** / kost /

ساحل / sâhel / **shore** / shor /

ساحل / sâhel / **bank** / bank /

ساخت / sâkht / **make** / meyk /

ساختمان / sâkhtemân / **block** / blâk /

ساختمان / sâkhtemân / **building** / bilding /

ساختن / sâkhtan / **to build** / to bild /

ساختن / sâkhtan / **to construct** / to kânstrâk /

ساختن / sâkhtan / **to make** / to meyk /

ساده / sâde / **simple** / simpel /

ساده لوح / sâde loh / **naïve** / nây-iiv /

سازگار کردن / sâzegâr kardan / **to adapt** / to edapt /

سازمان / sâzemân / **organization** / organâyzeyshen /

سازمان دادن / sâzemân dâdan / **to organize** /
to organâyz /

سازمان ملل متحد / sâzemâne melale mottahed /
United Nations / yunâyted neyshenz /

ساعت / sâat / **clock** / klâk /

ساعت / sâat / **hour** / aor /
ساعت / sâat / **o' clock** / oklâk /
ساعت / sâat / **watch** / wâch /
ساكت / sâket / **quite** / kwâyet /
ساكت / sâket / **silent** / sâylent /
ساكن / sâkene / **inhabitant** / inhabitent /
سال / sâl / **year** / yer /
سالاد / sâlâd / **salad** / salad /
سالگرد / sâlgard / **anniversary** / aniverseri /
سالم / sâlem / **healthy** / helthi /
سالم / sâlem / **safe** / seyf /
سالم / sâlem / **safely** / seifli /
سالن / sâlon / **hall** / hol /
سالن / sâlon / **saloon** / saloon /
سالن (استراحت) / sâlone esterâhat / **lounge** / laonj /
سالیانه / sâliyâne / **annual** / anyuel /
سانتیمتر / sântimetr / **centimeter** / sentimeter /
سایه / sâye / **shade** / sheyd /
ساكن شدن / sâken shodan / **to settle** / to setel /
سبد / sabad / **basket** / baskit /
سبز / sabz / **green** / griin /
سبك / sabok / **light** / lâyt /
سبیل / sibil / **moustache** / mâstash /

سپاسگزار / sepâsgozâr / **grateful** / greytful /

سپتامبر / septâmr / **September** / September /

ستاره / stâre / **star** / stâr /

ستاره دنباله دار / setâreye donbâledâr / **comet** / kâmit /

ستون / sutun / **pillar** / piler /

سخاوتمند / sekhâvatmand / **generous** / jeneres /

سخت / sakht / **hard** / hârd /

سخت / sakht / **seriously** / siriyesli /

سختگیر / sakhtgir / **strict** / strikt /

سر / sar / **head** / hed /

سرانجام / saranjâm / **eventually** / ivenchuwâli /

سرب / sorb / **lead** / led /

سرباز / sarbâz / **soldier** / soljer /

سرتاسر / sartâsar / **along** / elâng /

سرخ کردن / sorkh kardan / **fried** / frâyd /

سرد / sard / **cold** / kold /

سردبیر / sardabir / **editor** / editer /

سردرد / sardard / **headache** / hedeyk /

سردرگمی / sardargomi / **confusion** / kânfyoozhen /

سرزنش کردن / sarzanesh kardan / **to reproach** / to riproch /

سرزنش کردن / sarzanesh kardan / **to blame** / to bleym /

سرطان / saratân / **cancer** / kanser /

سرعت / soraat / **speed** / spiid /

سرعت بخشیدن / soraat bakhshidan / **to accelerate** /
to akselereyt /

سرفراز / sarfarâz / **proud** / praod /

سرفه / sorfe / **cough** / kâf /

سرکوب کردن / sarkub kardan / **to suppress** / to sâpres /

سرگرم کردن / sargam kardan / **to amuse** / to amyooz /

سرگرمی / sargarmi / **pastime** / pastâym /

سرگرمی / sargarmi / **amusement** / amyoozment /

سرگرمی / sargarmi / **hobby** / hâbi /

سرما خوردگی / sarmâkhordegi / **cold** / kold /

سرمایه گذاری / sarmâye gozâri / **investment** /
investment /

سرمایه گذاری کردن / sarmâyegozâri kardan /
to invest / **to invest**

سرنخ / sarnakh / **clue** / kloo /

سرنوشت / sarnevesht / **destiny** / destini /

سرنیزه / sarneyze / **bayonet** / beyonit /

سرهنگ / sarhang / **colonel** / kernel /

سرود / surud / **anthem** / anthem /

سرود مزهبی / surude mazhabi / **hymn** / him /

سرود کریسمس / surude krismas / **carol** / karol /

سروصدا / sarosedâ / **noise** / noyz /

113

سری / series / seri / siriiz /

سرکوب / suppression / sarkub / sâpreshen /

سزاوار / worthy / sazâvâr / werdhi /

سزاوار بودن / deserve / sezâvâr budan / dizerv /

سُس گوجه فرنگی / ketchup / sose gojefarangi / kechâp /

سطح / level / sath / level /

سطح / surface / sath / serfis /

سطحی / superficial / sathi / sooperfishâl /

سطل (کاغذ باطله) / (satle (kaghaz bâtele /

wastepaper basket / weyst peyper baskit /

سعی کردن / to try / saay kardan / to trây /

سفارت / embassy / sefârat / embesi /

سفت / rigid / seft / rijid /

سفت / tough / seft / tâf /

سفر / journey / safar / jerni /

سفر / travel / safar / travel /

سفر تفریحی / outing / safare tafrihi / aoting /

سفر دریایی / voyage / safare daryâyi / voyij /

سفید / blank / sefid / blank /

سفید / white / sefid / wâyt /

سفیر کبیر / ambassador / safire kabir / ambaseder /

سقف / roof / saghf / roof /

سقوط / fall / seghut / fol /

114

سگو / sakku / **platform** / platform /

سکه / sekke / **coin** / koyn /

سکوت / sekut / **silence** / sâylens /

سگ / sag / **dog** / dâg /

سلاح / selâh / **gun** / gân /

سلاح / selâh / **weapon** / wepen /

سلام / salâm / **greeting** / griiting /

سلام / salâm / **hallo** / helo /

سلام / salâm / **hello** / helo /

سلام کردن / salâm kardan / **to greet** / to griit /

سلامت / salâmat / **health** / helth /

سلطنت / saltanat / **reign** / reyn /

سلطنتی / saltanati / **imperial** / impiriyâl /

سلطنتی / saltanati / **royal** / royâl /

سلطه / solte / **domination** / dâmineyshen /

سلف سرویس / self servis / **cafeteria** / kafitiriyâ /

سلف سرویس / self servis / **self-service** / self-servis /

سلمانی / salmâni / **barber** / bârber /

سلول / sellul / **cell** / sel /

سم / sam / **poison** / poyzen /

سمّی / sammi / **poisonous** / poyzenes /

سن / sen / **age** / eyj /

سنت گرا / sonnatgarâ / **conformist** / kânformist /

سنتی / sonnati / **traditional** / tradishenâl /

سنجاب / sanjâb / **squirrel** / skwirel /

سنجاق / sanjâgh / **pin** / pin /

سنجاق قفلی / sanjâghe ghofli / **safety pin** / seyfti pin /

سند / sanad / **document** / dâkyument /

سنگ / sang / **rock** / râk /

سنگ / sang / **stone** / ston /

سنگواره / sangvâre / **fossil** / fâsl /

سنگین / sangin / **heavy** / hevi /

سنگی / sangi / **stony** / stoni /

سنت / sonnat / **tradition** / tradishen /

سه / se / **three** / thrii /

سه شنبه / seshanbe / **Tuesday** / tyoozdi /

سهم / sahm / **share** / sher /

سو / su / **Sioux** / soo /

سوار / savâr / **aboard** / ebord /

سوار شدن / savâr shodan / **to board** / to bord /

سوار شدن / savâr shodan / **to ride** / to râyd /

سوارکاری / savârkâri / **riding** / râyding /

سوپ / sup / **soup** / soop /

سوت / sut / **whistle** / wisel /

سوخت / sukht / **fuel** / fyoo-el /

سوختن / sukhtan / **to blaze** / to bleyz /

سوختن sukhtan / **to burn** / to bern /

سود sud / **benefit** / benifit /

سود sud / **profit** / prâfit /

سودمند sudmand / **beneficial** / benifishl /

سوراخ surâkh / **hole** / hol /

سوراخ کردن surâkh kardan / **to pierce** / to piyers /

سوزن suzan / **needle** / nidl /

سوسک susk / **beetle** / bitl /

سوسیالیست sasiyalist / **socialist** / soshâlist /

سوسیس sosis / **sausage** / sâsij /

سوگواری sogvâri / **mourning** / morning /

سوم sevvom / **third** / therd /

سی si / **thirty** / therti /

سیاست siyâsat / **politics** / pâlitiks /

سیاسی siyâsi / **political** / pâlitikâl /

سیاه siyâh / **black** / blak /

سیاه پوست siyâhpust / **negro** / niigro /

سیاه پوستان siyah pustân / **Blacks** / blaks /

سیاهرگ siyâhrag / **vein** / vein /

سیب sib / **apple** / apel /

سیب زمینی sibzamini / **potato** / poteyto /

سیبر siber / **cyber** / sâyber /

سیر sir / **garlic** / gâlik /

سیرک / **circus** / sirk / serkes /

سیزده / **thirteen** / sizdah / thertiin /

سیزدهمین / **thirteenth** / sizdahomin / thertiinth /

سیگار / **cigarette** / sigâr / sigaret /

سیگار برگ / **cigar** / sigâre barg / sigâr /

سیلندر / **cylinder** / silinder / silinder /

سیلی زدن / **to slap** / sili zadan / to slap /

سیم / **wire** / sim / wâyer /

سینما / **cinema** / sinamâ / sinimâ /

سینما / **movies** / sinamâ / mooviz /

سینی / **tray** / sini / trey /

سیّاره / **planet** / sayyâre / planit /

سکونت / **occupation** / sekunat / âkyupeyshen /

ش

شاخه / shâkhe / **branch** / brânch /

شاد / shâd / **cheerful** / chiyerful /

شاد / shâd / **delighted** / dilâytid /

شاد / shâd / **gay** / gey /

شاد / shâd / **merry** / meri /

شادمان / shâdemân / **joyous** / joyes /

شادی / shâdi / **joy** / joy /

شاعر / shâeer / **poet** / po-it /

شاگرد / shâgerd / **pupil** / pyoopil /

شام / shâm / **dinner** / diner /

شام / shâm / **supper** / sâper /

شام خوردن / shâm khordan / **to dine** / to dâyn /

شامل / shâmel / **consist** / kânsist /

شامل / shâmel / **inclusive** / inkloosiv /

شامل بودن / shâmel budan / **to comprise** / to kemprâyz /

شامل بودن / shâmel budan / **to include** / to inklood /

شانزده / shânzdah / **sixteen** / sikstiin /

شانزدهمی / shânzdahomi / **sixteenth** / sikstiinth /

شانس / shâns / **change** / cheynj /

شانس / shâns / **luck** / lâk /
شانه / shâne / **comb** / kom /
شانه / shâne / **shoulder** / sholder /
شاهپور / shahpur / **prince** / prins /
شاهد / shâhed / **witness** / witnis /
شاهراه / shâhrâh / **highway** / hâywey /
شاید / shâyad / **may** / mey /
شاید / shâyad / **maybe** / meybi /
شاید / shâyad / **perhaps** / perhaps /
شاید / shâyad / **possibly** / pâsibli /
شایعه / shâyee / **rumor** / roomer /
شب / shab / **night** / nâyt /
شباهت / shebâhat / **resemblance** / rizemblens /
شبیه / shabih / **alike** / elâyk /
شبیه / shabih / **like** / lâyk /
شبیه بودن / shabih budan / **to resemble** / to rizembel /
شتاب / shetâb / **acceleration** / akselereyshen /
شتاب / shetâb / **haste** / heyst /
شتر / shotor / **camel** / kaml /
شجاع / shojâ / **brave** / breyv /
شجاعت / shojâat / **courage** / kârij /
شخص / shakhs / **person** / persen /
شخصاً / shakhsan / **personally** / personâli /

/ persenâl / **personal** / shakhsi / شخصى

/ prâyvit / **private** / shakhsi / شخصى

/ karecter / **character** / shakhsiyyat / شخصيت

/ persenaliti / **personality** / shakshsiyyat / شخصيت

/ to bikâm / **to become** / shodan / شدن

/ intens / **intense** / shadid / شديد

/ tâytanik / **titanic** / shadid / شديد

/ siviyerli / **severely** / shahidan / شديداً

/ teribli / **terribly** / shadidan / شديداً

/ wâyn / **wine** / sharâb / شراب

/ serkâm-stansiz / **circumstances** / sharâyet / شرايط

/ termz / **terms** / sharâyet / شرايط

/ diskripshn / **description** / sharh / شرح

/ to diskrâyb / **to describe** / sharh dâdan / شرح دادن

/ bâyogrefi / **biography** / sharhezendegi / شرح زندگى

/ to bet / **to bet** / shartbandi kardan / شرط بندى كردن

/ iistern / **eastern** / sharghi / شرقى

/ ferm / **firm** / sherkat / شركت

/ esheymd / **ashamed** / sharmande / شرمنده

/ stârt / **start** / shuru / شروع

/ to bigin / **to begin** / shuru kardan / شروع كردن

/ to stârt / **to start** / shuru kardan / شروع كردن

/ pârtner / **partner** / sharik / شريك

121

شَست / thâm / **thumb** / shast /

شستن / to wâsh / **to wash** / shostan /

شش / siks / **six** / shesh /

شصت / sikstii / **sixty** / shast /

شطرنج / ches / **chess** / shatranj /

شعر / po-im / **poem** / sheer /

شعر / po-itrii / **poetry** / sheer /

شعله / fleym / **flame** / shoele /

شغل / keriyer / **career** / shoghl /

شفاف / kliyer / **clear** / shaffâf /

شفاهى / orâl / **oral** / shefâhi /

شك / daot / **doubt** / shak /

شکار کردن / to hânt / **to hunt** / shekâr kardan /

شکارچى / hânter / **hunter** / shekârchi /

شکاف / gap / **gap** / shekaf /

شکایت کردن / **to complain** / shekâyat kardan /
/ to kâmpleyn

شکر / shuger / **sugar** / shakar /

شکستن / to breyk / **to break** / shekastan /

شکل / format / **format** / shekl /

شکل / sheyp / **shape** / shekl /

شکل گیری / formeyshen / **formation** / shekl giri /

شکلات / châklit / **chocolate** / shokolât /

شکوفه / shekufe / **bloom** / blum /

شگفت / shegeft / **fantastic** / fantastik /

شگفتی / shegefti / **wonder** / wânder /

شل کردن / shol kardan / **to relax** / to rilaks /

شلوار / shalvâr / **trousers** / traozerz /

شلوارجین / shalvârejin / **jeans** / jiinz /

شلوغ / shulugh / **noisy** / noyzi /

شلوغی / shulughi / **rush hour** / râshaor /

شلیک / shellik / **shot** / shât /

شلیک / shellik / **shoot** / shot /

شلیک کردن / shellik kardan / **to fire** / to fâyer /

شما / shoma / **you** / yoo /

شماره گرفتن / shomâre gereftan / **to dial** / to dâyâl /

شمال / shomâl / **north** / north /

شمالی / shomâli / **northern** / nordhern /

شمردن / shemordan / **to count** / to kaont /

شمشیر / shamshir / **sword** / sord /

شمع / sham / **candle** / kandel /

شمول / shemul / **inclusion** / inkloozhen /

شنا کردن / shenâ kardan / **to swim** / to swim /

شناختن / shenâkhtan / **to identify** / to âydentifây /

شناختن / shenâkhtan / **to recognize** / to rekognâyz /

شناگر / shenâgar / **swimmer** / swimer /

123

شناورشدن / shenâvarshodan / **to float** / to flot /

شنبه / shanbe / **Saturday** / saterdi /

شنوایی / shenavâii / **audition** / odishen /

شنونده / shenavande / **listener** / listener /

شنی / sheni / **sandy** / sandi /

شنیدن / shenidan / **to hear** / to hiyer /

شهاب / shahâb / **meteor** / miitiyor /

شهر / shahr / **city** / siti /

شهر / shahr / **town** / taon /

شهرت / shohrat / **fame** / feym /

شهرت / shohrat / **publicity** / pâblisiti /

شهرت / shohrat / **reputation** / repyuteyshen /

شهرت / shohrat / **repute** / ripyoot /

شهرداری / shahrdâri / **municipality** / myunisipnleti /

شهری / shahri / **urban** / erben /

شوخی / shukhi / **humor** / hyoomer /

شوخی / shukhi / **jest** / jest /

شور / shur / **zeal** / zil /

شورا / shurâ / **council** / konsl /

شورش / shuresh / **rebellion** / ribelyen /

شورش کردن / shuresh kardan / **to revolt** / to rivolt /

شورشی / shureshi / **rebel** / rebel /

شوفاژ / shufâzh / **heating** / hiiting /

شومینه / shomine / **fireplace** / fâyerpleys /

شوهر / shohar / **husband** / hâzbend /

شیء / shey / **object** / âbjukt /

شیر / shir / **lion** / lâyen /

شیر / shir / **milk** / milk /

شیر / shir / **tap** / tap /

شیرجه / shirje / **dive** / dâyv /

شیرین / shirin / **sweet** / swii /

شیرینی / shirini / **pastry** / peystri /

شیشه / shishe / **glass** / glas /

شیطان / sheytân / **devil** / devl /

شیمی / shimi / **chemistry** / kemistri /

شیمی دان / shimidân / **chemist** / kemist /

شیمیایی / shimyâyi / **chemical** / kemikl /

شکایت / shekâyat / **complaint** / kâmpleynt /

شکست دادن / shekast dâdan / **to conquer** / to kânker /

شکست دادن / shekast dâdan / **to defeat** / to difiit /

شکنجه / shekanje / **torture** / torcher /

ص

صابون / sâbun / **soap** / sop /
صاحب بودن / sâheb budan / **to own** / to on /
صادرات / sâderât / **export** / eksport /
صادقانه / sâdeghâne / **faithfully** / feythfuli /
صادقانه / sâdeghâne / **honestly** / ânistli /
صادقانه / sâdeghâne / **sincerely** / sinsiyerli /
صاف / sâf / **smooth** / smoodh /
صافی / sâfi / **filter** / filter /
صبح / sobh / **morning** / morning /
صبحانه / sobhâne / **breakfast** / brekfast /
صبر / sabr / **patience** / peyshens /
صبرکردن / sabr kardan / **to wait** / to weyt /
صبور / sabur / **patient** / peyshent /
صبورانه / saburâne / **patiently** / peyshentl, /
صحبت / sohbat / **chat** / chat /
صحبت / sohbat / **talk** / tok /
صحنه / sahne / **scene** / siin /
صحنه / sahne / **stage** / steyj /
صد / sad / **hundred** / hândred /

126

صدا / sedâ / **voice** / voys /

صداکردن / sedâkardan / **call** / kol /

صدای پا / sadâye pâ / **footsteps** / futsteps /

صدمین / sadomin / **hundredth** / hândredth /

صرع / saree / **epilepsy** / epilepsi /

صریح / sarih / **definite** / definit /

صف / saf / **queue** / kyoo /

صفت / sefat / **adjective** / ajictiv /

صفحه / safhe / **page** / peyj /

صفر / sefr / **zero** / ziiro /

صلح / solh / **peace** / piis /

صلیب / salib / **cross** / krâs /

صمیمانه / samimâne / **sincerely** / sinceyerli /

صندلی / sandali / **chair** / cher /

صندلی / sandali / **seat** / siit /

صندلی دسته دار / sandaliye dastedâr / **armchair** /
ârmcher /

صندوق / sandugh / **chest** / chest /

صندوق پست / sandughe post / **letterbox** / leterbâks /

صندوق پست / sandughe post / **mailbox** / meylbâks /

صندوق عقب / sandughe aghab / **boot** / boot /

صندوقدار / sandughdâr / **teller** / teler /

صنعت / sanaat / **industry** / indâstri /

صنعتى / sanaati / **industrial** / indâstriyel /

صوت / sot / **sound** / saond /

صورت / surat / **face** / feys /

صورت / surat / **feature** / fiicher /

صورت / surat / **form** / form /

صورت غذا / surat ghazâ / **menu** / menyoo /

صورتى / surati / **pink** / pink /

صياد / sayyâd / **fisherman** / fisherman /

صياد / sayyad / **trapper** / traper /

ض

ضبط کردن / zabt kardan / **to record** / to rikord /

ضد آلرژی / zedde âlerzhi / **antihistamine** / antihistemin /

ضد میکروب / zedde mikrob / **antiseptic** / antiseptic /

ضرب المثل / zarbol masal / **proverb** / prâverb /

ضرب کردن / zarb kardan / **to multiply** / to mâltiplây /

ضربه / zarbe / **bang** / bang /

ضربه / zarbe / **blow** / blo /

ضربه مغزی / zarbeye maghzi / **concussion** / kânkâshen /

ضروری / zaruri / **essential** / isenshl /

ضعیف / zaiif / **feeble** / fiibel /

ضعیف / zaiif / **weak** / wiik /

ضیافت / ziyâfat / **feast** / fiist /

ط

طبقه / tabaghe / **class** / klas /
طبقه / tabaghe / **floor** / flor /
طبقه بالا / tabaghey'e bâlâ / **upstairs** / âpsterz /
طبل / tabl / **drum** / drâm /
طبیعت / tabiat / **nature** / neycher /
طبیعی / tabii / **natural** / nachrâl /
طبیعی / tabii / **normal** / normâl /
طراح / tarrâh / **designer** / dizâyner /
طرح / tarh / **design** / dizâyn /
طرح / tarh / **project** / prâjekt /
طرز / tarz / **manner** / maner /
طرز کار / tarze kâr / **operation** / âpereyshen /
طرف / taraf / **direction** / diekshen /
طرف / taraf / **side** / sâyd /
طعم / taam / **flavor** / fleyver /
طلا / talâ / **gold** / gold /
طلاق / talâgh / **divorce** / dives /
طلایی / talâyi / **golden** / golden /
طلوع / teluu / **sunrise** / sânrâyz /

130

طلوع کردن / teluu kardan / **to rise** / to râyz /

طناب / tanâb / **rope** / rop /

طنزآمیز / tanz âmiz / **ironic** / âyrânik /

ظ

ظالم / zâlem / **cruel** / kroo-el /
ظاهر / zâher / **appearance** / epiyerens /
ظاهر / zâher / **looks** / luks /
ظاهراً / zâheran / **apparently** / epareytes /
ظاهراً / zâheran / **obviously** / âbviyesli /
ظرافت / zerâfat / **delicacy** / delikasi /
ظرف / zarf / **container** / kânteyner /
ظرف / zarf / **dish** / dish /
ظرف / zarf / **pot** / pât /
ظريف / zarif / **delicate** / delikit /
ظهر / zohr / **midday** / middey /

ع

عابر پیاده / âbere piyâde / **pedestrian** / pidestriyen /

عادت / âdat / **habit** / habit /

عادى / âdi / **usual** / yoozhuwâl /

عاشق / âshegh / **lover** / lâver /

عاشقانه / âsheghâne / **romantic** / romantik /

عاطفه / âtefe / **emotion** / imoshen /

عالى / âli / **excellent** / ekselent /

عالى / âli / **magnificent** / magnifisent /

عالى / âli / **wonderful** / wânderful /

عبارت / ebârat / **phrase** / freiz /

عبرت / ebrat / **byword** / bâyved /

عبور کردن / ubur kardan / **to cross** / to krâs /

عجله کردن / ajale kardan / **to hurry** / to hâri /

عجله کردن / ajale kardan / **to rush** / to râsh /

عجله کردن / ajale kardan / **to hasten** / to heysen /

عجول / ajul / **hasty** / heysti /

عجیب / ajib / **queer** / kwiyer /

عجیب / ajib / **strange** / streynj /

عدالت / adâlat / **justice** / jâstis /

عدد / adad / **number** / nâmber /

عدد يك / adade yek / **one** / wân /

عدسى / adasi / **lens** / lenz /

عذاب دادن / azâb dâdan / **torment** / torment /

عذر / ozr / **excuse** / ikskyoos /

عرب / arab / **Arab** / arab /

عربى / arabi / **Arabian** / ereybiyan /

عربى / arabi / **Arabic** / arabik /

عرشه / arshe / **deck** / dek /

عرق / aragh / **perspiration** / perspireyshen /

عروسى / arusi / **wedding** / weding /

عروسك / arusak / **doll** / dol /

عزيز / aziz / **beloved** / bilâvd /

عزيز / aziz / **darling** / dârling /

عزيز / aziz / **dear** / diyer /

عسل / asal / **honey** / hâni /

عشق / eshgh / **love** / lâv /

عشق / eshgh / **passion** / pashen /

عصب / asab / **nerve** / nerv /

عصب شناسى / asab shenâsi / **neurology** / nu erâleji /

عصبانى / asabâni / **enrage** / inreyj /

عصبانى / asabâni / **furious** / fyriyes /

عصبى / asabi / **nervous** / nerves /

عصبى / asabi / **tense** / tens /

عضو / ozv / **member** / member /

عضويت / ozviyyat / **membership** / membership /

عطر / atr / **perfume** / perfyoom /

عظيم / azim / **huge** / hyooj /

عظيم / azim / **immense** / imens /

عفو / afv / **pardon** / pârden /

عقب / aghab / **back** / bak /

عقب / aghab / **rear** / riyer /

عقب مانده / aghab mânde / **backward** / bakword /

عقب نشينى كردن / aghabneshini kardan / **to retreat** /
/ to ritriit

عقرب / agharab / **scorpion** / skorpiyen /

عقل / aghl / **wisdom** / wizdem /

عقلانى / aghlâni / **intellectual** / intilekchuwâl /

عكس / aks / **photograph** / fotogrâf /

عكس / aks / **picture** / pikcher /

علاقه / alâghe / **affection** / afekshen /

علاقه / alâghe / **concern** / kânsern /

علاقه / alâghe / **interest** / intrist /

علاقه / alâghe / **liking** / lâyking /

علاقه مند / alâghemand / **interested** / intristid /

علامت / alâmat / **sign** / sâyn /

135

علامت / alâmat / **signal** / signâl /

علاوه براین / alâvebarin / **besides** / bisâydz /

علت / ellat / **cause** / koz /

علم / elm / **science** / sâyens /

علم اقتصاد / elme eghtesâd / **economics** / iikânâmiks /

علم وراثت / elme verâsat / **genetics** / jinetiks /

علمی / elmi / **scientific** / sâyentifik /

علیه / aleyhe / **against** / egenst /

عمداً / amdan / **deliberately** / diliberitli /

عمدتاً / omdatan / **mostly** / mostli /

عمدتاً / omdatan / **chiefly** / chiifly /

عمدتاً / omdatan / **mainly** / meynli /

عمده / omde / **main** / meyn /

عمده / omde / **principal** / prinsipâl /

عمر / omr / **lifetime** / lâyftâym /

عمق / omgh / **depth** / depth /

عمل / amal / **act** / akt /

عمل / amal / **practice** / praktis /

عملاً / amalan / **practically** / praktikli /

عملی / amali / **practical** / praktikâl /

عمومی / umumi / **general** / jenrâl /

عمیق / amigh / **deep** / diip /

عمیق / amigh / **intensive** / intensiv /

عنصر / onsor / **element** / eliment /

عنوان / onvân / **headline** / hedlâyn /

عنوان / onvân / **title** / tâytel /

عیب / eyb / **disadvantage** / disadvantij /

عیب / eeyb / **fault** / folt /

عینك / eynak / **glasses** / glasiz /

عینک آفتابی / eynake âftabi / **sunglasses** / sânglasiz /

عکاس / akkâs / **photographer** / fotâgrafer /

غ

غار / ghâr / **cave** / keiv /
غار / ghâr / **den** / den /
غاز / ghâz / **goose** / goos /
غایب / ghâyeb / **absent** / absent /
غدّه / ghodde / **gland** / gland /
غذا / ghazâ / **diet** / dâyet /
غذا / ghazâ / **food** / food /
غذا / ghazâ / **meal** / miil /
غذاخوری / ghazâkhori / **canteen** / kantiin /
غذای سبک / ghazâye sabok / **snack** / snak /
غرب / gharb / **west** / west /
غربی / gharbi / **western** / western /
غرش / ghorresh / **roar** / ror /
غرفه / ghorfe / **stand** / stand /
غرق کردن / gharh kardan / **to drown** / to draon /
غروب / ghurub / **sunset** / sânset /
غروب کردن / ghurub kardan / **to set** / to set /
غریبه / gharibe / **stranger** / streynjer /
غریزه / gharize / **instinct** / instink /

138

غزل / ghazal / **lyric** / lirik /

غصه دار / ghosse dâr / **unhappy** / ânhapi /

غضروف / ghozruf / **cartilage** / kâtilij /

غلتیدن / ghaltidan / **roll** / rol /

غلط / ghalat / **incorrect** / inkârekt /

غله / ghalle / **cereal** / siriyel /

غله / ghalle / **corn** / korn /

غمگین / ghamgin / **sad** / sad /

غمگین کردن / ghamgin kardan / **to depress** / to dipres /

غواص / ghavvâs / **diver** / dâyver /

غول / ghul / **giant** / jâyent /

غیبت / gheybat / **absence** / absens /

غیر بومی / gheyre bumi / **exotic** / igzâtik /

غیر ضروری / gheyre zaruri / **unnecessary** / ânneseseri /

غیر عادی / gheyre âdi / **eccentric** / iksentrik /

غیر قابل تحمل / gheyr ghâbele tahammul / **intolerable** / intâlerebel

غیر قابل درک / gheyr ghâbele dark / **inscrutable** / inskrootebel

غیر قانونی / gheyre ghânuni / **illegal** / iligl /

غیر منتظره / gheyr montazere / **unexpected** / ânikspektid

غیر منصفانه / gheyr monsefâne / **unfair** / ânfer /

139

غیرارادی / gheyrerâdi / **involuntary** / invâlentri /

غیرعادی / gheyreâdi / **unusual** / ânyoozhuwâl /

ف

فائق آمدن / fâegh âmadan / **to cope** / to kop /

فاتح / fâteh / **conqueror** / kânkerer /

فاسد / fâsed / **corrupt** / korâpt /

فاصله / fâsele / **intermission** / intermishen /

فاصله / fâsele / **interval** / intervâl /

فانوس / fânus / **lantern** / lantern /

فتح / fath / **conquest** / kânkwest /

فراتر رفتن / farâtar raftan / **exceed** / iksiid /

فرار کردن / farâr kardan / **escape** / iskeyp /

فرار کردن / farâr kardan / **flee** / flii /

فراری / farâri / **fugitive** / fyoojitiv /

فراصوتی / farâsoti / **supersonic** / soopersânik /

فراغت / farâghat / **leisure** / lezher /

فراموش کردن / farâmush kardan / **to forget** / to forget /

فرانسه / farânse / **France** / frâns /

فرانسوی / farânsavi / **French** / french /

فراوان / farâvân / **ample** / ampl /

فراوان / farâvân / **frequent** / friikwent /

فراوانی / farâvani / **multitude** / mâltiyood /

فرآیند / farâyand / **process** / prâses /

فردا / fardâ / **tomorrow** / tumâro /

فردی / fardi / **individual** / indivijuwâl /

فرستادن / frestâdan / **to send** / to send /

فرش / farsh / **carpet** / kârpit /

فرش کردن / farsh kardan / **to pave** / to peyv /

فرصت / forsat / **occasion** / âkeyzhen /

فرصت / forsat / **opportunity** / âportyooniti /

فرض کردن / farz kardan / **to presume** / to prizyoom /

فرض کردن / farz kardan / **to suppose** / to sâpoz /

فرق داشتن / fargh dâshtan / **to differ** / to difer /

فرمان / farmân / **steering wheel** / stiyering wiil /

فرمان / farmân / **command** / kâmmand /

فرماندار / farmândâr / **governor** / gâverner /

فرمانده / farmânde / **captain** / kaptin /

فرمانده / farmânde / **commander** / kâmander /

فرمول / formul / **formula** / fomyula /

فرهنگ / farhang / **culture** / kâlcher /

فرهنگ / farhang / **dictionary** / diksheneri /

فروبردن / furubordan / **to dip** / to dip /

فروختن / frukhtan / **to sell** / to sel /

فرود آمدن / furud âmadan / **to land** / to land /

فرودگاه / furudgâh / **airport** / erport /

فروش / furush / **sale** / seyl /

فروشگاه بزرگ / furusgâhe bozorg / **supermarket** /
soopermârkit /

فروشنده / furushande / **dealer** / diiler /

فریاد / faryâd / **cry** / krây /

فریاد / faryâd / **shout** / shaot /

فریاد کشیدن / faryâd keshidan / **to exclaim** / to ikskleym /

فریاد کشیدن / faryâd keshidan / **to cry** / to krây /

فریب / farib / **deceit** / disit /

فریب / farib / **deception** / disepshn /

فریب دادن / farib dâdan / **to deceive** / to disiiv /

فساد / fesâd / **corruption** / korâpshen /

فشار دادن / feshâr dâdan / **to press** / to pres /

فصل / fasl / **chapter** / chapter /

فصل / fasl / **season** / siizen /

فضا / fazâ / **space** / speys /

فعال / faâl / **active** / aktlv /

فعال / faaâl / **mover** / moover /

فعالیت / faâliyyat / **activity** / aktveti /

فقط / faghat / **merely** / miyerli /

فقیر / faghir / **poor** / pu-er /

فکر / fekr / **idea** / âydiyâ /

فکر / fekr / **thought** / thot /

143

فكر كردن / fekr kardan / **to think** / to think /

فلاش بك / flâshbak / **flashback** / flashbak /

فلز / felez / **metal** / metâl /

فلسفه / falsafe / **philosophy** / filâsofi /

فلسفى / falsafi / **philosophical** / filosâfikâl /

فلفل / felfel / **pepper** / peper /

فن شناسى / fanshenâsi / **technology** / teknâloji /

فنجان / fenjân / **cup** / kâp /

فندك / fandak / **lighter** / lâyter /

فهرست / fehrest / **list** / list /

فهميدن / fahmidan / **to understand** / to ânderstand /

فواره / favvâre / **fountain** / faotin /

فواره / favvâre / **jet** / jet /

فوتبال / futbâl / **football** / futbol /

فوراً / foran / **immediately** / imiidiyetli /

فورى / fori / **immediate** / imiidiyet /

فورى / fori / **urgent** / erjent /

فوريه / fevriye / **February** / februweri /

فوق العاده / fogholâde / **extremely** / ikstriimli /

فولاد / fulâd / **steel** / stiil /

فيزيكدان / fizikdân / **physicist** / fizisist /

فيزيولوژى / fiziyoloji / **physiology** / fiziyâloji /

فيزيك / fizik / **physics** / fiziks /

144

فیل / fil / **elephant** / elifent /
فیلسوف / filsuf / **philosopher** / filâsofer /
فیلم / film / **film** / film /
فکر کردن / fekr kardan / **to meditate** / to mediteyt /

ق

قائم / ghâem / **vertical** / vertikâl /

قاب / ghâb / **frame** / freym /

قابل / ghâbel / **able** / eybel /

قابل تبدیل / ghâbele tabdil / **convertible** / kânvertibe /

قابل رؤیت / ghâbele royat / **visible** / vizibel /

قابل شنیدن / ghâbele shenidan / **audible** / odibel /

قابل قبول / ghâbele ghabul / **acceptable** / akseptebel /

قابل مقایسه / ghabele moghâyese / **comparable** / kâmperebel /

قابل ملاحظه / ghâbele molâheze / **considerable** / kânsiderebel /

قاتل / ghâtel / **killer** / kiler /

قاتل / ghâtel / **murderer** / merderer /

قادر / ghâder / **capable** / keypebel /

قادر متعال / ghâdere motaâl / **almighty** / olmâyti /

قارچ / ghârch / **mushroom** / mâshrum /

قارّه / ghârre / **continent** / kântinent /

قاشق / ghâshogh / **spoon** / spoon /

قاصد / ghâsed / **messenger** / mesinjer /

146

قاضى / ghâzi / **judge** / jây /
قاعده / ghâeede / **base** / beys /
قاعده / ghâede / **rule** / rool /
قاليچه / ghâliche / **rug** / râg /
قانون / ghânun / **law** / lo /
قانونى / ghânuni / **lawful** / lofl /
قانونى / ghânuni / **legal** / ligl /
قايق / ghâyegh / **boat** / bot /
قايق نجات / ghâyeghe nejât / **lifeboat** / lâyfbot /
قبلاً / ghablan / **before** / bifor /
قبلاً / ghablan / **formerly** / formerli /
قبلى / ghabli / **former** / former /
قبول / ghabul / **admission** / edmishn /
قتل / ghatl / **murder** / merder /
قدرت / ghodrat / **strength** / strength /
قدردانى كردن / ghadrdâni kardan / **to appreciate** /
to epriishiyeyt /
قدرى / ghadri / **some** / sâm /
قدغن كردن / ghadaghan kardan / **to forbid** / to forbid /
قدم / ghadam / **pace** / peys /
قدم / ghadam / **step** / step /
قدم زدن / ghadaml zadan / **to walk** / to wok /
قديمى / ghadimi / **antique** / antiik /

قدیمی / ghadimi / **veteran** / veteren /

قرار(ملاقات) / gharâr (emolâghât) / **appointment** /
epoyntment /

قرارداد / gharârdâd / **bond** / bând /

قراردادن / gharâr dâdan / **to lay** / to ley /

قرآن / ghorân / **Koran** / Keran /

قربانت / ghorbânat / **yours** / yorz /

قربانی / ghorbâni / **victim** / viktim /

قرص / ghors / **pill** / pil /

قرص / ghors / **tablet** / tablit /

قرض / gharz / **debt** / det /

قرض دادن / gharz dâdan / **to lend** / to lend /

قرض گرفتن / gharz gereftan / **to borrow** / to bâro /

قرمز / ghermez / **red** / red /

قرن / gharn / **century** / senchri /

قرون وسطی / ghurune vostâ / **Middle Ages** / mideleyjiz /

قسم خوردن / ghasam khordan / **to swear** / to swer /

قسمت / ghesmat / **department** / dipârtment /

قسمت / ghesmat / **part** / pârt /

قسمت کردن / ghesmat kardan / **to divide** / to divâyd /

قشنگ / ghashang / **beautifully** / byootifuli /

قشنگ / ghashang / **charming** / chârming /

قشنگ / ghashang / **handsome** / hansâm /

قشنگ / ghashang / **pretty** / priti /

قصاب / ghassâb / **butcher** / bucher /

قصد / ghasd / **intention** / intenshen /

قصد داشتن / gasddâshtan / **aim** / eym /

قصه / ghesse / **fable** / feybel /

قصه گو / ghessegu / **narrator** / nareyter /

قطار / ghatâr / **train** / treyn /

قطب / ghotb / **pole** / pol /

قطب جنوب / ghotbe jonub / **Antarctic** / antârktik /

قطره / ghatre / **drop** / drâp /

قطع کردن / ghatee kardan / **interrupt** / interâpt /

قطعًا / ghataan / **surely** / shurli /

قطعی / ghatii / **decisive** / disâysiv /

قفس / ghafas / **cage** / keyj /

قفسه / ghafase / **bookcase** / bukkeys /

قفسه / ghafase / **cupboard** / kâbord /

قفل / ghofl / **lock** / lâk /

قلاب / ghollâb / **hook** / huk /

قلب / ghalb / **heart** / hârt /

قلعه / galee / **castle** / kâsel /

قلم / ghalam / **pen** / pen /

قلمرو / ghalamro / **territory** / teritori /

قهرمان / ghahramân / **champion** / champiyen /

قهرمان / ghahramân / **hero** / hiyero /

قهوه / ghahve / **coffee** / kâfi /

قهوه ای / ghahveii / **brown** / braon /

قوطی / ghuti / **can** / kan /

قوطی کبریت / ghutiye kebrit / **matchbox** / machbâks /

قول / ghol / **promise** / prâmis /

قول دادن / ghol dâdan / **to promise** / to prâmis /

قوی / ghavi / **powerful** / pawerful /

قوی / ghavi / **structure** / strâkcher /

قیاس / ghiyâs / **analogy** / enaleji /

قیچی / gheychi / **scissors** / sizerz /

قید / gheyd / **adverb** / edveb /

قیمت / gheymat / **cost** / kâst /

قیمت / ghaymat / **price** / prâys /

قیمتی / gheymati / **precious** / preshes /

کاوُچو / kauchu / **rubber** / râber /

کاباره / kâbâre / **cabaret** / kabare /

کابل / kâbl / **cable** / keybl /

کابوس / kâbus / **nightmare** / nâytmer /

کابین / kâbin / **cabin** / kabin /

کاپوت / kâput / **hood** / hud /

کاتولیك / kâtolik / **Catholic** / kathelik /

کادو / kâdo / **gift** / gift /

کار / kâr / **action** / akshn /

کار / kâr / **business** / biznis /

کار / kâr / **labor** / leyber /

کار / kâr / **task** / tâsk /

کار / kâr / **work** / werk /

کار / kâr / **job** / jâb /

کار کردن / kâr kardan / **to work** / to werk /

کار کردن / kâr kardan / **to serve** / to serv /

کاراته / kârâte / **karate** / karâti /

کارآگاه / kârâgâh / **detective** / ditektiv /

کارآموز / kârâmuz / **learner** / lerner /

کارآیی / kârâyi / **efficiency** / lfishensi /
کارت پستال / kartpostâl / **postcard** / postkârd /
کارتون / kârton / **cartoon** / kârtoon /
کارخانه / kârkhâne / **factory** / fakteri /
کارخانه / karkhâne / **mill** / mil /
کارد / kârd / **knife** / nâyf /
کارشناس / kârshenâs / **expert** / ekspert /
کارفرما / kârfarmâ / **employer** / imployer /
کارگر / kârgar / **worker** / werker /
کارگر / kârgar / **laborer** / leyberer /
کارگر / kârgar / **workman** / werkman /
کارمند / kârmand / **employee** / implyoii /
کاروان / kârâvân / **caravan** / karavan /
کاسه / kâse / **bowl** / bol /
کاسه / kâse / **basin** / beysin /
کاشتن / kâshtan / **plant** / plant /
کاشتن / kâshtan / **sow** / so /
کاغذ / kâghaz / **paper** / peyper /
کاغذنامه / kâghaznâme / **notepaper** / notpeyper /
کافه / kâfe / **cafe** / kafey /
کافی / kâfi / **adequate** / adikwit /
کافی / kâfi / **enough** / inâf /
کافی / kâfi / **sufficient** / sâfishent

كافيين / kâfeiin / **caffeine** / kafin /

كاكائو / kâkâu / **cocoa** / koko /

كالا / kâlâ / **goods** / gudz /

كالبد شناسی / kâlbod shenâsi / **anatomy** / enatemi /

كالبدگشایی / kâlbod goshâyi / **autopsy** / otapsi /

كالسکه / kaleskeh / **coach** / coch /

كامپیوتر زانویی / kâmpiotere zânuyi / **laptop** / laptâp /

كامل / kâmel / **complete** / kâmpliit /

كامل / kâmel / **perfect** / perfikt /

كامل / kâmel / **total** / totâl /

كامل كردن / kâmel kardan / **to complete** / to kâmpliit /

كاملاً / kâmelan / **quit** / kwâyt /

كاملاً / kâmelan / **totally** / totâli /

كاملاً / kâmelan / **absolutely** / absolootli /

كاملاً / kâmelan / **completely** / kâmpliitli /

كاملاً / kâmelan / **entirely** / intâyrli /

كاملاً / kâmelan / **fully** / fuli /

كاملاً / kâmelan / **perfectly** / perfektli /

كامیون / kâmyon / **truck** / trâk /

كاناپه / kânâpe / **couch** / kaoch /

كانادا / kânâdâ / **Canada** / kanada /

كانادایی / kânâdâyi / **Canadian** / kaneydiyan /

كانون / kânun / **focus** / fokes /

كاه / kâh / **straw** / stro /

كاهش / kâhesh / **decline** / siklâyn /

كاهش / kâhesh / **reduction** / ridâkshen /

كاوش / kâvosh / **exploration** / eksploreyshen /

كاوش كردن / kâvosh kardan / **to explore** / to iksplor /

كباب / kabâb / **kebab** / kebab /

كباب پز / kabâbpaz / **grill** / gril /

كباب كردن / kabâb kardan / **to roast** / to rost /

كبد / kabad / **liver** / liver /

كبريت / kebrit / **match** / mach /

كبوتر / kabutar / **dove** / dâv /

كبوتر / kabutar / **pigeon** / pijin /

كُت / kot / **jacket** / jakit /

كتاب / ketâb / **book** / buk /

كتاب فروشى / ketâb furushi / **bookshop** / bukshâp /

كتاب مقدس / ketâbe moghaddas / **Bible** / bâybel /

كتابخانه / ketâbkhâne / **library** / lâybreri /

كترى / ketri / **kettle** / ketel /

كتك زدن / kotak zadan / **to beat** / to biit /

كثافت / kesâfat / **dirt** / dert /

كثيف / kasif / **dirty** / derti /

كجا / kojâ / **where** / wer /

كُد / kod / **code** / kod /

كدام / wich / **which** / kodam /

كدپستى / zip kod / **zip code** / kode posti /

كر / def / **deaf** / kar /

كراوات / tây / **tie** / krâvât /

كرايه / fer / **fare** / kerâye /

كرايه كردن / to hâyr / **to hire** / kerâye kardan /

كراكر / krakerz / **crackers** / krâker /

كربن / kârben / **carbon** / karbon /

كردن / doo / **do** / kardan /

كره / bâter / **butter** / kare /

كره اى / bâtery / **buttery** / kareii /

كريسمس / krismas / **X-mas** / kirismas /

كريسمس / krismas / **Christmas** / krismas /

كسب كردن / to geyn / **to gain** / kasb kardan /

كسى / eniwân / **anyone** / kasi /

كسى / sâmbâdi / **somebody** / kasi /

كسى / sâmwân / **someone** / kasi /

كش سان / ilastik / **elastic** / keshsân /

كشاورزى / agriculture / **agriculture** / keshâvarzi /

كشتزار / planteyshen / **plantation** / keshtzâr /

كشتن / to kil / **to kill** / koshtan /

كشتى / ship / **ship** / kashti /

كشف / ditekshn / **detection** / kashf /

كشف / kashf / **discovery** / diskâveri /

كشف كردن / kasf kardan / **to discover** / to diskâver /

كِشو / kesho / **drawer** / dror /

كشور / keshvar / **country** / kântri /

كشيدن / keshidan / **to pull** / to pul /

كشيدن / keshidan / **to stretch** / to strech /

كف زدن / kafzadan / **to clap** / to klap /

كفايت كردن / kefâyet kardan / **to suffice** / to sâfâys /

كفش / kafsh / **shoe** / shoo /

كلاس / kelâs / **classroom** / klasrum /

كلاسيك / klâsik / **classical** / klasikâl /

كلاغ / kalâgh / **crow** / kro /

كلان / kalân / **huge** / huje /

كلانتر / kalântar / **sheriff** / sherif /

كلانترى / kalântari / **police station** / poliissteyshen /

كلانشهر / kalânshahr / **megalopolis** / megalopolis /

كلاه / kolâh / **hat** / hat /

كلاه / kolâh / **cap** / kap /

كلبه / kolbe / **hut** / hât /

كلبه / kolbe / **cottage** / kâtij /

كلسيم / kalsyum / **calcium** / kalsiem /

كلفت / koloft / **thick** / thik /

كلك / kalak / **trick** / trik /

كلم / kalam / **cabbage** / kabij /

كلمه / kalame / **word** / werd /

كلوب شبانه / klube shabâne / **nightclub** / nâyklâb /

كلوچه / koluche / **cookie** / kuki /

كليد / kelid / **key** / kii /

كليسا / kelisâ / **church** / cherch /

كليه / koliye / **kidney** / kidni /

كليه شناس / koliye shenâs / **urologist** / yurolojist /

كم شدن / kam shodan / **decrease** / dikriis /

كم كردن / kam kardan / **to reduce** / to ridyoos /

كمتر / kamtar / **less** / les /

كمترين / kamtarin / **least** / liist /

كمد / komod / **closed** / klâzit /

كمدى / komedi / **comedy** / kâmidi /

كمك / komak / **help** / help /

كمونيسم / komonism / **communism** / kâmyunizem /

كمياب / kamyâb / **scarce** / skers /

كميته / komite / **committee** / kâmiti /

كميّت / kamiyyat / **quantity** / kwântiti /

كمك / komak / **contribution** / kântribyooshen /

كنار / kanâr / **aside** / esâyd /

كناردريا / kanâredaryâ / **beach** / biich /

كناردريا / kanâredaryâ / **seaside** / siisâyd /

157

كنجكاو / konjkav / **curious** / kyuriyes /

كندن / kandan / **to dig** / to dig /

كنسرت / konsert / **concert** / kânsert /

كنسروشده / konservshode / **canned** / kand /

كنسول / konsul / **consul** / kânsel /

كنسولگری / konsulgari / **consulate** / kânsyulit /

كهربا / kahrabâ / **amber** / amber /

كهنه / kohne / **rag** / rag /

كوتاه / kutâh / **brief** / briif /

كوتاه / kutah / **low** / lo /

كوتاه / kutâh / **short** / short /

كوچك / kuchak / **junior** / jooniyer /

كوچك / kuchak / **little** / litel /

كوچك / kuchek / **small** / smol /

كوچه / kuche / **alley** / ali /

كوچك شدن / kuchak shodan / **to shrink** / to shrink /

كودك / kudak / **baby** / beybi /

كودك / kudak / **infant** / infent /

كور / kur / **blind** / blâynd /

كور / kur / **sightless** / sâytlis /

كورى / kuri / **blindness** / blâyndnis /

كوسه / kuse / **shark** / shârk /

كوشش / kushesh / **effort** / efort /

كوشيدن / kushidan / **attempt** / atempt /

كوه / kuh / **mountain** / maontin /

كوهان / kuhân / **hump** / hâmp /

كى / ki / **who** / hoo /

كيسه / kise / **sack** / sak /

كيسه خواب / kiseye khâb / **sleeping bag** / sliiping bag /

كيش ومات / kishomât / **checkmate** / chekmeyt /

كيف / kif / **bag** / bag /

كيف بغلى / kife baghali / **wallet** / wâlit /

كيف پول / kife pul / **purse** / pers /

كيفيت / keyfiyat / **quality** / kwâliti /

كيك / keyk / **cake** / keyk /

كيلو / kilo / **kilo** / kiilo /

كيلومتر / kilometr / **kilometer** / kilemiiter /

كينه / kine / **spite** / spâyt /

كيك / keyk / **bun** / bân /

گاری / gâri / **wagon** / wagen /

گاز / gâz / **bite** / bâyt /

گاز گرفتن / gâz gereftan / **to bite** / to bâyt /

گاه به گاه / gâh be gâh / **occasionally** / âkeyzhenâli /

گاو / gâv / **cow** / kao /

گاو / gâv / **ox** / âks /

گچ تحریر / gache tahrir / **chalk** / chok /

گدایی کردن / gedâyi kardan / **to beg** / to beg /

گذاشتن / gozâshtan / **to put** / to put /

گذر / gozar / **to pass** / to pas /

گذرنامه / gozarnâme / **passport** / pasport /

گذشتن / gozâshtan / **to pass** / to pas /

گذشته / gozashte / **past** / past /

گران / gerân / **costly** / kâstli /

گران / gerân / **expensive** / ikspensiv /

گربه / gorbe / **cat** / kat /

گرد / gerd / **round** / raond /

گرد وخاك / gardokhâk / **dust** / dâst /

گردان / gardân / **battalion** / bateliyen /

گرداننده / gardânande / **operator** / âpereyter /
گرداننده / gardânande / **organizer** / organâyzer /
گردگرفته / gard gerefte / **dusty** / dâsti /
گردن / gardan / **neck** / nek /
گرسنه / gorosne / **hungry** / hângri /
گرفتار کردن / gereftâr kardan / **to involve** / to invâlv /
گرفتن / gereftan / **to capture** / to kapcher /
گرفتن / gereftan / **to catch** / to kach /
گرفتن / gereftan / **to get** / to get /
گرفتن / gereftan / **to grip** / to grip /
گرفتن / gereftan / **to hold** / to hold /
گرفتن / gereftan / **to overtake** / to everteyk /
گرفتن / gereftan / **to take** / to teyk /
گرگ / gorg / **wolf** / wulf /
گرم / garm / **warm** / worm /
گره / gereh / **knot** / nât /
گروه / guruh / **band** / band /
گروه / guruh / **group** / groop /
گروه / guruh / **team** / tiim /
گروهبان / guruhbân / **sergeant** / sârjent /
گریپفر / giripfer / **grapefruit** / greypfroot /
گریه کردن / gerye kardan / **to weep** / to wiip /
گزارش دادن / gozâresh dâdan / **to report** / to riport /

گزیده / gozide / **extract** / ekstrakt /

گسترده / gostarde / **comprehensive** / kâmprihensiv /

گشت / gasht / **patrol** / patrol /

گشتن / gashtan / **to range** / to reynj /

گشتن / gashtan / **to turn** / to tern /

گفتار / goftâr / **speech** / spiich /

گفتگو / goftegu / **conversation** / kânverseyhen /

گفتگو / goftegu / **dialogue** / dâyelog /

گفتن / goftan / **to say** / to sey /

گفتن / goftan / **to tell** / to tel /

گل / gol / **flower** / flaower /

گل / gel / **mud** / mâd /

گل سرخ / gole sorkh / **rose** / roz /

گلابی / golâbi / **pear** / per /

گلخانه / golkhâne / **greenhouse** / griinhaos /

گلو / galu / **throat** / throt /

گلوله / golule / **bullet** / bulit /

گلوله برف / gululeye barf / **snowball** / snobol /

گله‌ٔ گاو / gale gâv / **cattle** / katel /

گم کردن / gom kardan / **to lose** / to looz /

گمرک / gomrok / **customs** / kâstemz /

گناه / gonâh / **guilt** / gilt /

گناهکار / gonâhkâr / **guilty** / gilti /

گنبد / gonbad / **dome** / dom /

گنج / ganj / **treasure** / trezher /

گواهی / govâhi / **certificate** / certifikit /

گوجه / goje / **plum** / plâm /

گوجه فرنگی / gojefarangi / **tomato** / tomeyto /

گور / gur / **grave** / greyv /

گوراسب / gureasb / **zebra** / zibre /

گوزن / gavazn / **deer** / dier /

گوسفند / gusefand / **sheep** / shiip /

گوش / gush / **ear** / iyer /

گوش به زنگ / gush be zang / **watchful** / wâchful /

گوش دادن / gush dâdan / **to listen** / to lisen /

گوشت / gusht / **flesh** / flesh /

گوشت (قرمز) / gusht (e ghermez) / **meat** / miit /

گوشت خوک / gushte khuk / **pork** / pork /

گوشت گاو / gushtegâv / **beef** / biif /

گوشت گوسفند / gushte gusefand / **mutton** / mâten /

گوشه / gushe / **corner** / korner /

گوشواره / gushvâre / **earring** / iyering /

گوناگون / gunâgun / **diverse** / dâyves /

گوناگون / gunâgun / **various** / veriyes /

گونه / gune / **cheek** / chiik /

گوینده / guyande / **announcer** / anaonser /

گیاه / giyâh / **plant** / plant /

گیاه / giyâh / **vegetable** / vejitable /

گیاه خردل / giyâhe khardal / **mustard** / mâsterd /

گیتار / gitâr / **guitar** / gitâr /

گیج / gij / **stupid** / styoopid /

گیج / gich / **absentminded** / absentmâyndid /

گیج کننده / gij konande / **confusing** / kânfiyoozing /

گیج کردن / gich kardan / **to confuse** / to kânfiyooz /

گیرنده / girende / **recipient** / risipiyent /

گیلاس / gilâs / **cherry** / cheri /

ل

لات / lât / **hooligan** / hooligen /
لازم / lâzem / **necessary** / neseseri /
لاغر / lâghar / **thin** / thin /
لامپ / lâmp / **bulb** / bâlb /
لامپ / lâmp / **bulb** / bâlb /
لامسه / lâmese / **touch** / tâch /
لانه / lâne / **nest** / nest /
لایق / lâyegh / **efficient** / ifishent /
لب / lab / **lip** / lip /
لباس / lebâs / **clothes** / klodhz /
لباس / lebâs / **dress** / dres /
لباس زیر / lebâse zir / **underwear** / ânderwer /
لباس فرم / lebâse form / **uniform** / yooniform /
لبخند / labkhand / **smile** / smâyl /
لبنیاتی / labaniyâti / **dairy** / deri /
لبه / labe / **edge** / ej /
لحظه / lahze / **moment** / moment /
لخت / lokht / **bare** / ber /
لخت / lokht / **naked** / neykid /

165

/ injoyment / **enjoyment** / lazzat bordan / لذت بردن
/ to shiver / **to shiver** / larzidan / لرزیدن
/ to trembel / **to tremble** / larzidan / لرزیدن
/ feyver / **favor** / lotf / لطف
/ pliiz / **please** / lotfan / لطفاً
/ jok / **joke** / latife / لطیفه
/ kers / **curse** / laanat / لعنت
/ dam / **damn** / laanat kardan / لعنت کردن
/ slip / **slip** / laghzesh / لغزش
/ to slâyd / **to slide** / laghzidan / لغزیدن
/ to slip / **to slip** / laghzidan / لغزیدن
/ maothful / **mouthful** / loghme / لقمه
/ kik / **kick** / lagad / لگد
/ to tâch / **to touch** / lams kardan / لمس کردن
/ anker / **anchor** / langar / لنگر
/ to limp / **to limp** / langidan / لنگیدن
/ to krâsh / **to crush** / leh kardan / له کردن
/ dâyâlekt / **dialect** / lahje / لهجه
/ biin / **bean** / lubyâ / لوبیا
/ indâlj / **indulge** / lus kardan / لوس کردن
/ pâyp / **pipe** / lule / لوله
/ tyoob / **tube** / lule / لوله
/ leyzer / **laser** / leyzer / لیزر

لیسیدن / **to lick** / to lik /

لیف / **fiber** / fâyber /

لیموترش / **lemon** / limutorsh /

لیموناد / **lemonade** / limunâd /

م

ما / mâ / **we** / wii /

ماتیک / mâtik / **lipstick** / lipstik /

ماجرا / mâjarâ / **adventure** / edvencher /

ماجراجو / mâjarâju / **adventurer** / edvencherer /

ماجراجو / mâjarâju / **adventurous** / advencheres /

مادّه / mâdde / **material** / matiriyel /

مادّه / mâdde / **matter** / mater /

مادّه / mâdde / **stuff** / stâf /

مادر / mâdor / **mother** / mâder /

مادر بزرگ / mâdar bozorg / **grandmother** / granmâder /

مادر پدر / mâdar pedar / **parent** / perent /

ماده / mâde / **female** / fiimeyl /

مار / mâr / **snake** / sneyk /

مارا / mârâ / **us** / âs /

مارس / mârs / **March** / mârch /

ماست / mâst / **yogurt** / yogert /

ماسه / mâse / **sand** / sand /

ماشین لباسشویی / mâshine lebâs-shuii / **washer** / wâsher /

ماشین / mâshin / **automobile** / otomobiil /

ماشین / mâshin / **machine** / meshiin /

ماشین تحریر / mâshine tahrir / **typewriter** / tâyprâyter /

ماشین نویس / mâshin nevis / **typist** / tâypist /

مال آنها / mâle ânhâ / **theirs** / dherz /

مال او / mâle u / **his** / hiz /

مال کی / mâle ki / **whose** / hooz /

مال ما / mâle mâ / **ours** / aorz /

مال من / mâle man / **mine** / mâyn /

مال تو / mâle to / **yours** / yorz /

مالك / mâlek / **owner** / oner /

مالکیت / mâlekiyyat / **possession** / pozeshen /

مالیات / mâliyât / **tax** / taks /

مالیات بر درآمد / mâliyât bardarâmad / **income tax** /
inkâmtaks /

مایل / meyl / **mile** / mâyl /

ماما / mâ mâ / **midwife** / midvâyf /

مامان / mâmân / **mom** / mâm /

مامور آتش نشانی / mamure âtash neshani / **fireman** /
fâyerman /

مأموریت / mamuriyyat / **mission** / mishn /

ماندن / mândan / **to remain** / to rimeyn /

ماندن / mândan / **to stay** / to stey /

مانع / mânee / **obstacle** / âbstakel /

مانند / mânand / **as** / az /

ماه / moon / **moon** / mâh

ماه عسل / hânimun / **honeymoon** / mâhe asal

ماهواره / satelâyt / **satellite** / mâhvâre

ماهی / fish / **fish** / mâhi

ماهیچه / mâsel / **muscle** / mâhiche

ماهیگیری / fishing / **fishing** / mâhigiri

ماهی تابه / frâying pan / **frying pan** / mâhitâbe

ماهی دودی / kiper / **kipper** / mâhi dudi

مایع / likwid / **liquid** / mâyee

مایه / vaksin / **vaccine** / mâye

مأیوس / disapoyntid / **disappointed** / maayus

مبادله / ikscheyj / **exchange** / mobâdele

مبادله کردن / **to exchange** / mobâdleh kardan /
to ikscheynj

مبالغه کردن / **to exaggerate** / mubâleghe kardan /
to igzajereyt

مبلغ / sâm / **sum** / mablagh

مبله / fernisht / **furnished** / moble

متأسف / sâri / **sorry** / motassef

متأسفانه / ânforchunitli / **unfortunately** / motassefâne

متحد / alâyd / **allied** / mottahed

متحد / alây / **ally** / mottahed

متحد / kânfederit / **confederate** / mottahed

متحد شدن / mottahed shodan / **to unite** / to yoonâyt /

متحدد / mottahed / **united** / yoonâytid /

متحرك / motaharrek / **mobile** / mobâyl /

متخصص / motakhasses / **specialist** / speshâlist /

متخصص شدن / motakhasses shodan / **to specialize** / to speshâlâyz

متداول / motadâvel / **common** / kâmân /

متر / metr / **meter** / miiter /

مترو / metro / **subway** / sâbwey /

متشکرم / motashakkeram / **thanks** / thanks /

متصل کردن / mottasel kardan / **to join** / to joyn /

متصل کننده / mottasel konande / **modem** / modem /

متظاهر / motazâher / **pretentious** / pritenshes /

متفاوت / motafâvet / **different** / difrent /

متفکر / motafakker / **thoughtful** / thotful /

متقاعد کردن / motaghâeed kardan / **to convince** / to kânvins

مُتل / motel / **motel** / motel /

متمایل بودن / motamâyel budan / **to tend** / to tend /

متمدن کردن / motamadden kardan / **to civilize** / to sivilâye

متمرکز کردن / motamarkez kardan / **to centralize** / to sentrâlâyz

متمرکزکردن / motamarkez kardan / **to concentrate** /
/ to kânsentreyt

متن / matn / **text** / tekst /

مته / mate / **drill** / dril /

متوقف کردن / motavaghghef kardan / **to stop** / to stâp /

متولد / motavalled / **born** / born /

متکبر / motakabber / **snobbish** / snâbish /

مثال / mesâl / **example** / igzâmpel /

مثال / mesâl / **instance** / instans /

مثلاً / masalan / **for instance** / forinstance /

مثلث / mosallas / **triangle** / trâyangel /

مجادله کردن / mojâdele kardan / **to contend** / to kentend /

مجادله کردن / mojâdele kardan / **to contest** / to kântest /

مجبور کردن / majbur kardan / **to force** / to fors /

مجبور کردن / majbur kardan / **to oblige** / to âblâyj /

مجتمع / mojtamee / **complex** / kâmpleks /

مجرم / mojrem / **criminal** / kriminâl /

مجروح کردن / majruh kardan / **to injure** / to injer /

مجسمه / mojassame / **statue** / stachoo /

مجسمه سازی / mojassame sâzi / **sculpture** / skâlpcher /

مجلس / majles / **assembly** / asembli /

مجلس شورا / majlese shurâ / **parliament** / pârliment /

مجله / majalle / **magazine** / magaziin /

مجله فكاهى / majalleye fokâhi / **comics** / kâmiks /

مجمع / majmaa / **congress** / kongres /

مجموع / majmuu / **total** / total /

مجهز كردن / mojahhaz kardan / **equip** / ikwip /

مچ / moch / **wrist** / rist /

مچ پا / mochepâ / **ankle** / ankel /

محاصره / mohâsere / **blockade** / blâkeyd /

محافظ / mohâfez / **protector** / protektor /

محافظت / mohâfezat / **protection** / protekshen /

محافظت كردن / mohâfezat kardan / **to protect** / to protekt /

محافظه كارى / muhafeze kâr / **conservatism** /
kânservatizem /

محاكمه / mohâkeme / **trial** / trâyâl /

محبوب / mahbub / **favorite** / feyverit /

محبوب / mahbub / **popular** / pâpyuler /

محترم / mohtaram / **decent** / diisent /

محترم / mohtaram / **respectable** / rispektebel /

محتمل / mohtamal / **likely** / lâykli /

محتوا / mohtevâ / **content** / kântent /

محدود كردن / mahdud kardan / **to restrict** / to ristrikt /

محدوديت / mahdudiyyat / **restriction** / ristrikshen /

محرمانه / mahramâne / **secretly** / siikritli /

محصول / mahsul / **product** / prâdâkt /

محكم / mohkam / **firm** / ferm /

محكم / mohkam / **steady** / stedi /

محكم / mohkam / **tight** / tâyt /

محل / mahal / **site** / sâyt /

محلّى / mahalli / **local** / lokâl /

محوطه دانشگاه / mohavvateye dâneshgâh / **campus** /
kampes /

محيط / mohit / **environment** / invârenment /

محكم / mohkam / **firmly** / fermli /

محكم / mohkam / **grasp** / grasp /

محكوم كردن / mahkum kardan / **to condemn** /
to kândem /

محكوميت / mahkumiyyat / **condemnation** /
kândemneyshen /

مخالف / mokhâlef / **opposite** / apozit /

مخالفت / mokhâlefat / **opposition** / âpozishen /

مخالفت كردن / mokhâlefat kardan / **to oppose** / to opoz /

مخالفت كردن / mokhâlefat kardan / **to disagree** /
to disagrii /

مختصر / mokhtasar / **brief** / briif /

مختلف / mokhtalef / **heterogeneous** / heterojilinieys /

مخصوص / makhsus / **special** / speshâl /

مخصوصاً / makhsusan / **especially** / ispeshâli /

مخصوصًا / makhsusan / **specially** / speshâli /

مخصوصًا / makhsusan / **particularly** / pârtikyulerli /

مخفی کردن / makhfi kardan / **to hide** / to hâyd /

مخلوط / makhlut / **cocktail** / kâkteyl /

مخلوط / makhlut / **mixture** / mikscher /

مخلوط کردن / makhlut kardan / **to mix** / to miks /

مخمل / makhmal / **velvet** / velvit /

مد / mod / **style** / stâyl /

مُد / mod / **fashionable** / fashenebel /

مداد / medâd / **pencil** / pensil /

مدار / madâr / **circuit** / serkit /

مدار / madâr / **orbit** / orbit /

مداعی / modâii / **defensive** / difensiv /

مدافع / modâfee / **defender** / difender /

مدام / modâm / **endlessly** / endlisli /

مدرسه / madrase / **school** / skool /

مدل / model / **model** / mâdel /

مدنی / madani / **civil** / sivil /

مدیر / modir / **director** / directer /

مدیر / modir / **manager** / manijer /

مدیریت / modiriyyat / **management** / manijment /

مرا / marâ / **me** / mii /

مراسم / marâsem / **ceremony** / serimoni /

175

مراقبت / morâghebat / **care** / ker /

مربا / morabba / **jam** / jam /

مربای پرتقال / morabbâye portaghâl / **marmalade** /

mârmeleyd /

مربع / morabbaa / **square** / skwer /

مربوط / marbut / **relative** / reletiv /

مرتب / morattab / **regular** / regyuler /

مرتب / morattab / **regularly** / regyulârli /

مرتب / morattab / **tidy** / tâydi /

مرتب کردن / morrattab kardan / **to arrange** / to areynj /

مرتکب شدن / mortâkeb shodan / **to commit** / to kâmit /

مرجع / marjaa / **reference** / referens /

مرد / mard / **fellow** / felo /

مرد / mard / **guy** / gây /

مرد / mard / **man** / man /

مردم / mardom / **folk** / fok /

مردم / mardom / **people** / piipel /

مردم / mardom / **public** / pâblik /

مردن / mordan / **die** / dây /

مرده / morde / **dead** / ded /

مرز / marz / **border** / border /

مرز / marz / **frontier** / frântiyer /

مرسوم / marsum / **conventional** / kânvenshenal /

176

مرطوب / martub / **damp** / damp /

مرکز / markaz / **center** / senter /

مرکزی / markazi / **central** / sentrâl /

مرکّب / morakkab / **ink** / ink /

مرگ / marg / **death** / deth /

مرموز / marmuz / **mysterious** / mistiriyes /

مرور / murur / **review** / rivyu /

مزاحم شدن / mozâhem shodan / **to disturb** / to disterb /

مزایده / mozâyede / **auction** / âkshn /

مزرعه / mazrae / **farm** / fârm /

مزرعه / mazrae / **field** / fiild /

مزرعه دار / mazraedâr / **farmer** / fârmer /

مزه / maze / **zest** / zest /

مژگان / mozhgân / **eyelash** / âylash /

مسئله / masale / **problem** / prâblem /

مسؤلیّت / masuuliyyet / **responsibility** / rispânsibiliti /

مسئول / masuul / **responsible** / rispânsibel /

مسابقه / mosâbeghe / **match** / mach /

مسابقه / mosâbeghe / **race** / reys /

مسابقه دوی ماراتون / mosâbegheye doe mârâton /
marathon / marathân /

مسافت / masâfat / **distance** / distans /

مسافر / mosâfer / **passenger** / pasinjer /

177

مسافر / **traveler** / mosâfer / travler /

مسافر / **voyager** / mosâfer / voyejer /

مسافرت / **trip** / mosâferat / trip /

مسافرخانه / **inn** / mosâfer khâne / in /

مست / **drunk** / mast / drânk /

مستطیل / **rectangle** / mostatil / rektangel /

مستعد / **apt** / mostaeed / apt /

مستعمر / **colony** / mostaamar / kâleni /

مستقیم / **direct** / mostaghim / direkt /

مستقیم / **right** / mostaghim / râyt /

مستقیماً / **directly** / mostaghiman / direktli /

مستمری / **pension** / mostamari / penshen /

مسجد / **mosque** / masjed / mâsk /

مسری / **infectious** / mosri / infekshes /

مسکن / **sedative** / mosakken / sedativ /

مسلح / **armed** / mosallah / ârmd /

مسلح کردن / **to arm** / mosallah kardan / to ârm /

مسلط بودن / **to dominate** / mosallat budan / to dâmineyt /

مسلم / **undisputed** / mosallam / ândispyootid /

مسلمان / **Muslim** / mosalmân / mâzlem /

مسواك / **toothbrush** / mesvâk / toothbrâsh /

مسیحیت / **Christianity** / masihiyyat / kristiyaniti /

مسیر / **course** / masir / kors /

178

مسکونی / maskuni / **built-up** / biltâp /

مشاهده / moshâhede / **observation** / âbzerveyshen /

مشاهده کردن / moshâhede kardan / **to observe** /
to âbzerv /

مشاهده کننده / moshâhede konande / **observer** /
âbzerver /

مشت / mosht / **fist** / fist /

مشتاق / moshtagh / **eager** / iiger /

مشتری / moshtari / **client** / klâyent /

مشتری / moshtari / **customer** / kâstemer /

مشروب فروشی / mashrubfrushi / **bar** / bâr /

مشغول / mashghul / **busy** / bizi /

مشکل / moshkel / **difficult** / difikâlt /

مشهور / mashhur / **famous** / feymes /

مشکل / moshkel / **choosy** / choozi /

مشکل / moshkel / **difficulty** / difikâlti /

مصاحبت / mosâhebat / **company** / kâmpani /

مصاحبه / mosâhebe / **interview** / interviyoo /

مصادره کردن / mosâdere kardan / **to seize** / to siiz /

مصالحه / mosâlehe / **compromise** / kâmpromâyz /

مصر / mesr / **Egypt** / iijipt /

مصرف کننده / masraf konande / **user** / yoozer /

179

مصرف کردن / masraf kardan / **to consume** /
to kânsyoom /

مصرف کننده / masraf konande / **consumer** /
kânsyoomer /

مصنوعی / masnoii / **artificial** / ârtifishâl /

مضر / mozer / **harmful** / hârmful /

مضر / mozer / **pernicious** / pernishes /

مضطرب کردن / moztareb kardan / **to agitate** / to ajiteyt /

مضطربانه / moztarebâne / **anxiously** / ankshesli /

مطالعه / motâlee / **study** / stâdi /

مطلع کردن / mottalee kardan / **to inform** / to inform /

مطمئن / motmaeen / **confident** / kânfident /

مطمئن / motmaen / **sure** / shur /

معالجه کردن / moâleje kardan / **to treat** / to triit /

معامله / moâmele / **bargain** / bâgin /

معاون / moââven / **assistant** / esistent /

معاینه / moâyene / **inspection** / inspekshen /

معبد / maabad / **temple** / templ /

معتبر / motabar / **valid** / valid /

معدن / maadan / **mine** / mâyn /

معدنچی / madanchi / **miner** / mâyner /

معده / meede / **stomach** / stâmak /

معدود / maadud / **few** / fyoo /

معدودی / maadudi / **handful** / handful /

معرفی / moarrefi / **introduction** / introdâkshen /

معرفی کردن / moarrefi kardan / **to introduce** / to introdyoos /

معلم / moallem / **instructor** / instâkter /

معلم / moallem / **teacher** / tîlcher /

معمار / meemâr / **architect** / ârkitekt /

معماری / meemâri / **architecture** / ârkitekcher /

معمولاً / mamulan / **generally** / jenrâli /

معمولاً / mamulan / **normally** / normâli /

معمولاً / mamulan / **usually** / yoozhuwâli /

معمولی / maamuli / **ordinary** / ordineri /

معنی دادن / maani dâdan / **to mean** / to miin /

معنی / maani / **meaning** / miining /

معین کردن / moayyan kardan / **to determine** / to ditermin /

معکوس / maakus / **reverse** / rivers /

مغازه / maghâze / **shop** / shâp /

مغازه دار / maghâzedâr / **shopkeeper** / shâpkiiper /

مغرضانه / moghrezâne / **malicious** / melishes /

مغرور / maghrur / **imperious** / impiriyes /

مغز / maghz / **brain** / breyn /

مفصل / mafsal / **joint** / joynt /

مفید / mofid / **helpful** / helpful /

مفید / mofid / **useful** / yoosful /

مقاله / maghâle / **article** / ârtikel /

مقاومت / moghavemat / **resistance** / rizistens /

مقاومت کردن / moghavemat kardan / **to resist** / to rizist /

مقایسه / moghâyese / **compare** / kâmper /

مقایسه / moghâyese / **comparison** / kamparisen /

مقایسه / moghâyese / **to contrast** / to kântrâst /

مقایسه کردن / moghâyese kardan / **contrast** / kântrâst /

مقدار / megdâr / **amount** / emaunt /

مقدار / meghdâr / **bulk** / bâlk /

مقدار / meghdâr / **deal** / diil /

مقدس / maghaddas / **holy** / geuly /

مقدماتی / moghaddamâti / **elementary** / elimentri /

مقرری / mogharrari / **allowance** / elao-ens /

مقیاس / meghyâs / **measure** / mezher /

مکاتبه / mokâtebe / **correspondence** / kârispândens /

مکانیسم / mekanism / **mechanism** / mekanizim /

مکث / maks / **pause** / poz /

مکعب / mokaab / **cube** / kyoob /

مگر این که / magarinke / **unless** / ânles /

مگس / magas / **fly** / flây /

ملاقات کردن / molâghat kardan / **to meet** / to miit /

/ to incorporate / molhagh kardan / ملحق کردن /
/ to inkorporeyt

/ kwiin / **queen** / malake / ملکه
/ neyshen / **nation** / mellat / ملت
/ nahnâl / **national** / melli / ملی
/ nashenaliti / **nationality** / melliyat / ملیت
/ nashenalizem / **nationalism** / melligarâyi / ملی گرایی
/ seyler / **sailor** / malavân / ملوان
/ pâsibel / **possible** / momken / ممکن
/ to ban / **to ban** / mamnuu kardan / ممنوع کردن
/ ây / **I** / man / من
/ risorsiz / **resources** / manâbee / منابع
/ kânviiniyent / **convenient** / monâseb / مناسب
/ fit / **fit** / monâseb / مناسب
/ prâper / **proper** / monâseb / مناسب
/ to soot / **to suit** / monâseb budan / مناسب بودن
/ sootebel / **suitable** / monâseb / مناست
/ sors / **source** / manbaa / منبع
/ kritik / **critic** / montaghed / منتقد
/ kânvey / **convey** / montaghel / منتقل
/ ikstremiti / **extremity** / montahâ daraje / منتها درجه
/ to strey / **to stray** / monharef shodan / منحرف شدن
/ ârijin / **origin** / manshaa / منشا

183

منشی / monshi / **clerk** / klerk /

منشی / monshi / **secretary** / sekreteri /

منصف / monsef / **fair** / fer /

منصوب کردن / mansub kardan / **to appoint** / to epoynt /

منطق / mantegh / **logic** / lâjik /

منطقه / mantaghe / **area** / eryâ /

منطقه / mantaghe / **region** / rijen /

منطقه / mantaghe / **zone** / zon /

منطقه ای / mantagheyi / **zonal** / zonl /

منطقی / manteghi / **logical** / lâjikl /

منطقی / manteghi / **reasonable** / riizenebel /

منظره / manzare / **landscape** / landskeyp /

منظره / manzare / **panorama** / panorâmâ /

منظور / manzur / **purpose** / perpes /

منع / manee / **prohibition** / prohibishn /

منع کردن / manee kardan / **to prohibit** / to prohibit /

منعکس کردن / monaakes kardan / **to reflect** / to riflekt /

منفجرکردن / monfajer kardan / **to explode** / to iksplod /

منفی / manfi / **negative** / negetiv /

منقار / menghâr / **bill** / bil /

مه / meh / **fog** / fâg /

مه / meh / **May** / mey /

مه / meh / **mist** / mist /

مه آلود / mehâlud / **foggy** / fâgi /

مهاجر / mohâjer / **emigrant** / emigrent /

مهاجر / mohâjer / **immigrant** / imigrent /

مهاجر / mohâjer / **settler** / setler /

مهاجرت / mohâjerat / **immigration** / imigreyshen /

مهاجرت کردن / mohâjerat kardan / **to emigrate** /
to emigreyt /

مهاجم / mohâjem / **attacker** / etaker /

مهارت / mahârat / **skill** / skil /

مهارت / mahârat / **technique** / tekniik /

مهربان / mehrebân / **gentle** / jentel /

مهربان / mehrabân / **gracious** / greyshes /

مهربان / mehrabân / **kind** / kâynd /

مهربانی / mehrabâni / **kindness** / kâyndnis /

مهلک / mohlek / **fatal** / feytal /

مهم / mohem / **important** / importent /

مهمان / mehmân / **guest** / gest /

مهمان نوازی / mehmân navâzi / **hospitality** / hâspitaliti /

مهماندار / mehmândâr / **hostess** / hostis /

مهماندار / mehmândâr / **steward** / styuwerd /

مهماندار زن / mehmândâre zan / **stewardess** /
styuwerdis /

مهیج / mohayyej / **exciting** / iksâyting /

185

مو / mu / **hair** / her /

مواظب / movâzeb / **attentive** / atentiv /

مواظب / movâzeb / **careful** / kerful /

مواظب بودن / movâzeb budan / **to beware** / to biwer /

مواظب بودن / movâzeb budan / **to mind** / to mâynd /

موافقت کردن / movâfegat kardan / **to agree** / to egrii /

موبور / mubor / **blond** / blând /

موتور / motor / **engine** / enjin /

موتور / motor / **motor** / motor /

موتور / motor / **scooter** / skooter /

موتورسیکلت / motorsiklet / **motorcycle** / motorsâykel /

موتورسیکلت / motorsikelet / **motorbike** / motorbâyk /

مؤثر / moasser / **effective** / ifectiv /

موج / moj / **wave** / weyv /

موج گیر / mojgir / **antenna** / antene /

موجود / mojud / **creature** / kriicher /

موجود زنده / mojude zende / **organism** / organizem /

موجودی / mojudi / **stock** / stâk /

مؤدب / moaddab / **polite** / polâyt /

مورچه / murche / **ant** / ant /

موز / muz / **banana** / banânâ /

موزه / muze / **museum** / myooziyem /

مؤسسه / moassese / **institute** / instityoot /

موسمی / mosemi / **seasonal** / sizenl /

موسیقی / museghi / **music** / myoozik /

موش / mush / **mouse** / maos /

موش / mush / **rat** / rat /

موشك / mushak / **rocket** / râkit /

موشک / mushak / **missile** / misâyl /

موضعی / mozeii / **locally** / lokâli /

موضوع / mozu / **proposition** / prâpozishen /

موضوع / mozuu / **subject** / sâbjikt /

موضوع / mozu / **topic** / tâpik /

موفق / movaffagh / **prosperous** / prâspres /

موفق / movaffagh / **successful** / sâksesful /

موفق شدن / movaffagh shodan / **to prosper** / to prâsper /

موفق شدن / movaffagh shodan / **to succeed** / to sâksiid /

موفقیت / movaffaghiyat / **success** / sâkses /

موقعی که / mogheii ke / **while** / wâyl /

موقت / movaghghat / **provisional** / provishenâl /

مولد / movalled / **generator** / jenereyter /

موم / mum / **wax** / waks /

میان / miyân / **among** / emâng /

میانگین / miyângin / **average** / averij /

میدان / meydân / **plaza** / plâzâ /

میدان / meydân / **square** / skwer /

میراث / mirâs / **heritage** / heritij /

میز / miz / **desk** / desk /

میز / miz / **table** / teybel /

میل / meyl / **rod** / râd /

میلیون / milyon / **million** / milyen /

میلیونر / milyoner / **millionaire** / milyener /

میمون / meymun / **monkey** / mânki /

مینا / minâ / **enamel** / inaml /

مینیاتور / minyâtur / **miniature** / minicher /

میوه / mive / **fruit** / froot /

میوه مغزدار / miveye maghzdâr / **nut** / nât /

میکروفن / mikrofon / **microphone** / mâykrofon /

مکالمه / mokâleme / **dialogue** / dâyâlâg /

مکانیک / mekânik / **mechanic** / mikanik /

مکانیکی / mekâniki / **mechanical** / mikanikâl /

ن

نا آگاه / nâ âgâh / **ignorant** / ignorent /

نا برابری / nâbarâbari / **inequality** / inikwâliti /

نا محدود / nâ mahdud / **unlimited** / ânlimitid /

نا مناسب / nâ monâseb / **awkward** / okword /

نابغه / nâbeghe / **genius** / jinies /

نابودی / nâbudi / **extinction** / ikstinkshen /

ناپدید شدن / nâpadid shodan / **to disappear** /
to disapiyer /

ناپدید شدن / nâpadid shodan / **to vanish** / to vanish /

ناتوان / nâtavân / **incapable** / inkeypebel /

ناتوان / nâtavân / **unable** / âneybel /

ناخن / nâkhon / **nail** / neyl /

ناخوشایند / nâ khoshâyand / **unpleasant** / ânplezent /

نادر / nâder / **rare** / rer /

نادرست / nâdorost / **dishonest** / disânist /

ناراحت / nârâhat / **uncomfortable** / ânkâmftebel /

ناراحت کردن / nârâhat kardan / **to annoy** / to anoy /

ناراحت کردن / nârâhat kardan / **to bother** / to bâdher /

ناراحت کردن / nârâhat kardan / **to worry** / to wâri /

ناسالم / nâsâlâm / **unhealthy** / ânhelthi /

ناشناخته / nâshenâkhte / **unknown** / ânnoon /

ناشناس / nâshenâs / **unidentifield** / ânâydenifâyd /

ناشی دانستن از / nâshi dânestan az / **attribute** / etibyoot /

ناشی شدن از / nâshi shodan az / **result** / rizâlt /

نافرمانی کردن / nâ farmâni kardan / **to disobey** /

to disobey /

ناگهان / nâgahân / **suddenly** / sâdenli /

ناگهانی / nâgahâni / **abrupt** / ebrâpt /

ناگهانی / nâgahâni / **sudden** / sâden /

ناگهانی / nâgahâni / **abruptly** / ebrâptli /

نالایق / nâ lâyegh / **incompetent** / inkâmpitent /

ناله کردن / nâle kardan / **to moan** / to mon /

نام خانوادگی / nâme khânevâdegi / **surname** / sermeym /

نامرئی / nâmarii / **invisible** / invizibel /

نامرد / nâmard / **coward** / kâved /

نامزد / nâmzad / **engaged** / ingeyjd /

نامزدی / nâmzadi / **engagement** / ingeyjiment /

نامشروع / nâ mashruu / **bastard** / basterd /

نامطلوب / nâmatlub / **adverse** / advers /

ناممکن / nâmomken / **impossible** / impâsibel /

نامه / nâme / **letter** / leter /

نان / nân / **bread** / bred /

نانوا / nânvâ / **baker** / beyker /

ناهار / nâhâr / **lunch** / lânch /

ناهموار / nâhamvâr / **rough** / râf /

ناوگان / nâvgân / **armada** / ârmâdâ /

نایلون / nâylon / **nylon** / nâylân /

نبرد / nabard / **battle** / batel /

نترس / natars / **fearless** / fiyerlis /

نتیجه / natije / **consequence** / kânsikwens /

نتیجه / hatije / **result** / rizâlt /

نجات دادن / nejât dâdan / **to rescue** / to reskyoo /

نجات دادن / nejât dâdan / **to rid** / to rid /

نجات دادن / nejat dâdan / **to save** / to seyv /

نجوا کردن / najvâ kardan / **to whisper** / to wisper /

نخ / nakh / **string** / string /

نخست وزیر / nokhost vazir / **prime minister** /
prâymminister /

نخستین / nokhostin / **original** / orijinâl /

نخستین / nokhostin / **primary** / prâymeri /

نخود / nokhod / **pea** / pii /

نداشتن / nadâshtan / **lack** / lak /

نر / nar / **male** / meyl /

نرخ / nerkh / **rate** / reyt /

نردبان / nardebân / **ladder** / lader /

191

نرم / narm / **soft** / sâft /

نزاع / nezââ / **dispute** / dispyut /

نزدیك / nazdik / **close** / klos /

نزدیك / nazdik / **near** / niyer /

نزدیكِ / nazdike / **by** / bây /

نزدیك شدن / nazdik shodan / **to approach** / to eproch /

نزدیك / nazdik / **adjacent** / ejeysnt /

نژاد / nazhâd / **race** / reys /

نژادی / nazhâdi / **racial** / reyshâl /

نساجی / nassâji / **textile** / tekstâyl /

نسبت / nesbat / **relation** / rileyshn /

نسبتًا / nesbatan / **pretty** / piriti /

نسبتًا / nesbatan / **relatively** / reletivli /

نسخه / noskhe / **copy** / kâpi /

نسخه / noskhe / **prescription** / priskripshen /

نشان / neshân / **badge** / baj /

نشان / neshân / **indication** / indikeyshen /

نشان / neshân / **mark** / mârk /

نشان / neshân / **medal** / medâl /

نشان دادن / neshân dâdan / **demonstration** / demonstreyshen /

نشان دادن / neshân dâdan / **to display** / to displey /

نشان دادن / neshân dâdan / **to expose** / to ikspoz /

نشان دادن / neshân dâdan / **to indicate** / to indikeyt /

نشان دادن / neshân dâdan / **to produce** / to prodyoos /

نشان دادن / neshân dâdan / **to represent** / to reprizent /

نشان دادن / neshân dâdan / **to reveal** / to riviil /

نشان دادن / neshân dâdan / **to show** / to sho /

نشانی / neshâni / **address** / edres /

نشتن / neshastan / **sit** / sit /

نشریه / nashriye / **journal** / jernâl /

نصب / nasb / **installation** / instoleyshen /

نصب کردن / nasb kardan / **to fix** / to fiks /

نصب کردن / nasb kardan / **to install** / to instol /

نصف / nesf / **half** / hâf /

نصیحت / nasihat / **advice** / advâys /

نظارت / nezârat / **control** / kentrol /

نظافت چی / nezâfatchi / **cleaner** / kliiner /

نظام / nezâm / **system** / sistem /

نظامی / nezâmi / **military** / militeri /

نظر / nazar / **comment** / kâment /

نظر / nazar / **opinion** / opinyen /

نظریه / nazariye / **theory** / tieri /

نظم / nazm / **arrangement** / areynjment /

نعلبکی / naalbaki / **saucer** / soser /

نفتکش / naftkesh / **oil tanker** / oyl tanker /

نفرت / nefrat / **disgust** / disgâst /

نفرت انگیز / nefrat angiz / **disgusting** / disgvsting /

نفرت انگیز / nefrat angiz / **repulsive** / ripâlsiv /

نفرت انگیز / nefrat angiz / **abominable** / ebâminebel /

نفس / nafas / **breath** / breth /

نفس کشیدن / nafas keshidan / **to breathe** / to briidh /

نفوذ / nefuz / **influence** / influ-ens /

نقاش / naghghâsh / **painter** / peynter /

نقاشی / naghghâshi / **drawing** / dro-ing /

نقاشی / naghghâshi / **painting** / peynting /

نقره / noghre / **silver** / silver /

نقش / naghsh / **role** / rol /

نقشه / naghshe / **map** / map /

نقشه / naghshe / **plan** / plan /

نقص / naghs / **defect** / diifekt /

نقص / naghs / **handicap** / handikap /

نقطه / noghte / **dot** / dât /

نقطه / noghte / **point** / poynt /

نقل / naghl / **narration** / nareyshen /

نقل کردن / naghl kardan / **narrate** / nareyt /

نگارخانه / negârkhâne / **gallery** / galeri /

نگاه / negâh / **to look** / to luk /

نگاه کردن / negâh kardan / **look** / luk /

نگاهبان / negahbân / **guard** / gârd /

نگران / negarân / **anxious** / ankshes /

نگران / negarân / **concerned** / kânsernd /

نگرش / negaresh / **attitude** / atityood /

نگه داشتن / negah dâshtan / **to keep** / to kiip /

نگهداری / negahdâri / **reservation** / rezerveyshen /

نماد / nemâd / **symbol** / simbel /

نمایان شدن / nemâyân shodan / **emerge** / imerj /

نمایش / nemâyesh / **revue** / rivioo /

نمایش / nemâyesh / **show** / sho /

نمایش دادن / nemâyesh dâdan / **to exhibit** / to egzibit /

نمایشگاه / nemâyeshgâh / **exhibition** / eksibishen /

نمایشی / nemâyeshi / **dramatic** / dramatik /

نماینده / nemâyande / **agent** / eyjent /

نمره دادن / nomre dâdan / **to mark** / to mârk /

نمك / namak / **salt** / solt /

نمودار / nemudâr / **graph** / grâf /

نمونه / nemune / **typical** / tipikâl /

نه / na / **no** / no /

نه / na / **nope** / nop /

نه / na / **not** / nât /

نه / noh / **nine** / nâyn /

نهارخوری / nâhârkhori / **dining room** / dâyning-rum /

195

ن Farsi-English

نهایی / nahâii / **extreme** / ikstriim /
نهایی / nehâyi / **final** / fâynâl /
نوار / navâr / **ribbon** / riben /
نوار / navâr / **stripe** / strip /
نوار / navâr / **tape** / teyp /
نوازنده / navâzande / **musician** / myoozishen /
نوامبر / novâmbr / **November** / november /
نوجوان / nojavân / **teenager** / tiineyjer /
نوجوانی / nojavâni / **teenage** / tiineyj /
نود / navad / **ninety** / nâynti /
نور / nur / **light** / lâyt /
نوزده / nuzdah / **nineteen** / nâyntiin /
نوزدهمی / nuzdahomi / **nineteenth** / nâyntiinth /
نوسان / navasân / **fluctuation** / fluctuation /
نوسان کردن / navasân kardan / **to fluctuate** / to fluctuate /
نوشابه / nushâbe / **drink** / drink /
نوشتن / neveshtan / **to write** / to râyt /
نوشته / neveshte / **inscription** / inskripshen /
نوشته / neveshte / **writing** / râyting /
نوع / noe / **kind** / kâynd /
نوع / noe / **make** / meyk /
نوع بشر / noee bashar / **mankind** / mankâynd /
نوک / nuk / **top** / tâp /

196

نوه ها / **grandchildren** / navehâ / granchildren /
نویسنده / **author** / nevisande / other /
نویسنده / **writer** / nevisande / râyter /
نیاز / **need** / niyâz / niid /
نیرو / **energy** / niru / enerji /
نیرو / **power** / niru / pawer /
نیروی دریایی / **navy** / niruye daryâyi / neyvi /
نیز / **too** / niz / too /
کنیسه / **synagogue** / kanise / sinâgâg /
نیش / **sting** / nish / sting /
نیمه / **mid** / nime / mid /
نیمه شب / **midnight** / nimeshab / midnâyt /
نیک بین / **optimist** / nikbin / âptimist /

هاکی / hockey / hâki / hâki /
هتل / hotel / hotel / hotel /
هجا / syllable / silâbel / hejâ /
هجی / spelling / speling / hejji /
هجی کردن / spell / spel / hejji kardan /
هدایت / steering / stiyering / hedâyat /
هدایت کردن / to steer / to stiyer / hedâyat kardan /
هدف / goal / gol / hadaf /
هدف / target / târgit / hadaf /
هدیه / present / prezent / hadiye /
هر / each / iich / har /
هر / every / evri / har /
هر / per / per / har /
هراسان / frantic / frantic / harâsân /
هرج و مرج / anarchy / aneki / harjomarj /
هرجاکه / wherever / werever / harjâke /
هرچند / however / haoever / harchand /
هرچیز / everything / evrithing / harchiz /
هردو / both / both / hardo /

هرطرف / hartaraf / **around** / eraond /

هرکس / harkas / **anybody** / enibâdi /

هرکس / harkas / **everybody** / evribâdi /

هرکس / harkas / **everyone** / evriwân /

هرگز / hargez / **never** / never /

هروقت / harvaght / **whenever** / wenever /

هزار / hezâr / **thousand** / thaozend /

هزینه / hazine / **expense** / ikspens /

هزینه پست / hazineye post / **postage** / postij /

هستم / hastam / **am** / am /

هسته ای / hasteii / **nuclear** / nyookliyer /

هستی / hasti / **existence** / igzistens /

هشت / hasht / **eight** / yet /

هشتاد / hashtâd / **eighty** / eyti /

هشدار دادن / hoshdâr dâdan / **to warn** / to worn /

هضم / hazm / **digestion** / dijeschen /

هضم کردن / hazm kardan / **to digest** / to dijest /

هفت / haft / **seven** / seven /

هفتاد / haftâd / **seventy** / seventi /

هفتگی / haftegi / **weekly** / wiikli /

هفتمین / haftomin / **seventh** / seventh /

هفته / hafte / **week** / wiik /

هفده / hefdah / **seventeen** / seventiin /

199

هفده همین / **seventeenth** / hefdahomin / seventiinth /

هلو / **peach** / hulu / piich /

هم / **also** / ham / olso /

هم میهن / **compatriot** / ham mihan / kâmpatriyet /

همان / **same** / haman / seym /

همانند / **similar** / hamânand / similâr /

همدردی / **sympathy** / hamdardi / simpathi /

همسایه / **neighbor** / hamsâye / neyber /

همسایگی / **neighborhood** / hamsâyegi / neyberhud /

همکاری / **association** / hamkâri / asosiyeyshen /

همه / **all** / hame / ol /

همه / **whole** / hame / hol /

همه جا / **everywhere** / hamejâ / evriwer /

همه گیر / **epidemic** / hamegir / epidemic /

هموار / **flat** / hamvâr / flat /

همیشگی / **frequent** / hamishegi / frikvent /

همیشگی / **perpetually** / hamishegi / perpechuwâli /

همیشه / **always** / hamishe / olweyz /

همیشه / **forever** / hamishe / forever /

همکار / **colleague** / hamkâr / kâliig /

هند / **India** / hend / indiyâ /

هندی / **Indian** / hendi / indiyen /

هنر / **art** / honar / ârt /

200

هنرپیشه / honarpishe / **actor** / akter /

هنرمند / honarmand / **artist** / ârtist /

هنری / honari / **artistic** / âtistic /

هنوز / hanuz / **still** / stil /

هنوز / hanuz / **yet** / yet /

هوا / havâ / **air** / er /

هوا / havâ / **weather** / wedher /

هوا پیمایی / havâ peymâyi / **airline** / erlâyn /

هواپیما / havâpeymâ / **airplane** / erpleyn /

هواپیما / havâpeymâ / **aircraft** / erkrâft /

هواپیما / havâpeyma / **plane** / pleyn /

هواپیمایی / havâpeymâyi / **aviation** / eyvlieyshn /

هواسنج / havâsanj / **barometer** / beromiter /

هواپیما ربایی / havâpeymâ robâii / **hijack** / hâyjak /

هواپیماربا / havâpeymârobâ / **hijacker** / hâyjaker /

هوایی / havâyi / **aerial** / eriel /

هورا / hura / **hooray** / hoorey /

هوش / hush / **intelligence** / intelijens /

هولناک / holnâk / **fearful** / fiyrful /

هویج / havich / **carrot** / karot /

هویّت / hoviyyat / **identity** / âydentiti /

هیچ چیز / hich chiz / **nothing** / nâthing /

هیاهو / hayâhu / **fuss** / fâs /

هیپی / **hippie** / hipi / هیپی

هیجان / **excitement** / iksâytment / هیجان

هیجان زده / **excited** / iksâytid / heyejânzade

هیجده / **eighteen** / eytiin / hijdah

هیجدهمین / **eighteenth** / eytinth / hijdahomin

هیچ / **any** / eni / hich

هیچ جا / **nowhere** / nower / hichjâ

هیچ کدام / **neither** / nâydher / hich kodâm

هیچکس / **nobody** / nobâdi / hichkas

هیچوقت / **ever** / ever / hichvaght

هیچیک / **none** / nân / hichyek

هیدروژن / **hydrogen** / hâydrojen / hidrojen

هیس! / **hush!** / hâsh / his

هیستری / **hysteria** / histeriyâ / histeri

هیولا / **monster** / mânster / hayulâ

و

و / va / **and** / and /

وابسته / vâbaste / **dependent** / dipendent /

وابسته بودن / vâbaste budan / **depend** / dipend /

وارد شدن / vâred shodan / **to enter** / to enter /

وارد کردن / vared kardan / **to import** / to import /

واردات / vâredât / **importation** / importeyshen /

وارونه کردن / vârune kardan / **to invert** / to invert /

واژگان / vâzhgân / **vocabulary** / vekabyuleri /

واقعًا / vâghean / **really** / riyeli /

واقعی / vâghei / **actual** / akchuwâl /

واقعی / vâgheii / **objective** / âbjectiv /

واقعی / vâgheii / **real** / riyel /

واقعیت / vâgheiyyat / **fact** / fakt /

واکنش / vâkonesh / **reaction** / rlakshen /

واگذاری / vâgozâri / **session** / seshen /

وانت / vânet / **van** / van /

وانیل / vânil / **vanilla** / vânilâ /

وبا / vabâ / **cholera** / kolere /

وجود داشتن / vujut dâshtan / **exist** / igzist /

وحدت / vahdat / **unity** / yooniti /

وحشت / vahshat / **horror** / hârer /

وحشت / vahshat / **panic** / panik /

وحشت / vahshat / **terror** / terer /

وحشتناك / vahshatnâk / **awful** / oful /

وحشتناك / vahshatnâk / **horrible** / hâribel /

وحشتناك / vahshatnâk / **terrible** / teribel /

وحشتناک / vahshatnâk / **terrifying** / terifâying /

وحشی / vahshi / **wild** / wâyld /

وحشیانه / vahshiyâne / **savagely** / savijli /

وحشیگری / vahshigari / **wildness** / wâyldnis /

وحشی / vahshi / **savage** / savij /

ورزش / varzesh / **athletics** / athletiks /

ورزش / varzesh / **sport** / sport /

ورزشکار / varzeshkâr / **athlete** / atlit /

ورزشگاه / varzeshgâh / **stadium** / steydiyem /

ورزشی / varzeshi / **athletic** / athletik /

ورود / vurud / **entry** / entri /

ورودی / vurudi / **entrance** / entrens /

وزارت / vezârat / **ministry** / ministri /

وزغ / vazagh / **frog** / frog /

وزن / vazn / **weight** / weyt /

وزن کردن / vazn kardan / **to weigh** / to wey /

وزیدن / vazidan / **to blow** / to blo /

وزیر / vazir / **minister** / minister /

وسایل خانه / vasâyele khâne / **furniture** / fernicher /

وسط / az vasat / **across** / ekros /

وسط / vasat / **middle** / midel /

وسیله / vaslle / **instrument** / instrument /

وسیله / vasile / **means** / miininz /

وسیله نقلیه / vasileye naghliye / **vehicle** / viyikel /

پوشاندن / pushândan / **to conceal** / to kânsiil /

وضع / vaz / **position** / pozishen /

وضع / vazee / **state** / steyt /

وضع اضطراری / vazee ezterâri / **emergency** / imerjensi /

وضعیت / vaziyat / **condition** / kândishen /

وضعیّت / vaziyyat / **situation** / sichuweyshen /

وطن پرست / vatanparast / **nationalist** / nashenalist /

وطن پرست / vatanparast / **patriot** / patriyât /

وظیفه / vazife / **duty** / dyooti /

وظیفه / vazife / **obligation** / abligeyshen /

وفادارانه / vafâdârâne / **loyally** / loyâli /

وفادار / vafâdâr / **loyal** / loyâl /

وفور / vefur / **plenty** / plenti /

وقفه / vaghfe / **break** / breyk /

وقفه / vaghfe / **interruption** / interâpshen /

وکیل / vakil / **lawyer** / loyer /

ولت / volt / **volt** / volt /

ولخرج / velkharj / **extravagant** / ikstravagent /

ویتامین / vitâmin / **vitamin** / vâytemin /

ویدئو / video / **video** / video /

ویرایش کردن / virâyesh kardan / **to edit** / to edit /

ویروس / virus / **virus** / vâyres /

ویژگی / vizhegi / **attribute** / atribyoot /

ویسکی / viski / **whisky** / wiski /

ویلن / viyolen / **violin** / vâyelin /

ي

یا / either / yâ / âydher /

یا / or / or / yâ /

یاد دادن / instruct / yâd dâdan / instâkt /

یاد دادن / to teach / yâd dâdan / to tiich /

یادآوری کردن / to remind / yâdâvari kardan / to rimâynd /

یادآوری / reminding / yâdâvari / rimâynding /

یادداشت / note / yaddâsht / not /

یادداشت / record / yâddâsht / rekord /

یادگاری / souvenir / yâdegâri / sooveniyer /

یادگرفتن / to learn / yâdgereftan / to lern /

یازده / eleven / yâzdah / ilevn /

یازدهمین / eleventh / yâzdahomin / ilevnth /

یاقوت کبود / sapphire / yâghute kabud / safâyr /

یخ / ice / yakh / âys /

یخ بستن / to freeze / yakh bastan / to friiz /

یخبندان / frost / yakhbandan / frâst /

یقه / collar / yaghe / kâler /

یقیناً / definitely / yaghinan / definitli /

یقیناً / certainly / yaghinan / sertenli /

یک / a / yek / e /

207

/ kworter / **quarter** / yek châhârom / یك چهارم

/ tenth / **tenth** / yekdahom / یك دهم

/ thertiyeth / **thirtieth** / yeksiyom / یك سی ام

/ nâynth / **ninth** / yeknohom / یك نهم

/ wâns / **once** / yekbâr / یكبار

/ sâmhao / **somehow** / yekjuri / یكجورى

/ âydentikâl / **identical** / yeksân / یكسان

/ siksth / **sixth** / yeksheshom / یكششم

/ sândi / **Sunday** / yekshanbe / یكشنبه

/ an / **an** / yeki / یكى

/ joo / **Jew** / yahudi / یهودى

/ joo-ish / **Jewish** / yahudi / یهودى

/ slo / **slow** / yavâsh / یواش

/ yuro / **euro** / yuro / یورو

/ yoge / **yoga** / yugâ / یوگا

/ griis / **Greece** / yunân / یونان

/ griik / **Greek** / yunâni / یونانى

/ fiftiinth / **fifteenth** / yek pânezdahom / یك پانزدهم

/ fiftiyeth / **fiftieth** / yek panjâhom / یك پنجاهم

/ fortiinth / **fourteenth** / yek châhârdahom / یك چهاردهم

/ forth / **fourth** / yek châhârom / یك چهارم

/ fortiyeth / **fortieth** / yek chehelom / یك چهلم

/ eyth / **eighth** / yek-hashtom / یك هشتم

ENGLISH-FARSI

DICTIONARY

A

a / e / *ind.art* یك / yek/

able / eybel / *adj* قابل / ghâbel/

aboard / ebord / *adv* سوار / savâr/

abominable / ebâminebel / *adj* نفرت انگیز / nefrat angiz/

about / ebaot / *adv* درحدود / darhudude/

above / ebâv / *adv* در بالا / dar bâlâ/

abrupt / ebrâpt / *adj* ناگهانی / nâgahâni/

abruptly / ebrâptlii / *adv* ناگهان / nâgahân/

absence / absens / *n* غیبت / gheybat/

absent / absent / *adj* غایب / ghâyeb/

absentminded / absentmâyndid / *adj* گیج /gich/

absolutely / absolootlii / *adv* کاملاً / kâmelan/

absorb / absorb / *vt* جذب کردن / jazb kardan/

accelerate / akselereyt / *vt* سرعت بخشیدن / soraat bakhshidan/

acceleration / akselereyshen / *n* شتاب / shetâb/

accept / aksept / *vt* پذیرفتن / paziroftan/

acceptable / akseptebel / *adj* قابل قبول / ghâbele ghabul/

accident / aksident / *n* تصادف / tasâdof/

acclaim / ekleym / *vt* تحسین کردن / tahsin kardan/

ache / eyk / *vi* درد کردن / dard kardan/

achieve / echiv / *vt* انجام دادن / anjâm dâdan/

achievement / echivment / *n* انجام / anjâm/

acid / asid / *adj* ترش / torsh/

acidity / esidetii / *n* ترشی / torshi/

acne / aknii / *n* جوش صورت / jushe surat/

acquire / ekvayer / *vt* به دست آوردن / bedast âvardan/

across / ekros / *prep* از وسط / az vasat/

act / akt / *n* عمل / aamal/

action / akshen / *n* کار / kâr/

active / aktiv / *adj* فعال / faâl/

activity / aktivetii / *n* فعالیت / faâliyyat/

actor / akter / *n* هنرپیشه / honarpishe/

actual / akchuwâl / *adj* واقعی / vâghei/

actually / akchuwâlii / *adv* درواقع / darvâghe/

acute / ekyut / *adj* تیز / tiz/

adapt / edapt / *vt* سازگار کردن / sâzegâr kardan/

add / ad / *vt* جمع کردن / jam kardan/

addition / edishen / *n* جمع / jam/

address / edres / *n* نشانی / neshâni/

adequate / adikwit / *adj* کافی / kâfi/

adhere / edhier / *vi* چسبیدن / chasbidan/

adhesive / edhisiv / *adj* / چسبنده / chasbande/
adjacent / ejeysent / *adj* / نزدیک / nazdik/
adjective / ajictiv / *n* / صفت / sefat/
administer / edminister / *vt* / اداره کردن / edâre kardan/
administration / edministreshen / *n* / اداره / edâre/
administrative / edministreytiv / *adj* / اداری / edâri/
admirable / admerebl / *adj* / پسندیده / pasandide/
admiral / admiral / *n* / دریاسالار / daryâsâlâr/
admiration / admireyshen / *n* / تحسین / tahsin/
admire / admâyr / *vt* / تحسین کردن / tahsin kardan/
admission / edmishen / *n* / قبول / ghabul/
admit / edmit / *vt* / پذیرفتن / paziroftan/
adolescent / adelesnt / *adj* / بالغ / bâlegh/
adoption / edâpshn / *n* / اختیار / ekhtiyâr/
adore / edor / *vt* / پرستیدن / parastidan/
adult / adâlt / *n* / بزرگسال / bozorgsâl/
advance / advâns / *vi* / پیشرفت کردن / pishraft kardan/
advantage / advântij / *n* / امتیاز / emtiyâz/
adventure / edvencher / *n* / ماجرا / mâjarâ/
adventurer / edvencherer / *n* / ماجراجو / mâjarâju/
adventurous / advencheres / *adj* / ماجراجو / mâjarâju/
adverb / edverb / *n* / قید / gheyd/
adversary / adverseri / *n* / دشمن / doshman/

adverse / advers / *adj* نامطلوب / nâmatlub/

advertise / advertâyz / *vt* آگهی کردن / âgahi kardan/

advertise / advertâyz / *n* آگهی دادن / âgahi dâdan/

advertisement / advertâyzment / *v* آگهی / âgahi/

advertisement / advertisment / *n* آگهی / âgahi/

advertiser / advertâyzer / *n* آگهی دهنده / âgahi dahande/

advice / advâys / *n* نصیحت / nasihat/

advise / advâyz / *vt* توصیه کردن / tosiye kardan/

aerial / eriel / *adj* هوایی / havâyi/

airplane / erpleyn / *n* هواپیما / havâpeymâ/

affect / afekt / *vt* تاثیر گذاشتن / tasir gozâshtan/

affectation / afecteyshen / *n* تظاهر / tazâhor/

affection / afekshen / *n* علاقه / alâghe/

affirm / eferm / *vt* تایید کردن / tayid kardan/

affirmative / affirmative / *adj* مثبت / mosbât/

affirmation / afermeyshen / *n* اثبات / esbât/

affluence / afluwens / *n* ثروت / servat/

affluent / afluwent / *adj* فراوان / faravân /

afford / eford / *vt* توانستن / tavânestan/

afraid / efreyd / *adj* ترسیدن / tarsidan/

Africa / afrikâ / *n* افریقا / âfrikâ/

African / afriken / *adj,n* افریقایی / âfrighâii/

after / âfter / *adv* بعد از / baad az /

afternoon / âfternoon / *n* / بعد ازظهر / baad azzohr/

afterwards / âfterwordz / *adv* / بعدًا / baadan/

again / egen / *adv* / دوباره / dobâre/

against / egenst / prep / برعلیه / aleyhe/

age / eyj / *n* / سن / sen/

agent / eyjent / *n* / نماینده / nemâyande/

aggression / egreshen / *n* / تجاوز / tajâvoz/

aggressive / agresiv / *adj* / جسور / jasur/

agile / ajâyl / *adj* / چابک / châbok/

agility / ejilitii / *n* / چابکی / châboki/

agitate / ajiteyt / *vt* / مضطرب کردن / moztareb kardan/

ago / ego / *adv* / پیش / pish/

agree / egrii / *vi* / موافقت کردن / movâfegat kardan/

agreement / egriiment / *n* / توافق / tavâfog/

agriculture / agrikulchur / *n* / کشاورزی / keshâvarzi/

ahead / ehed / *adv* / پیش / pish/

AIDS / eydz / *n* / ایدز / eydz/

aim / eym / *vt* / قصد داشتن / gasddâshtan/

air / er / *n* / هوا / havâ/

airline / erlâyn / *n* / هوا پیمایی / havâ peymâyi/

airport / erport / *n* / فرودگاه / furudgâh/

airway / erwey / *n* / خط هوایی / khatte havâii/

alarm / elâm / *n* / آژیر / âzhir/

alien / eylien / *adj* بیگانه / bigâne/

alien / eylien / *n,adj* خارجی / khâreji/

alike / elâyk / *adj* شبیه / shabih/

alive / elâyv / *adj* زنده / zende/

all / ol / *adj* همه / hame/

allergy / alerji / *n* آلرژی / âlerzhi/

alley / ali / *n* کوچه / kuche/

allied / alâyd / *adj* متحد / mottahed/

allow / elao / *vt* اجازه دادن / ejâzedâden/

allowance / elao-ens / *n* مقرری / mogharrari/

ally / alây / *n* متحد / mottahed/

almighty / âlmâyti / *adj* قادر متعال / ghâdere motaâl/

almost / âlmost / *adv* تقریباً / taghriban/

alone / elon / *adj* تنها / tanhâ/

along / elâng / *prep* سرتاسر / sartâsar/

alphabet / alfabet / *n* الفبا / alefbâ/

already / alredi / *adv* تاحالا / tâhâlâ/

also / âlso / *adv* هم / ham/

alteration / altereyshen / *n* تغییر / taghyir/

although / âldho / *conj* اگرچه / agarche/

altitude / altitud / *n* بلندی / bolandi/

altogether / âltegeter / *adv* به کلی / be kolli/

aluminium / aloominum / *n* آلومینیوم / âlominyum/

always / âlweyz / *adv* / همیشه / hamishe/

a.m. (ante meridiem) / eyem / *adj* / پیش از ظهر /
pish az zohr/

am / am / *v* / هستم / hastam/

amateur / amater / *n* / آماتور / âmâtor/

ambassador / ambaseder / *n* / سفیر کبیر / safire kabir/

amber / amber / *n* / کهربا / kahrabâ/

ambulance / ambyulens / *n* / آمبولانس / âmbulâns/

America / emerikâ / *n* / امریکا / âmerikâ/

American / emeriken / *adj,n* / امریکایی / âmrikâyi/

ammonia / emonya / *n* / آمنیاک / âmonyâk/

among / emâng / *prep* / میان / miyân/

amount / emaont / *n* / مقدار / meghdâr/

amphibian / amfibiien / *n* / دوزیست / dozist/

ample / ampl / *adj* / فراوان / farâvân/

amuse / amyooz / *vt* / سرگرم کردن / sargam kardan/

amusement / amyoozment / *n* / سرگرمی / sargarmi/

an / an / *indef.art.* / یکی / yeki/

analogy / enalejii / *n* / قیاس / ghiyâs/

analyze / analâyz / *vt* / تجزیه کردن / tajziye kardan/

analysis / enalisis / *n* / تجزیه / tajziye/

anarchy / anerkii / *n* / هرج ومرج / harjomarj/

anatomy / enatomi / *n* / کالبد شناسی / kâlbod shenâsi/

ancestor / ansester / *n* / جد / jad/

anchor / anker / *n* / لنگر / langar/

ancient / eynshent / *adj* / باستانی / bâstâni/

and / and / *conj* / و /va/

anger / anger / *n* / خشم / khashm/

angle / angel / *n* / زاویه / zâviye/

angrily / angrilii / *adv* / با خشم / bâ khashm/

angry / angrii / *adj* / خشمگین / khashmgin/

animal / animâl / *n* / جانور / jânevar/

ankle / ankel / *n* / مچ پا / mochepâ/

anniversary / aniverseri / *n* / سالگرد/ sâlgard/

announce / anaons / *vt* / اعلام کردن / eelâmkardan/

announcer / anaonser / *n* / گوینده / guyande/

annoy / ânoy / *vt* / ناراحت کردن / nârâhatkardan/

annual / anyooal / *adj* / سالیانه / sâliyâne/

another / enâdher / *adj* / دیگر / digar/

answer / ânser / *n* / جواب / javâp/

answer / ânser / *vt* / جواب دادن / javâp dâdan/

ant / ant / *n* / مورچه / murche/

antagonism / antagonizem / *n* / دشمنی / doshmani/

Antarctic / antârktik / *n, adj* / قطب جنوب / ghotbe jonub/

antenna / antenâ / *n* / موج گیر / mojgir/

anthem / anthem / *n* / سرود / surud/

anticipate / antisipeyt / *vt* / پیش بینی کردن / pish bini kardan/

anticipation / antisipeyshen / *n* پیش بینی / pish bini/

antihistamine / antihistemiin / *adj* / ضد آلرژی / zedde âlerzhi/

antique / antiik / *adj* قدیمی / ghadimi/

antiquity / antikwitii / *n* دوران باستان / dorâne bâstan/

antiseptic / antiseptik / *n* ضد میکروب / zedde mikrob/

anxiety / angzâyetii / *n* اضطراب / ezterâb/

anxious / ankshes / *adj* نگران / negarân/

anxiously / anksheslii / *adv* مضطربانه / moztarebâne/

any / eni / *adj* هیچ / hich/

anybody / eniibâdi / *pron* هرکس / harkas/

anyhow / eniihao / *adj* درهرصورت / darharsurat/

anymore / eniimor / *adj* دیگر / digar/

anyone / eniiwân / *pron* کسی / kasi/

anything / eniithing / *pron* چیزی / chizi/

anyway / enilwey / *adv* به هرحال / beharhâl/

anywhere / eniiwer / *adv* جایی / jâyi/

apart / epârt / *adv* جدا از هم / joda az ham/

apartment / epârtment / *n* آپارتمان / âpârtemân/

apologize / epâlojâyz / *vi* / پوزش خواستن / puzesh khâstan/

apology / epolejii / *n* پوزش / puzesh/

apparatus / apareytes / *n* دستگاه / dastgâh/

apparent / eparent / *adj* آشکار / âshekâr/

apparently / epareytes / *adv* / ظاهراً / zâheran/

appear / epiyer / *vi* / آشکار شدن / âshekâr shodan/

appearance / epiyerens / *n* / ظاهر / zâher/

appetite / appetayt / *n* / اشتها / eshtehâ/

apple / apel / *n* / سیب / sib/

appliance / aplâyens / *n* / اسباب / asbâb/

application / aplikeyshen / *n* / درخواست / darkhâsh/

apply / eplây / *vt* / تقاضا کردن / taghâzâ kardan/

appoint / epoynt / *vt* / منصوب کردن / mansub kardan/

appointment / epoyntment / *n* / قرار(ملاقات) / gharâr (emolâghât)/

appreciate / epriishiyeyt / *vt* / قدردانی کردن / ghadrdâni kardan/

approach / eproch / *vt* / نزدیک شدن / nazdik shodan/

approval / aproovâl / *vt* / تصویب / tasvib /

approve / aproov / *n* / پذیرفتن / paziroftan/

apricot / eyprikât / *n* / زردآلو / zardâlu/

April / eypril / *n* / آوریل / âvril/

apron / eypren / *n* / پیشبند / pishband/

apt / apt / *adj* / مستعد / mostaeed/

aptitude / aptitud / *n* / استعداد / esteedâd/

aquatic / ekwatik / *adj* / آبی / âbi/

Arab / arab / *n* / عرب / arab/

Arabian / ereybiyan / *adv* / *n* عربی / arabi/

Arabic / arabik / *adj* عربی / arabi/

archaeology / arkiiolejii / *n* باستان شناسی /
bâstân shenâni/

architect / ârkitekt / *n* معمار / meemâr/

architecture / ârkitekcher / *n* معماری / meemâri/

area / eryâ / *n* منطقه / mantaghe/

argue / ârgyoo / *vi* جروبحث کردن / jarrobahs kardan/

argument / ârgyooment / *n* جروبحث / jarrobahs/

arise / erâyz / *vi* پیش آمدن / pish âmadan/

aristocracy / aristâkrasi / *n* اشراف / ashrâf/

aristocrat / aristokrat / *n* اشراف زاده / ashrâf zâde/

aristocratic / aristokratik / *adj* اشرافی / ashrâfi/

arithmetic / arithmetik / *n* حساب / hesab/

arm / ârm / *n* دست / dast/

arm / ârm / *vt* مسلح کردن / mosallah kardan/

armada / ârmâdâ / *n* ناوگان / nâvgân/

armchair / ârmcher / *n* صندلی دسته دار /
sandaliye dastedâr/

armed / ârmd / *adj* مسلح / mosallah/

army / ârmii / *n* ارتش / artesh/

aroma / erome / *n* بوی خوش / buye khosh/

aromatic / aromatik / *adj* خوشبو / khoshbu/

around / eraond / *adv* هرطرف / hartaraf/

arrange / areynj / *vt* مرتب کردن / morrattab kardan/

arrangement / areynjment / *n* / نظم / nazm/

arrest / erest / *vt* / دستگیر کردن / dastgir kardan/

arrival / erâyvâl / *n* / رسیدن / residan/

arrive / erâyv / *vi* / رسیدن / residan/

arrow / aro / *n* / تیر / tir/

art / ârt / *n* / هنر / honar/

article / ârtikel / *n* / مقاله / maghâle/

artificial / ârtifishâl / *adj* / مصنوعی / masnoii/

artillery / ârtilerii / *n* / توپخانه / tupkhâne/

artisan / âtizen / *n* / آفزارمند / afzarmand/

artist / ârtist / *n* / هنرمند / honarmand/

artistic / ârtistik / *adj* / هنری / honari/

as / az / *prep* / مانند / mânand/

ascend / âsend / *vt* / بالا رفتن / bâlâ raftan/

ascending / asending / *adj* / به ترتیب / be tertib/

ascent / asent / *n* / بالا رفتن / bâlâ raftan/

ash / ash / *n* / خاکستر / khâkestar/

ashamed / âsheymd / *adj* / شرمنده / sharmande/

ashore / âshor / *adv* / به ساحل / be sâhel/

ashtray / ashtrey / *n* / زیرسیگاری / zirsigâri/

Asian / eyshen / *adj* / آسیایی / âsiyâyi/

aside / esâyd / *adv* / کنار / kanâr/

ask / âsk / *vt* / پرسیدن / porsidan/

222

asleep / âsliip / *adj* / خوابیده / khâbide/
aspect / aspekt / *n* / جنبه / janbe/
asphalt / asfolt / *n* / اسفالت / âsfâlt/
aspirin / asprin / *n* / آسپرین / âspirin/
assault / âsolt / *n* / حمله / hamle/
assemble / asembel / *vi* / جمع شدن / jam shodan/
assembly / asembli / *n* / مجلس / majles/
assistant / asistent / *adj* / دستیار / dastyâr/
assistant / asistent / *n* / معاون / moââven/
associate / asoshiyet / *vt* / پیوند دادن / peyvand dâdan/
association / âsosiyeyshen / *n* / همکاری / hamkâri/
assurance / âshurens / *n* / بیمه / bime/
asthma / azme / *n* / تنگی نفس / tangiye nafas/
at / at / *prep* / در / dar/
athlete / atliit / *n* / ورزشکار / varzeshkâr/
athletic / athletik / *adj* / ورزشی / varzeshi/
athletics / athletiks / *n* / ورزش / varzesh/
atmosphere / atmosfiyer / *n* / جَوَّ / javv/
atom / atem / *n* / اتم / atom/
attach / âtach / *vt* / چسباندن / chasbândan/
attack / âtak / *n* / حمله / hamle/
attacker / âtaker / *n* / مهاجم / mohâjem/
attempt / âtempt / *vt* / کوشیدن / kushidan/

attend / âtend / *vt* توجه کردن / tavajjoh kardan/

attention / âtenshen / *n* توجه / tavajjoh/

attentive / âtentiv / *adj* مواظب / movâzeb/

attitude / atityood / *n* نگرش / negaresh/

attract / âtrakt / *vt* جذب کردن / jazb kardan/

attractive / âtraktiv / *adj* جذاب / jazb/

attraction / âtrakshen / n جذابیت / jazzâbiyat/

attribute / atribyoot / *vt* ناشی دانستن از /
nâshi dânestan az/

attribute / atribyoot / *n* ویژگی / vizhegi/

auction / âkshn / *n* مزایده / mozâyede/

audible / âdibel / *adj* قابل شنیدن / ghâbele shenidan/

audition / âdishen / *n* شنوایی / shenavâii/

August / âgest / *n* اوت / out/

aunt / ânt / *n* خاله،عمه / Ameh, Khâle/

austere / âustiir / *adj* جدی / jeddi/

Australia / âstreyliyâ / *adj* استرالیا / ostorâliyâ/

Australian / âstreyliyen / *n* استرالیایی / ostorâliyâyi/

author / âther / *n* نویسنده / nevisande/

authority / âthâriti / *n* اقتدار / eghtedâr/

autobiography / âtobâyâgrafi *n* زندگی نامه شخصی /
zendeginâmeye shâkhsi/

autograph / âtogrâf / *n* امضا / emzâ/

automatic / âtomatik / *adj* خودکار / khodkâr/

automobile / âtomobiil / *n* ماشين / mâshin/

autonomy / âtânemi / *n* خودمختارى / khodmokhtâri/

autopsy / âtapsi / *n* كالبدگشايى / kâlbod goshâyi/

autumn / âtem / *n* پاييز / pâyiz/

available / eveylebel / *adj* دردسترس / dardastras/

avenue / avenyoo / *n* خيابان / khiyâbân/

average / averij / *n* ميانگين / miyângin/

Avesta / âvestâ / *n* اوستا / avestâ/

aviation / eyviieyshn / *n* هواپيمايى / havâpeymâyi/

avoid / âvoyd / *vt* خودداری کردن / khoddâri kardan/

awake / âweyk / *vt* بيدار شدن / bidâr shodan/

awake / âweyk / *adj* بيدار / bidâr/

awaken / âweyken / *vt* بيدار کردن / bidâr kardan/

aware / âwer / *adj* باخبر / bâkhaber/

away / âwey / *adv* دور / dur/

awful / âful / *adj* وحشتناك / vahshatnâk/

awfully / âfuli / *adv* خيلى خيلى / kheyli kheyli/

awkward / âkword / *adj* نا مناسب / nâ monâseb/

ax / aks / *n* تبر / tabar/

axis / aksis / *n* آسه / âse/

B

baby / beybii / *n* كودك / kudak/

back / bak / *adv* عقب / aghab/

back / bak / *n* پشت / posht/

back / bak / *vi* برگشتن / bargashtan/

background / bakgrownd / *n* سابقه / sâbeghe/

backward / bakword / *adj* عقب مانده / aghab mânde/

bacon / beyken / *n* ژامبون / zhâmbon/

bacteria / baktiiriiâ / *n* باکتری / bâkteri/

bad / bad / *adj* بد / bad/

badge / baj / *n* نشان / neshân/

badly / badlii / *adv* بدجوری / badjuri/

bag / bag / *n* کیف / kif/

baggage / bagij / *n* بار / bâr/

bake / beyk / *vt* پختن / pokhtan/

baker / beyker / *n* نانوا / nânvâ/

baksheesh / bahkshiish / *n* بخشش / bakhshesh/

balance / balens / *n* ترازو / tarâzu/

balcony / balkonii / *n* بالکن / bâlkon/

ball / bol / *n* توپ / tup/

ballet / baley / *n* باله / bâle/

balloon / bâloon / *n* / بادكنك / badkonak/

ban / ban / *vt* / ممنوع كردن / mamnuu kardan/

banana / bânanâ / *n* / موز / muz/

band / band / *n* / گروه / guruh/

bandage / bandij / *n* / باند / bând/

bandit / bandit / *n* / دزد مسلح / dozde mosallah/

bang / bang / *n* / ضربه / zarbe/

bank / bank / *n* / بانك / bânk/

bank / bank / *n* / ساحل / sâhel/

banknote / banknot / *n* / اسكناس / eskenâs/

bar / bahr / *n* / مشروب فروشی / mashrubfrushi/

barber / bahrbâr / *n* / سلمانی / salmâni/

bare / ber / *adj* / لخت / lokht/

bargain / bargin / *n* / معامله / moâmele/

bark / bark / *vi* / پارس كردن / pars kardan/

barley / bahrlii / *n* / جو / jo/

barometer / beromiter / *n* / هواسنج / havâsanj/

base / beys / *n* / پايگاه / pâygâh/

base / beys / *vt* / اساس قرار دادن / asâsgharâr dadan/

base / beys / *n* / قاعده / ghâeede/

baseball / beysbol / *n* / بيس بال / beysbâl/

basement / beysment / *n* / زيرزمين / zirzamin/

basic / beysik / *adj* / اساسی / asâsi/

basin / beysin / n کاسه / kâse/
basis / beysis / n اساس / asâs/
basket / baskit / n سبد / sabad/
basketball / baskitbol / n بسکتبال / basketbâl/
bat / bat / n چوگان / chogân/
bath / bath / n حمام / hamâm/
bathe / beydh / vi آبتنی کردن / âbtani kardan/
bathhouse / bathhâus / n حمام / hamâm/
battalion / bâtalyon / n گردان / gardân/
batter / bater / n توپ زن / tupzan/
battery / baterii / n باتری / bâtri/
battle / batel / n نبرد / nabard/
bay / bey / n خلیج / khalij/
bayonet / beyonit / n سرنیزه / sarneyze/
be / bii / vi بودن / budan/
beach / biich / n کناردریا / kanâredaryâ/
beam / biim / n تیر / tir/
bean / biin / n لوبیا / lubyâ/
bear / ber / vi حمل کردن / haml kardan/
bear / ber / n خرس / khers/
beard / biyerd / n ریش / rish/
bearing / bering / n بردباری / bordbâri/
beast / biist / n چهارپا / châhârpâ/

beat / biit / *vt* / كتك زدن / kotak zadan/

beautiful / byootiful / *adj* / زیبا / zibâ/

beautifully / byootifulii / *adv* / قشنگ / ghashang/

beauty / byootii / *n* / زیبایی / zibâyi/

because / bikâz / conj / چونکه / chonke/

become / bikâm / *vi* / شدن / shodan/

bed / bed / *n* / تختخواب / takhtekhâb/

bedroom / bedroom / *n* / اتاق خواب / otag hekhâb/

bee / bii / *n* / زنبورعسل / zanbureasal/

beef / biif / *n* / گوشت گاو / gushtegâv/

beer / biyer / *n* / آبجو / âbjo/

before / bifor / *adv* / قبلاً / ghablan/

beg / beg / *vi* / گدایی کردن / gedâyi kardan/

begin / bigin / *vt* / شروع کردن / shuru kardan/

beginning / bigining / *n* / اول / avval/

behalf / bihaf / *n* / حق / hagh/

behave / biheyv / *vi* / رفتار کردن / raftâr kardan/

behaviour / biheyviyer / *n* / رفتار / raftâr/

behind / bihâynd / *adv* / از عقب / azaghab/

being / bii-ing / *n* / آدم / âdam/

Belgian / beljen / *adj* / بلژیکی / belzhiki/

Belgium / beljem / *n* / بلژیک / belzhiki/

belief / biliif / *n* / اعتقاد / eeteghâd/

believe / biliiv / *vt* / باور کردن / bâvar kardan/

bell / bel / *n* / زنگ / zang/

belong / bilâng / *vi* / تعلق داشتن / taallogh dâshtan/

beloved / bilâvd / *adj* / عزیز / aziz/

below / bilo / *adv* / زیر / zir/

bend / bend / *n* / پیچ / pich/

bend / bend / *vi* / خم کردن / kham kardan/

beneficial / benifishl / *adj* / سودمند / sudmand/

benefit / benifit / *n* / سود / sud/

bent / bent / *n* / تمایل / tamâyol/

berry / berii / *n* / دانه / dâne/

beside / bisâyd / *prep* / درکنار / darkenâre/

besides / bisâydz / *adv* / علاوه براین / alâvebarin/

best / best / *adj* / بهترین / behtarin/

bet / bet / *vt* / شرط بندی کردن / shartbandi kardan/

better / beter / *adj* / بهتر / behtar/

between / bitwiin / *prep* / بین / beyne/

beverage / beverij / *n* / آشامیدنی / âshâmidani/

beware / biwer / *vi* / مواظب بودن / movâzeb budan/

beyond / biyând / *prep* / آن طرف / ân tarafe/

bib / bib / *n* / پیش گیر / pishgir/

bible / bâybel / *n* / کتاب مقدس / ketâbe moghaddas/

bicycle / bâysikel / *n* / دوچرخه / docharkhe/

big / big / *adj* بزرگ / bozorg/

bike / bâyk / *n* دوچرخه / docharkhe/

biker / bâyker / *n* دوچرخه سوار/ docharkhesavâr/

bilingual / bâylinguel / *adj* دوزبانه / dozabâne/

bill / bil / *n* اسکناس / eskenâs/

bill / bil / *n* منقار / menghâr/

bind / bâynd / *vt* بستن / bastan/

biography / bâyogrefii / *n* شرح زندگی / sharhezendegi/

biology / bâyâlâjii / *n* زیست شناسی / zistshenâsi/

biopsy / bayopsii / *n* بافت برداری / bâft bardâri/

bird / berd / *n* پرنده / parande/

birth / berth / *n* تولد / tavallod/

birthday / berth-dey / *n* روزتولد / ruzetavallod/

biscuit / biskit / *n* بیسکویت / biskuvit/

bit / bit / *n* تکه / tekke/

bite / bâyt / *n* گاز / gâz/

bite / bâyt / *vt* گاز گرفتن / gâz gereftan/

bitter / biter / *adj* تلخ / talkh/

black / blak / *adj* سیاه / siyâh/

blackboard / blâkbord / *n* تخته (سیاه) / takhte (siyah)/

Blacks / blaks / *n* سیاه پوستان / siyah pustân/

blame / bleym / *vt* سرزنش کردن / sarzanesh kardan/

blank / blank / *adj* سفید / sefid/

blanket / blankit / *n* / پتو / patu/

blaze / bleyz / *vi* / سوختن / sukhtan/

bleed / bliid / *vi* / خون آمدن / khun âmadan/

blind / blâynd / *adj* / کور / kur/

blind / blâynd / *n* / پرده کرکره / parde ker kere/

blindness / blâyndnis / *n* / کوری / kuri/

blink / blink / *vi* / چشمک زدن / chesmak zadan/

block / blâk / *n* / ساختمان / sâkhtemân/

block / blâk / *n* / بستن / bastan/

blockade / blâkeyd / *n* / محاصره / mohâsere/

blond / blând / *adj* / موبور / mubor/

bloody / blâdi / *adj* / خونین / khunin/

bloom / blum / *n* / شکوفه / shekufe/

blouse / blaoz / *n* / بلوز / buluz/

blow / blo / *vi* / وزیدن / vazidan/

blow / blo / *n* / ضربه / zarbe/

blue / bloo / *adj* / آبی / âbi/

board / bord / *n* / تخته / takhte/

board / bord / *vt* / سوار شدن / savâr shodan/

boarding house / bording haos / *n* / پانسیون / pânsiyon/

boast / bost / *vt* / پز دادن / poz dâdan/

boat / bot / *n* / قایق / ghâyegh/

body / bâdii / *n* / تن / tan/

boil / boyl / *vi* / جوشیدن / jushidan/

boiler / boyler / *n* / دیگ / dig/

bold / bold / *adj* / دلیر / dalir/

bomb / bâm / *n* / بمب / bomb/

bomber / bâmer / *n* / بمب افکن / bomb afkan/

bombing / bâming / *n* / بمباران / bombârân/

bond / bând / *n* / قرارداد / gharârdâd/

bone / bon / *n* / استخوان / ostokhân/

bonfire / bânfâyer / *n* / آتش بزرگ / âtashe bozorg/

bonny / bâni / *adj* / خوشگل / khoshgel/

book / buk / *n* / کتاب / ketâb/

bookcase / bukkeys / *n* / قفسه / ghafase/

booking-office / buking-âfis / *n* / باجه فروش بلیت /
bajeye furushe belit/

bookshop / bukshâp / *n* / کتاب فروشی / ketâb furushi/

boot / boot / *n* / چکمه / chakme/

boot / boot / *n* / صندوق عقب / sandughe aghab/

border / border / *n* / مرز / marz/

bore / bor / *vt* / سوراخ کردن / sorakh kardan/

bored / bord / *adj* / خسته / khaste/

boring / boring / *adj* / خسته کننده / khaste konande/

born / bord / *vi* / متولد / motavalled/

borrow / bâro / *vt* / قرض گرفتن / gharz gereftan/

boss / bâs / *n* / رییس / rais/

both / both / _adj_ هردو / hardo/

bother / bâdher / _vt_ ناراحت کردن / nârâhat kardan/

bottle / bâtel / _n_ بطری / botri/

bottom / bâtem / _n_ ته / tah/

bounce / baons / _vt_ برگشتن / bargashtan/

bound / baond / _vt_ پریدن / paridan/

bowl / bol / _n_ پرتاب کردن / partâb kardan/

bowl / bol / _n_ کاسه / kâse/

bowler / boler / _n_ کلاه لگنی / kolâhe Lagani/

box / bâks / _n_ جعبه / jaabe/

boxing / bâksing / _n_ بوکس / boks/

boy / boy / _n_ پسر / pesar/

boyfriend / boyfrend / _n_ دوست پسر / duste pesar/

brag / brag / _vi_ پزدادن / poz dâdan/

brain / breyn / _n_ مغز / maghz/

brake / breyk / _n_ ترمز / tormoz/

branch / brânch / _n_ شاخه / shâkhe/

brass / brâs / _n_ برنج / berenj/

brave / breyv / _adj_ شجاع / shojâ/

Brazil / brezil / _n_ برزیل / berezil/

Brazilian / brezilyen / _adj_ برزیلی / berezili/

bread / bred / _n_ نان / nân/

break / breyk / _n_ وقفه / vaghfe/

break / breyk / *vt* / شکستن / shekastan/

breakdown / breykdaon / *n* / خرابی / kharâbi/

breakfast / brekfast / *n* / صبحانه / sobhâne/

break-in / breyk-in / *n* / به زور وارد شدن /
bezur vâred shodan/

breath / breth / *n* / نفس / nafas/

breathe / briidh / *vi* / نفس کشیدن / nafas keshidan/

breathless / brethlis / *adj* / از نفس افتاده / az nafas oftâdan/

breathtaking / brethteyking / *adj* / خیره کننده /
khire konande/

breed / briid / *vt* / تولید مثل کردن / tolide nesl kardan/

brick / brik / *n* / آجر / âjor/

bridge / bridge / *n* / پل / pol/

brief / briif / *adj* / کوتاه / kutâh/

brief / briif / *adj* / مختصر / mokhtasar/

briefly / briiflii / *adv* / به طور اختصار / be tore ekhtesâr/

bright / brâyt / *adj* / روشن / roshan/

brightly / brâytli / *adv* / به روشنی / be roshani/

brilliant / brilyent / *adj* / درخشان / drakhshân/

bring / bring / *vt* / آوردن / âvardan/

Britain / briten / *n* / بریتانیا / beritâniyâ/

British / british / *adj* / بریتانیایی / beritâniyâyi/

Briton / briten / *n* / بریتانیایی / betitâniyâyi/

broad / brod / *adj* / پهن / pahn/

broadcast / brodkâst / *n* برنامه / barnâme/

broad-minded / brod-mâyndid / *adj* روشنفکر /
roshanfekr/

broad shouldered / brod-sholderd / *adj* چهارشانه /
châhârshâne/

broke / brok / *adj* بی پول / bi pul/

broken / broken / *adj* از هم پاشیده / az ham pâshide/

broker / broker / *n* دلال / dallâl/

bronchitis / brânkâytis / *n* برونشیت / bronshit/

broth / bros / *n* آبگوشت / âbgusht/

brother / brâdher / *n* برادر / barâdar/

brown / braon / *adj* قهوه ای / ghahveii/

brush / brâsh / *n* بُرس / boros/

brush / brâsh / *vt* تمیز کردن / tamiz kardan/

bubble / bâbl / *n* حباب / hobâb/

bud / bâd / *n* جوانه / javâne/

buffalo / bâfâlo / *n* بوفالو / bufâlo/

build / bild / *vt* ساختن / sâkhtan/

building / bilding / *n* ساختمان / sâkhtemân/

built-up / biltâp / *adj* مسکونی/maskuni/

bulb / bâlb / *n* لامپ / lâmp/

bulbous / bâlbes / *adj* پیازی / piyâzi/

bulk / bâlk / *n* مقدار / meghdâr/

bullet / bulit / *n* گلوله / golule/

bump / bâmp / *vi* / خوردن به / khordan be/

bun / bân / *n* / کیک / keyk/

burglar / bergler / *n* / دزد / dozd/

burn / bern / *vt* / سوختن / sukhtan/

burst / berst / *vi* / ترکیدن / tarakidan/

bury / beri / *vt* / دفن کردن / dafn kardan/

bus / bâs / *n* / اتوبوس / otobus/

bus driver / bâs drâyver / *n* / راننده اتوبوس / rânandeye otobus/

business / biznis / *n* / کار / kâr/

businessman / biznisman / *n* / بازرگان / bâzargân/

bus stop / bâsstâp / *n* / ایستگاه اتوبوس / istgâhe otobos/

busy / bizi / *adj* / مشغول / mashghul/

but / bât / *conj* / اما / ammâ/

butcher / bucher / *n* / قصاب / ghassâb/

butter / bâter / *n* / کره / kare/

butterfly / bâterflây / *n* / پروانه / parvâne/

buttery / bâtery / *adj* / کره ای / kareii/

button / bâten / *n* / دکمه / dokme/

buy / bây / *vt* / خریدن / kharidan/

buyer / bâyer / *n* / خریدار / kharidâr/

by / bây / *prep* / نزدیکِ / nazdike/

bye / bây / *intj* / خداحافظ / khodâhâfez/

byword / bâyved / *n* / عبرت / ebrat/

C

cab / kab / n / تاکسی / tâksi/
cabaret / kabarey / n / کاباره / kâbâre/
cabbage / kabij / n / کلم / kalam/
cabin / kabin / n / کابین / kâbin/
cable / keybl / n / کابل / kâbl/
cafeteria / kafiteriiyâ / n / سلف سرویس / self servis/
cafe / kafe / n / کافه / kâfe/
caffeine / kafeen / n / کافیین / kâfeiin/
cage / keyj / n / قفس / ghafas/
cake / keyk / n / کیک / keyk/
calcium / kalsiem / n / کلسیم / kalsyum/
calculate / kalkyuleyt / vt / حساب کردن / hesâb kardan/
calendar / kalinder / n / تقویم / taghvim/
call / kol / n / داد / dâd/
call / kol / vt / صداکردن / sedâkardan/
callbox / kolbâks / n / باجه تلفن / bâjeye telefon/
calm / kâm / adj / آرام / ârâm/
camel / kaml / n / شتر / shotor/
camera / kamerâ / n / دوربین / durbin/

camp / kamp / *n* اردو / ordu/

campus / kampes / *n* محوطه دانشگاه /
mohavvateye dâneshgâh/

can / kan / *v.aux* توانستن / tavânestan/

can / kan / *n* قوطی / ghuti/

Canada / kanada / *n* کانادا / kânâdâ/

Canadian / kaneydiyan / *adj* کانادایی / kânâdâyi/

canal / kanal / *n* آبراه / âbrâh/

cancel / kansel / *vt* به هم زدن / beham zadan/

cancer / kanser / *n* سرطان / saratân/

candle / kandel / *n* شمع / sham/

candy / kandii / *n* آب‌نبات / âbnabât/

canned / kand / *adj* کنسروشده / konservshode/

canteen / kantiin / *n* غذاخوری / ghazâkhori/

cap / kap / *n* کلاه کپی / kolâhe kapi/

capable / keypebel / *adj* قادر / ghâder/

cape / keyp / *n* دماغه / damâghe/

capital / kapitâl / *n* پایتخت / pâytakht/

captain / kaptin / *n* فرمانده / farmânde/

capture / kapcher / *vt* گرفتن / gereftan/

car / kâr / *n* اتومبیل / otomobil/

caravan / karavan / *n* کاروان / kârâvân/

carbon / kârben / *n* کربن / karbon/

cardigan / kârdigen / *n* ژاکت / zhâket/

cardinal / kârdinâl / *adj* / اصلى / asli/

care / ker / *n* / مراقبت / morâgheb/

care / ker / *vi* / اهميت دادن / ahammiyyet dâdan/

career / keriyer / *n* / شغل / shoghl/

careful / kerful / *adj* / مواظب / movâzeb/

carefully / kerfulii / *adv* / با احتياط / bâ ehtiyât/

careless / kerlis / *adj* / بى احتياط / bi ehtiyât/

carol / karol / *n* / سرود كريسمس / surude krismas/

carpet / kârpit / *n* / فرش / farsh/

carriage / karij / *n* / درشكه / doroshke/

carrot / karot / *n* / هويج / havich/

carry / kari / *vt* / حمل كردن / haml kardan/

cartilage / kârtilij / *n* / غضروف / ghozruf/

cartoon / kârtoon / *n* / كارتون / kârton/

case / keys / *n* / جعبه / jaabe/

cash / kash / *n* / پول نقد / pulenaghd/

castle / kâsel / *n* / قلعه / galee/

casual / kazhuwâl / *adj* / اتفاقى / ettefâghi/

casually / kazhuwali / *adv* / تصادفاً / tasâdofan/

cat / kat / *n* / گربه / gorbe/

catch / kach / *vt* / گرفتن / gereftan/

Catholic / kathelik / *n* / كاتوليك / kâtolik/

cattle / katel / *n* / گاو / gâv/

cause / koz / *n* / علت / ellat/

cave / keyv / *n* / غار / ghâr/

celebrate / celibreyt / *vt* / جشن گرفتن / jashn gereftan/

celebration / selibreyshen / *n* / جشن / jashn/

cell / sel / *n* / سلول / sellul/

cellar / celâr / *n* / زیرزمین / zirzamin/

center / senter / *n* / مرکز / markaz/

centimeter / sentimiiter / *n* / سانتیمتر / sântimetr/

central / sentrâl / *adj* / مرکزی / markazi/

centralize / sentrâlâyz / *vt* / متمرکزکردن / motamarkez kardan/

century / senchrii / *n* / قرن / gharn/

cereal / siriyel / *n* / غله / ghalle/

ceremony / serimonii / *n* / مراسم / marâsem/

certain / serten / *adj* / حتمی / hatmi/

certainly / sertenli / *adv* / یقیناً / yaghinan/

certificate / certifikit / *n* / گواهی نامه / govâhi nâme /

chain / choyn / *n* / زنجیر / zanjir/

chair / cher / *n* / صندلی / sandali/

chalk / châk / *n* / گچ تحریر / gache tahrir/

champion / champiyen / *n* / قهرمان / ghahramân/

change / cheynj / *n* / عوض کردن / avaz kardan/

channel / chanel / *n* / تنگه / tange/

chapter / chapter / *n* / فصل / fasl/

character / karecter / *n* / شخصيت / shakhsiyyat/

charcoal / chârkol / *n* / زغال / zoghâl/

charge / chârj / *n* / اتهام / ettehâm/

charm / chârm / *n* / زيبايى / zibâyi/

charming / chârming / *adj* / قشنگ / ghashang/

chase / cheys / *vt* / دنبال (كسى) دويدن /
donbâle (kasi) dovidan/

chase / cheys / *n* / تعقيب / taaghib/

chat / chat / *n* / صحبت / sohbat/

cheap / chiip / *adj* / ارزان / arzân/

check / chek / *n* / بازرسى / bâzrasi/

check / chek / *n* / چك / chak/

checkmate / chekmeyt / *n* / كيش ومات / kishomât/

cheek / chiik / *n* / گونه / gune/

cheer up / chiir âp / *vt* / خوشحال بودن / khoshhal budan/

cheerful / chiyerful / *adj* / شاد / shâd/

cheers! / chiirz / *intj* / به سلامتى! / besalâmati/

cheese / chiiz / *n* / پنير / panir/

chemical / kemikl / *adj* / شيميايى / shimyâyi/

chemist / kemist / *n* / شيمى دان / shimidân/

chemistry / kemistrii / *n* / شيمى / shimi/

cherry / cherii / *n* / گيلاس / gilâs/

chess / ches / *n* / شطرنج / shatranj/

chest / chest / *n* / صندوق / sandugh/

chew / choo / *vt, vi* / جویدن / javidan/

chicken / chikin / *n* / جوجه / juje/

chief / chiif / *n, adj* / رییس / raais/

chiefly / chiiflii / *adv* / عمداً / omdatan/

child / châyld / *n* / بچه / bachche/

childhood / châyl-hud / *n* / بچگی / bachchegi/

chimney / chimnii / *n* / دودکش / dudkesh/

chin / chin / *n* / چانه / châne/

China / châynâ / *n* / چین / chin/

chips / chips / *n* / چیپس / chips/

chocolate / châklit / *n* / شکلات / shokolât/

choice / chays / *n* / انتخاب / entekhâb/

cholera / kolere / *n* / وبا / vabâ/

choose / chooz / *vt* / انتخاب کردن / entekhâb kardan/

choosy / choozi / *adj* / مشکل / moshkel/

Christianity / kristiiyanitii / *n* / مسیحیت / masihiyyat/

Christmas / krismâs / *n* / کریسمس / krismas/

church / cherch / *n* / کلیسا / kelisâ/

cigar / sigâr / *n* / سیگار برگ / sigâre barg/

cigarette / sigaret / *n* / سیگار / sigâr/

cinema / sinimâ / *n* / سینما / sinamâ/

cinnamon / sinemen / *n* / دارچین / dârchin/

circle / serkel / *n* / دایره / dâyere/

circuit / serkit / *n* / مدار / madâr/

circumstances / serkâm-stansiz / *n* / شرایط / sharâyet/

circus / serkes / *n* / سیرک / sirk/

citizen / sitizn / *n* / تابع / tâbee/

city / sitii / *n* / شهر / shahr/

civil / sivil / *adj* / مدنی / madani/

civilization / sivilâyzeyshen / *n* / تمدن / tamaddon/

civilize / sivilâyz / *vt* / متمدن کردن / motamadden kardan/

claim / kleym / *vt* / درخواست کردن / darkhâst kardan/

claim / kleym / *n* / ادعا / eddeââ/

clap / klap / *vt* / کف زدن / kafzadan/

clash / klash / *vi* / درگیر شدن / dargir shodan/

clash / klash / *n* / بر خورد / bar khord/

class / klas / *n* / طبقه / tabaghe/

classical / klasikâl / *adj* / کلاسیک / klâsik/

classless / klaslis / *adj* / بی طبقه / bi tabaghe/

classroom / klasroom / *n* / کلاس / kelâs/

clean / kliin / *adj* / تمیز / tamiz/

cleaner / kliiner / *n* / نظافت چی / nezâfatchi/

clear / kliyer / *adj* / شفاف / shaffâf/

clearly / kliyerli / *adv* / روشن / roshan/

clergy / klerji / *n* / روحانیون / ruhâniyyun/

clergyman / klerjimen / *n* / روحانی / ruhâni/

clerk / klerk / *n* / منشی / monshi/

clever / klever / *adj* / باهوش / bâhush/

click / klik / *n* / تیلیک / tilik/

client / klâyent / *n* / مشتری / moshtari/

climate / klâymit / *n* / آب وهوا / âbohavâ/

climax / klâymaks / *n* / اوج / oj/

climb / klâym / *vt* / بالارفتن / bâlâraftan/

climber / klâymer / *n* / بالارونده / bâlâ ravande/

cling / kling / *vi* / چسبیدن به / chasbidan be/

clinic / klinik / *n* / درمانگاه / darmângâh/

cloakroom / klokroom / *n* / رخت کن / rakht kan/

clock / klâk / *n* / ساعت / sâat/

close / klos / *adj* / نزدیک / nazdik/

closet / klâzit / *n* / کمد / komod/

cloth / klod, klâth / *n* / پارچه / pârche/

clothes / klodhz / *n* / لباس / lebâs/

clothing / klodhing / *n* / پوشاک / pushâk/

cloud / klaod / *n* / ابر / abr/

cloudy / klaodii / *adj* / ابری / abri/

club / klâb / *n* / باشگاه / bâshgâh/

clue / kloo / *n* / سرنخ / sarnakh/

coach / coch / *n* / کالسگه / kâleske /

coal / kol / *n* / زغال سنگ / zoghâlesang/

coast / kost / *n* / ساحل / sâhel/

coat / kot / *n* / پالتو / pâlto/

cock / kâk / *n* / خروس / khurus/

cocktail / kâkteyl / *n* / نوشابه های مخلوط /
noshabehâi makhlut/

cocoa / koko / *n* / کاکائو / kâkâu/

code / kod / *n* / کُد / kod/

coffee / kâfi / *n* / قهوه / ghahve/

coffin / kâfin / *n* / تابوت / tâbut/

coin / koyn / *n* / سکه / sekke/

coincidence / koinsidens / *n* / اتفاق / ettefâgh/

cold / kold / *adj* / سرد / sard/

cold / kold / *n* / سرما خوردگی / sarmâkhordegi/

coldly / koldlii / *adv* / با سردی / bâ sardi/

collar / kâler / *n* / یقه / yaghe/

colleague / kâliig / *n* / همکار / hamkâr/

collect / kâlekt / *vt* / جمع کردن / jam kardan/

collection / kâlekshen / *n* / جمع آوری / jamâvari/

collector / kâlekter / *n* / کلکسیونر / koleksiyoner/

college / kâlij / *n* / دانشکده / dâneshkade/

colonel / kernel / *n* / سرهنگ / sarhang/

colonial / koloniiyâl / *adj* / استعماری / esteemâri/

colony / kâlenii / *n* / مستعمر / mostaamar/

color / kâler / *n* / رنگ / rang/

colored / kâlerd / *adj* رنگی / rangi/

comb / kom / *n* شانه / shâne/

combination / kâmbineyshn / *n* ترکیب / tarkib/

combine / kâmbâyn / *vt* ترکیب کردن / tarkib kardan/

come / kâm / *vi* آمدن / âmadan/

comedy / kâmldll / *n* کمدی / komodi/

comet / kâmit / *n* ستاره دنباله دار / setâreye donbâledâr/

comfort / kâmfort / *n* آسایش / âsâyesh/

comfortable / kâmfterbel / *adj* راحت / râhat/

comfortably / kâmfterblii / *adv* براحتی / be râhati/

comic / kâmik / *adj* خنده دار / khandedâr/

comics / kâmiks / *n* مجله فکاهی / majalleye fokâhi/

command / kâmand / *n* دستور / dastur/

commander / kâmander / *n* فرمانده / farmânde/

comment / kâment / *n* نظر / nazar/

commentary / kâmenteri / *n* تفسیر / tafsir/

commerce / kâmers / *n* بازرگانی / bâzargâni/

commercial / kâmershâl / *adj* بازرگانی / bâzargâni/

commit / kâmit / *vt* مرتکب شدن / mortâkeb shodan/

committee / kâmitii / *n* کمیته / komite/

common / kâmân / *adj* متداول / motadâvel/

communication / kâmyoonikeyshen / *n* ارتباط / ertebât/

communism / kâmyoonizem / *n* کمونیسم / komonism/

community / kâmyoonitii / *n* / اجتماع / ejtemââ/

company / kâmpanii / *n* / مصاحبت / mosâhebat/

comparable / kâmperebel / *adj* / قابل مقایسه /
ghabele moghâyese/

compare / kâmper / *vt* / مقایسه / moghâyese/

comparison / kâmparisen / *n* / مقایسه / moghayese/

compatriot / kâmpatriyet / *n* / هم میهن / ham mihan/

compete / kâmpiit / *vi* / رقابت کردن / reghâbat kardan/

competition / kâmpitishen / *n* / رقابت / reghâbat/

competitive / kâmpetitiv / *adj* / رقابتی / reghâbati/

complain / kâmpleyn / *vi* / شکایت کردن / shekâyat kardan/

complaint / kâmpleynt / *n* / شکایت / shekâyat/

complete / kâmpliit / *adj* / کامل / kâmel/

complete / kâmpliit / *vt* / کامل کردن / kâmel kardan/

completely / kâmpliitlii / *adv* / کاملاً / kamelan/

complex / kâmpleks / *adj* / مجتمع / mojtamee/

complicate / kâmplikeyt / *vt* / پیچیده تر کردن /
pichidetar kardan/

comply / kemplây / *vi* / پذیرفتن / paziroftan/

compose / kâmpoz / *vt* / تشکیل دادن / tashkil dâdan/

composer / kâmpozer / *n* / آهنگساز / âhangsâz/

composition / kâmpozishen / *n* / ترکیب / tarkib/

comprehensive / kâmprihensiv / *adj* / گسترده / gostarde/

comprise / kemprâyz / *vt* / شامل بودن / shâmel budan/

compromise / kâmpromâyz / *n* / مصالحه / mosâlehe/

compulsory / kâmpâlserii / *adj* / اجباری / ejbâri/

compute / kâmpyoot / *vt* / حساب کردن / hesab kardan/

computer / kâmpyooter / *n* / رایانه / râyâne/

conceal / kânsiil / *vt* / پوشاندن / pushândan/

conceive / kânsllv / *vt* / تصورکردن / tasavvor kardan/

concentrate / kânsentreyt / *vt* / متمرکزکردن /
motamarkez kardan/

concentration / kânsentreyshen / *n* / دقت / deghghat/

concern / kânsern / *n* / علاقه / alâghe/

concerned / kânsernd / *adj* / نگران / negarân/

concert / kânsert / *n* / کنسرت / konsert/

conclusion / kânkloozhen / *n* / پایان / pâyân/

concrete / kânkriit / *n* / بتون / beton/

concussion / kânkâshen / *n* / ضربه مغزی /
zarboyo maghzi/

condemn / kândern / *vt* / محکوم کردن / mahkum kardan/

condemnation / kândemneyshen / *n* / محکومیت /
mahkumiyyat/

condition / kândishen / *n* / وضعیت / vaziyat/

conduct / kândâkt / *n* / رفتار / raftâr/

conductor / kândâkter / *n* / رهبر / rahbar/

confederacy / kânfederasii / *n* / اتحاد / ettehâd/

confederate / kânfederit / *adj* / متحد / mottahed/

confide / kânfâyd / *vt* اعتماد کردن / eetemâd kardan/

confidence / kânfidens / *n* اعتماد / eetemâd/

confident / kânfident / *adj* مطمئن / motmaeen/

confirm / kenferm / *vt* تأیید کردن / taayid kardan/

confirmation / kânfermeyshen / *n* تأیید / taiid/

conflict / kânflikt / *n* برخورد / barkhord/

conformist / kânformist / *vt* سنت گرا / sonnatgarâ/

confound / kânfaond / *vt* اشتباه کردن / eshtebâh kardan/

confuse / kânfiyooz / *vt* گیج کردن / gich kardan/

confused / kânfiyoozd / *adj* آشفته / âshofte/

confusing / kânfiyoozing / *adj* گیج کننده / gij konande/

confusion / kânfyoozhen / *n* سردرگمی / sardargomi/

congratulation / kângrachuleyshen / *n* تبریک / tabrik/

congress / kângres / *n* مجمع / majmaa/

connect / kânekt / *vt* ارتباط داشتن / ertebât dâshtan/

connection / kânekshen / *n* ارتباط / ertebât/

conquer / kânker / *vt* شکست دادن / shekast dâdan/

conqueror / kânkerer / *n* فاتح / fâteh/

conquest / kânkwest / *n* فتح / fath/

consequence / kânsikwens / *n* نتیجه / natije/

conservation / kânserveyshen / *n* حفاظت / hefâzat/

conservatism / kânservatizem / *n* محافظه کاری / muhafeze kâr/

conserve / kânserv / *vt* حفظ کردن / hefz kardan/

consider / kânsider / *vt* درنظر گرفتن / darnazar gereftan/

considerable / kânsiderebel / *adj* قابل ملاحظه /
  ghâbele molâheze/

consist / kânsist / *vi* شامل / shâmel/

console / kensol / *vt* تسلی دادن / tasalli dâdan/

constable / kânstebel / *n* پاسبان / pâsbân/

constant / kânstant / *adj* ثابت / sâbet/

construction / kânstrukshen / *n* ساختن / sâkhtan/

consul / kânsul / *n* کنسول / konsul/

consulate / kânsyulit / *n* کنسولگری / konsulgari/

consume / kânsyoom / *vt* مصرف کردن / masraf kardan/

consumer / kânsyoomer / *n* مصرف کننده /
  masraf konande /

contact / kontakt / *n* تماس / tamâs/

contain / kânteyn / *vt* حاوی بودن / hâvi budan/

container / kânteyner / *n* ظرف / zarf/

contempl / kântempt / *n* تنفر / tanaffor/

contend / kentend / *vi* مجادله کردن / mojâdele kardan/

content / kântent / *adj* راضی / râzi/

content / kântent / *n* محتوا / mohtevâ/

contest / kântest / *n* رقابت / reghâbat/

contest / kântest / *vt* مجادله کردن / mojâdele kardan/

continent / kântinent / *n* قارّه / ghârre/

continue / kântinyoo / *vt* ادامه دادن / edâme dâdan/

continuity / kântinyoowitii / *n* پیوستگی / peyvastegi/

continuous / kântinyuwes / *adj* پیوسته / peyvaste/

contract / kântrakt / *n* پیمان / peymân/

contrary / kântrerii / *adj* مخالف / mokhâlef/

contrast / kântrâst / *n* مقایسه / moghâyese/

contrast / kântrâst / *vt* مقایسه کردن / moghâyese kardan/

contribution / kântribyooshen / *n* کمک / komak/

control / kântrol / *n* تسلط / tasallot/

control / kentrol / *n* نظارت / nezârat/

convenience / kânviiniyens / *n* راحتی / râhati/

convenient / kânviiniyent / *adj* مناسب / monâseb/

convention / kânvenshen / *n* پیمان نامه / payman nâme /

conventional / kânvenshenal / *adj* مرسوم / marsum/

conversation / kânverseyhen / *n* گفتگو / goftegu/

convert / kânvert / *vt* تبدیل کردن / tabdil kardan/

convertible / kânvertibel / *adj* قابل تبدیل / ghâbele tabdil/

convey / kânvey / *vt* انتقال دادن / enteghâl dâdan/

convince / kânvins / *vt* متقاعد کردن / motaghâeed kardan/

cook / kuk / *vt* آشپزی کردن / âshpazi kardan/

cooker / kuker / *n* اجاق / ojâgh/

cookie / kukii / *n* کلوچه / koluche/

cooking / kuking / *n* آشپزی / âshpazi/

cool / kool / *adj* خنک / khonak/

cop / kâp / *n* / پاسبان /pâsbân/

cope / kop / *vi* / فائق آمدن / fâegh âmadan/

copy / kâpii / *n* / نسخه /noskhe/

corn / korn / *n* / غله / ghalle/

corner / korner / *n* / گوشه / gushe/

correct / korekt / *adj* / درست /dorost/

correspond / korispând / *vi* / تطبیق کردن / tatbigh kardan/

correspondence / korispândens / *n* / مکاتبه / mokâtebe/

correspondent / korispândent / *n* / خبرنگار / khabarnegâr/

corrupt / korâpt / *adj* / فاسد / fâsed/

corruption / korâpshen / *n* / فساد / fesâd/

cost / kâst / *n* / قیمت / gheymat/

costly / kâstlii / *adj* / گران / gerân/

cottage / kâtij / *n* / کلبه / kolbe/

couch / kaoch / *n* / کاناپه / kânâpe/

cough / kâf / *n* / سرفه / sorfe/

council / kaonsl / *n* / شورا / shurâ/

count / kaont / *vt* / شمردن / shemordan/

counter / kaonter / *n* / پیشخوان / pishkhân/

country / kântrii / *n* / کشور / keshvar/

countryman / kântriiman / *n* / روستایی / rustâii/

couple / kâpel / *n* / جفت / joft/

courage / kurij / *n* / شجاعت / shojâat/

course / kors / *n* مسیر / masir/

court / kort / *n* دادگاه / dâdgâh/

cover / kâver / *n* پوشش / pushesh/

cow / kao / *n* گاو / gâv/

coward / kâowerd / *n* نامرد / nâmard/

cowboy / kaoboy / *n* گاوچران / gâvcherân/

crackers / krakerz / *n* کراکر / krâker/

craft / kraft / *n* پیشه / pishe/

crash / krash / *n* تصادف / tasâdof/

crazy / kreyzii / *adj* دیوانه / divâne/

cream / kriim / *n* خامه / khâme/

create / kriyeyt / *vt* آفریدن / âfaridan/

creation / kriyeyshen / *n* آفرینش / âfarinesh/

creative / kriyeytiv / *adj* خلاق / khallâgh/

creator / kriyeyter / *n* آفریننده / âfarinande/

creature / kriicher / *n* مخلوق / makhlogh /

creep / kriip / *vi* خزیدن / khazidan/

crew / kroo / *n* خدمه کشتی / khadame kashti /

crime / krâym / *n* جرم / jorm/

criminal / kriminâl / *n* مجرم / mojrem/

crisis / krâysis / *n* بحران / bohrân/

critic / kritik / *n* منتقد / montaghed/

critical / kritikâl / *adj* بحرانی / bohrâni/

criticism / kritisizem / *n* انتقاد / enteghâd/

criticize / kritisâyz / *vt* انتقاد کردن / enteghâd kardan/

cross / krâs / *n* صلیب / salib/

cross / krâs / *vt* عبور کردن / ubur kardan/

crossing / krâsing / *n* تقاطع / taghâto/

crossroads / krâsrodz / *n* تقاطع / taghâto/

crow / kro / *n* کلاغ / kalâgh/

crowd / kraod / *n* جمعیت / jamiyyat/

crowded / kraodid / *adj* پرجمعیت / porjamiyet/

crown / kraon / *n* تاج / tâj/

cruel / kroo-el / *adj* ظالم / zâlem/

cruelty / kroo-eltii / *n* بیرحمی / birahmi/

crush / krâsh / *vt* له کردن / leh kardan/

crutch / krâch / *n* چوب زیربغل / chube zirbaghal/

cry / krây / *n* فریاد / faryâd/

cry / krây / *vi* فریاد کشیدن / faryâd keshidan/

crystal / kristl / *n* بلور / blur/

cube / kyoob / *n* مکعب / mokaab/

cucumber / kyookâmber / *n* خیار / khiyar/

culture / kâlcher / *n* فرهنگ / farhang/

cup / kâp / *n* فنجان / fenjân/

cupboard / kâbord / *n* قفسه / ghafase/

curious / kyuriyes / *adj* کنجکاو / konjkav/

currency / kârensii / *n* پول / pul/

current / kârent / *adj* جاری / jâri/

curse / kers / *n* لعنت / laanat/

curtain / kerten / *n* پرده / parde/

curve / kerv / *vt* پیچیدن / pichidan/

custom / kâstem / *n* رسم / rasm/

customer / kâstemer / *n* مشتری / moshtari/

customs / kâstemz / *n* گمرك / gomrok/

cut / kât / *vt* بریدن / boridan/

cyber / sâyber / *pref* سیبر / siber/

cycle / sâykel / *n* گردش / gardesh /

cylinder / silinder / *n* سیلندر / silinder/

cylindrical / silindrikâl / *adj* استوانه ای / ostovâneii/

D

daddy / dadii / *n* / بابا / bâbâ/

daily / deylii / *adj* / روزانه / ruzâne/

dairy / derii / *n* / لبنیاتى / labaniyâti/

damage / damij / *n* / خسارت / khesârat/

damp / damp / *adj* / مرطوب / martub/

dance / dans / *n* / رقص / raghs/

danger / deynjer / *n* / خطر / khatar/

dangerous / deynjeres / *adj* / خطرناك / khatarnâk/

dare / der / *vi* / جرات کردن / joraat kardan/

dark / dârk / *adj* / تاريك / târik/

darkness / dârknis / *n* / تاریکى / târiki/

darling / dârling / *adj* / عزيز / aziz/

darn / dârn / *vt* / رفوکردن / refu kardan/

dart / dârt / *n* / تير / tir/

dash / dash / *n* / خط تيره / khatte tire/

date / deyt / *n* / تاريخ / târikh/

daughter / doter / *n* / دختر / dokhtar/

day / dey / *n* / روز / ruz/

daylight / deylâyt / *n* / روز / ruz/

dead / ded / *adj* / مرده / morde/

deaf / def / *adj* / کر / kar/

deal / diil / *n* / مقدار / meghdâr/

dealer / diiler / *n* / فروشنده / furushande/

dear / diir / *adj* / عزیز / aziz/

death / deth / *n* / مرگ / marg/

debate / dibeyt / *n, vi* / بحث / bahs/

debt / det / *n* / قرض / gharz/

deceit / disiit / *n* / فریب / farib/

deceive / disiiv / *vt* / فریب دادن / farib dâdan/

December / disember / *n* / دسامبر / desâmbr/

decent / diisint / *adj* / محترم / mohtaram/

deception / disepshn / *n* / فریب / farib/

decide / disâyd / *vt* / تصمیم گرفتن / tasmim gereftan/

decision / disizhen / *n* / تصمیم / tasmim/

decisive / disâysiv / *adj* / قطعی / ghatii/

deck / dek / *n* / عرشه / arshe/

declaration / deklereyshen / *n* / اعلام / eelâm/

declare / dikler / *vt* / اعلام کردن / eelâm kardan/

decline / diklâyn / *n* / کاهش / kâhesh/

decorate / dekereyt / *vt* / آرایش / ârâyesh/

decoration / dekoreyshen / *n* / تزیین / taziin/

decrease / dikriis / *vi* / کم شدن / kam shodan/

dedicate / dedikeyt / *vt* / اهدا کردن / ehdâ kardan/

dedication / dedikeyshn / *n* / اهدا / ehdâ/

deep / diip / *adj* / عمیق / amigh/

deer / dier / *n* / گوزن / gavazn/

defeat / difiit / *vt* / شکست دادن / shekast dâdan/

defcot / diifokt / *n* / نقص / naghs/

defend / difend / *vt* / دفاع کردن / defââ kardan/

defender / difender / *n* / مدافع / modâfee/

defense / difens / *n* / دفاع / defâ/

defensive / difensiv / *adj* / مداعی / modâii/

definite / definit / *adj* / صریح / sarih/

definitely / definitlii / *adv* / یقیناً / yaghinan/

degree / digrii / *n* / درجه / daraje/

delay / diley / *vi* / تاخیر / taakhir/

deliberately / diliberitlii / *adv* / عمداً / omdatan/

delicacy / delikasii / *n* / ظرافت / zerâfat/

delicate / delikit / *adj* / ظریف / zarif/

delicious / dilishes / *adj* / خوشمزه / khoshmaze/

delighted / dilâytid / *adj* / شاد / shâd/

deliver / diliver / *vt* / رساندن / resândan/

delivery / diliverii / *n* / تحویل / tahvil/

demand / dimând / *n* / درخواست / darkhâst/

demonstrate / demonstreyt / *vt* / ثابت کردن / sâbet kardan/

demonstration / demonstreyshen / *n* / نشان دادن / neshân dâdan/

demonstrative / dimânstrativ / *adj* / احساساتی / ehsâsâti/

den / den / *n* / غار / ghâr/

dentist / dentist / *n* / دندانپزشك / dandânpezeshk/

deny / dinây / *vt* / انکار کردن / enkâr kardan/

depart / dipart / *vi* / حرکت کردن / harakat kardan/

department / dipârtment / *n* / قسمت / ghesmat/

departure / dipârcher / *n* / حرکت / harekat/

depend / dipend / *vi* / وابسته بودن / vâbaste budan/

dependent / dipendent / *adj* / وابسته / vâbaste/

deport / diport / *vt* / تبعید کردن / tabiid kardan/

depress / dipres / *vt* / غمگین کردن / ghamgin kardan/

depression / dipreshen / *n* / افسردگی / afsordegi/

depth / depth / *n* / عمق / omgh/

describe / diskrâyb / *vt* / شرح دادن / sharh dâdan/

description / diskripshen / *n* / توصیف / tosif/

description / diskripshn / *n* / شرح / sharh/

desert / dezert / *n* / بیابان / biyâbân/

deserve / dizerv / *vt* / سزاوار بودن / sezâvâr budan/

design / dizâyn / *n* / طرح / tarh/

designer / dizâyner / *n* / طراح / tarrâh/

desire / dizâyer / *n* / آرزو / ârezu/

desk / desk / *n* / میز / miz/

destiny / destinii / *n* / سرنوشت / sarnevesht/

destroy / distroy / *vt* / خراب کردن / kharâb kardan/

destruction / distrâkshen / *n* / خرابی / kharâbi/

detach / ditach / *vt* / باز کردن / bâz kardan/

detail / diiteyl / *n* / جزئیات / joziyyât/

detection / ditekshn / *n* / کشف / kashf/

detective / ditektiv / *n* / کارآگاه / kârâgâh/

determination / ditermineyshn / *n* / تعیین / taayin/

determine / ditermin / *vt* / معین کردن / moayyan kardan/

develop / divelop / *vt* / رشد کردن / roshd kardan/

development / divelopment / *n* / رشد / roshd/

devil / devil / *n* / شیطان / sheytân/

devout / divaot / *adj* / دیندار / dindâr/

diabetes / dâyebiitiiz / *n* / بیماری قند / bimâriye ghand/

dial / dâyâl / *vt* / شماره گرفتن / shomâre gereftan/

dialect / dâyâlekt / *n* / لهجه / lahje/

dialogue / dâyâlâg / *n* / مکالمه / mokâleme/

dialogue / dâyelog / *n* / گفتگو / goftegu/

diamond / dâyemend / *n* / الماس / almâs/

diaper / dayper / *n* / پوشک / pushâk/

dictate / dikteyt / *vt* / دیکته گفتن / dikte goftan/

dictator / dikteyter / *n* / دیکتاتور / diktâtor/

dictionary / diksherii / *n* / فرهنگ / farhang/

die / dây / *vi* / مردن / mordan/

diet / dâyet / *n* / غذا / ghazâ/

differ / difer / *vi* / فرق داشتن / fargh dâshtan/

difference / difrens / *n* / تفاوت / tafâvot/

different / difrent / *adj* / متفاوت / motafâvet/

difficult / difikâlt / *adj* / مشکل / moshkel/

difficulty / difikâltii / *n* / مشکل / moshkel/

dig / dig / *vt* / کندن / kandan/

digest / dâyjest / *n* / خلاصه / kholâse/

digest / dijest / *vt* / هضم کردن / hazm kardan/

digestion / dijeschen / *n* / هضم / hazm/

dimension / dimenshn / *n* / اندازه / andâze/

dine / dâyn / *vi* / شام خوردن / shâm khordan/

dining room / dâyning-rum / *n* / نهارخوری / nâhârkhori/

dinner / diner / *n* / شام / shâm/

dip / dip / *vt* / فروبردن / furubordan/

diploma / diplomâ / *n* / دیپلم / diplom/

direct / direkt / *adj* / مستقیم / mostaghim/

direction / direkshen / *n* / طرف / taraf/

directly / direktlii / *adv* / مستقیماً / mostaghiman/

director / directer / *n* / مدیر / modir/

directory / directerii / *n* / دفتر راهنما / daftare râhnemâ/

dirt / dert / *n* / کثافت / kesâfat/

dirty / dertii / *adj* / كثيف / kasif/

disadvantage / disadvantij / *n* / عيب / eyb/

disagree / disagrii / *vi* / مخالفت كردن / mokhâlefat kardan/

disagreement / disagriiment / *n* / اختلاف / ekhtelâf/

disappear / disapiyer / *vi* / ناپديد شدن / nâpadid shodan/

disappointed / disapoyntid / *adj* / مأيوس / maayus/

disappointment / disapoyntment / *n* / دلسردى / delsardi/

discipline / disiplin / *n* / انضباط / enzebât/

disco / disko / *n* / ديسكو / disko/

discomfort / diskâmfort / *n* / درد / dard/

discount / diskaont / *n* / تخفيف / takhfif/

discourage / diskârij / *vt* / دلسرد كردن / delsard kardan/

discover / diskâver / *vt* / كشف كردن / kasf kardan/

discovery / diskâverii / *n* / كشف / kashf/

discuss / diskâs / *vt* / بحث كردن / bahs kardan/

discussion / diskâshen / *n* / بحث / bahs/

disease / diziiz / *n* / بيمارى / bImâri/

disguise / disgâyz / *vt* / تغيير دادن / tâghiir dâdan/

disgust / disgâst / *n* / نفرت / nefrat/

disgusting / disgusting / *adj* / نفرت انگيز / nefrat angiz/

dish / dIsh / *n* / ظرف / zarf/

dishonest / disânist / *adj* / نادرست / nâdorost/

dislike / dislâyk / *vt* / دوست نداشتن / dust nadâshtan/

disobey / disobey / *vt* ناقرمانی کردن / nâ farmâni kardan/

disorder / disorder / *n* بی نظمی / bi nazmi/

display / displey / *vt* نشان دادن / neshân dâdan/

dispute / dispyoot / *n* بحث / bahs/

distance / distans / *n* مسافت / masâfat/

distant / distant / *adj* دور / dur/

distinction / distinkshen / *n* تفاوت / tafâvot/

distribution / distribyooshen / *vt* توزیع کردن / tozii kardan/

disturb / disterb / *vt* مزاحم شدن / mozâhem shodan/

dive / dâyv / *n* شیرجه / shirje/

diver / dâyver / *n* غواص / ghavvâs/

diverse / dâyvers / *adj* گوناگون / gunâgun/

divide / divâyd / *vt* قسمت کردن / ghesmat kardan/

division / divizhen / *n* تقسیم / taghsim/

divorce / divors / *n* طلاق / talâgh/

do / doo / *vt* کردن / kardan/

dock / dâk / *vt* باراندازِ / bâr andâz/

doctor / dâkter / *n* دکتر / doktor/

document / dâkyument / *n* سند / sanad/

dog / dâg / *n* سگ / sag/

doll / dâl / *n* عروسک / arusak/

dollar / dâler / *n* دلار / dolâr/

dolphin / dâlfin / *n* دُلفین / dolfin/

dome / dom / *n* گنبد / gonbad/

dominate / dâmineyt / *vt* مسلط بودن / mosallat budan/

domination / dâmineyshen / *n* سلطه / solte/

door / dor / *n* در / dar/

doorway / dorwey / *n* راهرو / râhrou/

dot / dât / *n* نقطه / noghte/

double / dâbel / *adj* دوبرابر / dobarâbar/

doubt / daot / *n* شک / shak/

doubtless / daotlis / *adv* بی شک / bi shak/

dove / dâv / *n* کبوتر / kabutar/

down / daon / *adv* پایین / pâyin/

downward(s) / daonword(z) / *adv* به طرف پایین / betarafe pâyin/

dozen / dâzen / *adj* دوجین / dujin/

drama / drâme / *n* درام / drâm/

dramatic / dramatik / *adj* نمایشی / nemâyeshi/

draw / drâ / *vt* رسم کردن / rasm kardan/

drawer / dror / *n* کشو / kesho/

drawing / drâ-ing / *n* نقاشی / naghghâshi/

dread / dred / *vt* ترسیدن از / tarsidan az/

dream / driim / *n* رؤیا / royâ/

dress / dres / *n* لباس / lebâs/

drill / dril / *n* مته / mate/

drink / drink / *n* نوشابه / nushâbe/

drink / drink / *vt* / آشامیدن / âshâmidan/

drive / drâyv / *n* / رانندگی / rânandegi/

driver / drâyver / *n* / راننده / râdande/

drop / drâp / *n* / قطره / ghatre/

drop / drâp / *vi* / افتادن / oftâdan/

drown / draon / *vt* / غرق کردن / gharh kardan/

drug / drâg / *n* / دارو / dâru/

drugstore / drâgstor / *n* / داروخانه / dârukhâne/

drum / drâm / *n* / طبل / tabl/

drunk / drânk / *adj* / مست / mast/

dry / drây / *adj* / خشك / khoshk/

duck / dâk / *n* / اردك / ordak/

duke / dyook / *n* / دوک / duk/

dull / dâl / *adj* / تیره / tire/

dumb / dâm / *adj* / خنک / khonak/

during / dyuring / prep / درطول / dartule/

dust / dâst / *n* / گرد وخاك / gardokhâk/

dusty / dâstii / *adj* / گردگرفته / gard gerefte/

duty / dyootii / *n* / وظیفه / vazife/

dye / dây / *vt* / رنگ کردن / rang kardan/

dynamism / dâynamizem / *n* / اصالت نیرو / esâlat niro/

E

each / iich / *adj* / هر / har/

eager / iiger / *adj* / مشتاق / moshtagh/

ear / iyer / *n* / گوش / gush/

early / erlii / *adj* / زود / zud/

earn / ern / *vt* / درآمد داشتن / darâmed dâshtan/

earnestly / ernestlii / *adv* / جداً / jeddan/

earring / iyering / *n* / گوشواره / gushvâre/

earth / erth / *n* / زمین / zamin/

earthquake / ertkveyk / *n* / زلزله / zelzele/

easily / iizilii / *adv* / به آسانی / beâsâni/

east / iist / *n* / خاور / khâvar/

eastern / iistern / *adj* / شرقی / sharghi/

easy / iizii / *adj* / آسان / âsân/

eat / iit / *vt* / خوردن / khordan/

eccentric / iksentrik / *adj* / غیر عادی / gheyre âdi/

echo / eko / *n* / پژواك / pezhvâk/

ecology / iikâlojii / *n* / بوم شناسی / bumshenâsi/

economic / iikânâmik / *adj* / اقتصادی / eghtesâdi/

economical / iikânamikal / *adj* / باصرفه / bâsarfe/

economics / iikânâmiks / *n* / علم اقتصاد / elme eghtesâd/

economist / iikânemist / *n* / اقتصاددان / eghtesâddân/

economy / iikânamii / *n* / اقتصاد / eghtesâd/

edge / ej / *n* / لبه / labe/

edit / edit / *vt* / ویرایش کردن / virâyesh kardan/

edition / edishen / *n* / چاپ / châp/

editor / editer / *n* / سردبیر / sardabir/

educate / ejukeyt / *vt* / آموزش دادن / âmuzesh dâdan/

education / ejukeyshen / *n* / آموزش / âmuzesh/

educational / ejukeyshenl / *adj* / آموزشی / âmuzeshii/

effect / ifekt / *n* / اثر / asar/

effective / ifectiv / *adj* / مؤثر / moasser/

effeminate / ifeminit / *adj* / زنانه / zanâne/

efficiency / ifishensi / *n* / کارآیی / kârâyi/

efficient / ifishent / *adj* / لایق / lâyegh/

effort / efort / *n* / کوشش / kushesh/

egg / eg / *n* / تخم مرغ / tokhmemorgh/

Egypt / iijipt / *n* / مصر / mesr/

eight / eyt / *n, adj* / هشت / hasht/

eighteen / eytiin / *adj* / هیجده / hijdah/

eighteenth / eytiinth / *adj* / هیجدهمین / hijdahomin/

eighth / eyth / *adj* / یک هشتم / yek-hashtom/

eighty / eyti / *n, adj* / هشتاد / hashtâd/

either / âydher / *adj* / یا /yâ/

elastic / ilastik / *adj* / کش سان /keshsân/

elbow / elbo / *n* / آرنج /âranj/

elder / elder / *adj* / بزرگتر /bozorgtar/

eldest / eldist / *adj* / بزرگترین /bozorgtarin/

elect / ilekt / *vt* / انتخاب کردن /entekhâb kardan/

election / ilekshen / *n* / انتخابات /entekhâbât/

electric / ilektrik / *adj* / برقی /barghi/

electrical / ilektrikâl / *adj* / برقی /barghi/

electrician / ilektrishen / *n* / برق کار /bargh kar/

electricity / ilektrisitii / *n* / برق /bargh/

elegance / eligens / *n* / آراستگی /ârâstegi/

elegant / eligent / *adj* / آراسته /ârâste/

element / eliment / *n* / عنصر /onsor/

elementary / elimentrii / *adj* / مقدماتی /moghaddamâti/

elephant / elifent / *n* / فیل /fil/

elevate / eliveyt / *vt* / بلند کردن /boland kardan/

elevator / ellveyter / *n* / آسانسور /âsânsor/

eleven / ilevn / *n, adj* / یازده /yâzdah/

eleventh / ileventh / *adj* / یازدهمین /yâzdahomin/

eliminate / ilimineyt / *vt* / حذف کردن /hazf kardan/

else / els / *adv* / دیگر /digar/

elsewhere / elswer / *adv* / جای دیگر /jâyedigar/

e-mail / ii-meyl / *n* پست الکترونیکی / poste elektroniki/

emancipate / imânsipeyt / *vt* آزاد کردن / âzâd kardan/

embassy / embesi / *n* سفارت / sefârat/

embrace / imbreys / *vt* بغل کردن / baghal kardan/

emerge / imerj / *vi* نمایان شدن / nemâyân shodan/

emergency / imerjensi / *n* وضع اضطراری /
vazee ezterâri/

emigrant / emigrent / *n* مهاجر / mohâjer/

emigrate / emigreyt / *vi* مهاجرت کردن / mohâjerat kardan/

emotion / imoshen / *n* عاطفه / âtefe/

empire / empâyr / *n* امپراتوری / emprâturi/

employ / imploy / *vt* استخدام کردن / estekhdâm kardan/

employee / imployii / *n* کارمند / kârmand/

employer / imployer / *n* کارفرما / kârfarmâ/

employment / imployment / *n* استخدام / estekhdâm/

empty / emptii / *adj* خالی / khâli/

enable / ineybel / *vt* امکان دادن به / emkân dâdanm be/

enamel / inaml / *n* مینا / minâ/

encourage / inkârij / *vt* تشویق کردن / tashvigh kardan/

encouragement / inkârijment / *n* تشویق / tashvigh/

end / end / *n* پایان / pâyân/

endless / endlis / *adj* بی پایان / bi pâyân/

endlessly / endlislii / *adv* مدام / modâm/

endurance / indurans / *n* دوام / davâm/

endure / indyur / *vt* تحمل کردن / tahammol kardan/
enemy / enemi / *n* دشمن / doshman/
energy / enerjii / *n* نیرو / niru/
engage / ingeyj / *vt* استخدام کردن / estekhtam kardan/
engaged / ingeyjd / *adj* نامزد / nâmzad/
engagement / ingeyjment / *n* نامزدی / nâmzadi/
engine / enjin / *n* موتور / motor/
England / ingland / *n* انگلستان / engelestân/
English / inglish / *adj* انگلیسی / engilisi/
enjoyment / injoyment / *n* لذت بردن / lazzat bordan/
enormous / inormes / *adj* بزرگ / bozorg/
enough / inâf / *adj* کافی / kâfi/
enrage / inreyj / *vt* عصبانی کردن / asabâni kardan/
enter / enter / *vi* وارد شدن / vâred shodan/
enterprise / enterprâyz / *n* جسارت / jesârat/
entertain / enterteyn / *vt* پذیرایی کردن / pazirâii kardan/
entertainment / enterteynment / *n* تفریح / tafrih/
enthusiasm / inthyooziyazem / *n* اشتیاق / eshtiâgh/
entire / intâyr / *adj* تمام / tamam/
entirely / intâyrlii / *adv* کاملاً / kâmelan/
entrance / entrens / *n* ورودی / vurudi/
entry / entrii / *n* ورود / vurud/
envelop / invelop / *vt* پیچیدن / pichidan/

envelope / envelop / *n* / پاکت (نامه) / pâkat (nâme)/

envious / enviyes / *adj* / حسود / hasud/

environment / invârenment / *n* / محیط / mohit/

envy / envii / *n* / حسادت / hesâdat/

epidemic / epidemik / *adj* / همه گیر / hamegir/

epilepsy / epilepsii / *n* / صرع / saree/

episode / episod / *n* / حادثه / hâdese/

equal / iikwâl / *adj* / برابر / barâbar/

equality / ikwâlitii / *n* / برابری / barâbari/

equally / iikwâlii / *adv* / به یک اندازه / be yek andâze/

equip / ikwip / *vt* / مجهز کردن / mojahhaz kardan/

equipment / ikwipment / *n* / تجهیز / tajhiz/

equipped / ikwipt / *adj* / آماده / âmâde/

eraser / ireyser / *n* / پاک کن / pâkkon/

error / erer / *n* / اشتباه / eshtebâh/

escape / iskeyp / *vi* / فرار کردن / farâr kardan/

especially / ispeshâlii / *adv* / مخصوصاً / makhsusan/

essential / isenshl / *adj* / ضروری / zaruri/

establish / istablish / *vt* / تأسیس کردن / tasis kardan/

eternity / iternitii / *n* / ابدیت / abadiyat/

ethical / ethikl / *adj* / اخلاقی / akhlâghi/

euro / yuro / *n* / یورو / yuro/

Europe / yurop / *n* / اروپا / urupâ/

European / yuropiiyen / *adj* / اروپایی / urupâyi/

European Union / yuropiien yoonyen / *n* / اتحاد اروپا / ettehâde urupâ/

evacuate / ivakyooneyt / *vt* / تخلیه کردن / takhliye kardan/

evaluate / ivalyooneyt / *vt* / ارزیابی کردن / arzyâbi kardan/

even / iiven / *adv* / حتی / hattâ/

event / ivent / *n* / حادثه / hâdese/

eventful / iventful / *adj* / پرماجرا / por mâjarâ/

eventually / ivenchoowâlii / *adv* / سرانجام / saranjâm/

ever / ever / *adv* / هیچوقت / hichvaght/

every / evrii / *adj* / هر / har/

everybody / evriibâdii / *pron* / هرکس / harkas/

everyone / evriiwân / *pron* / هرکس / harkas/

everything / evriithing / *pron* / هرچیز / harchiz/

everywhere / evriiwer / *adv* / همه جا / hamejâ/

evil / iivel / *adj* / بد / bad/

evocation / evokeyshen / *n* / یادآوری / yâdâvari/

evoke / ivok / *vt* / به یاد آوردن / bo yâd âvardan/

evolution / evolooshen / *n* / تکامل / takâmol/

evolve / ivâlv / *vi* / تکامل یافتن / takâmol yâftan/

exact / igzakt / *adj* / دقیق / daghigh/

exactly / igzaktlii / *adv* / دقیقًا / daghighan/

exaggerate / igzajereyt / *vt* / مبالغه کردن / mubâleghe kardan/

exam / igzam / *n* / امتحان / emtehân/

examination / igzamineyshen / *n* / امتحان / emtehân/

examine / igzamin / *vt* / امتحان کردن / emtehân kardan/

example / igzâmpel / *n* / مثال / mesâl/

exceed / iksiid / *vt* / فراتر رفتن / farâtar kardan/

excellent / ekselent / *adj* / عالی / âli/

except / iksept / *prep* / بجز / bejoz/

exception / iksepshen / *n* / استثنا / estesnâ/

exchange / ikscheynj / *n* / مبادله / mobâdele/

exchange / ikscheynj / *vt* / مبادله کردن / mobâdele kardan/

excite / iksâyt / *vt* / به هیجان آوردن / be heyejân âvardan/

excited / iksâytid / *adj* / هیجان زده / heyejânzade/

excitedly / iksâytdlii / *adv* / با هیجان / bâ heyejân/

excitement / iksâytment / *n* / هیجان / hayajân/

exciting / iksâyting / *adj* / مهیج / mohayyej/

exclaim / ikskleym / *vt* / فریاد کشیدن / faryâd keshidan/

exclamation / eksklmeyshen / *n* / اظهار تعجب /
ezhâre taajjob/

excuse / ikskyoos / *n* / عذر / ozr/

excuse / ikskyooz / *vt* / بخشیدن / bakhshidan/

execute / eksikyoot / *vt* / اجرا کردن /ejrâ kardan/

executive / igzekyutiv / *adj* / اجرایی / ejrâyi/

exercise / eksersâyz / *n* / تمرین / tamrin/

exhibit / egzibit / *vt* / نمایش دادن / nemâyesh dâdan/

exhibition / eksibishen / n نمایشگاه / nemâyeshgâh/

exist / igzist / vi وجود داشتن / vujud dâshtan/

existence / igzistens / n هستی / hasti/

exit / eksit / n خروج / khuruj/

exotic / igzâtik / adj غیر بومی / gheyre bumi/

expect / ikspekt / vt انتظار داشتن / entezâr dâshtan/

expectation / ekspekteyshen / n انتظار / entezâr/

expense / ikspens / n هزینه / hazine/

expensive / ikspensiv / adj گران / gerân/

experience / ikspiiriiyens / n تجربه / tajrobe/

experienced / iksperiyenst / adj با تجربه / bâ tajrobe/

experiment / iksperiment / n آزمایش / âzmâyesh/

experiment / iksperiment / vt آزمایش کردن /
  âzemâyesh kardan/

experimental / iksperimentâl / adj آزمایشی / âzemâyeshi/

expert / ekspert / vt کارشناس / kârshenâs/

explain / ikspleyn / vt توضیح دادن / tozih dâdan/

explanation / eksplaneyshen / n توضیح / tozih/

explode / iksplod / vt منفجرکردن / monfajer kardan/

exploration / eksploreyshen / n کاوش / kâvosh/

explore / iksplor / vt کاوش کردن / kâvosh kardan/

explorer / iksplorer / n جهانگرد / jahângard/

explosion / iksplozhen / n انفجار / enfejâr/

export / eksport / n صادرات / sâderât/

expose / ikspoz / *vt* / نشان دادن / neshân dâdan/

express / ikspres / *vt* / بیان کردن / bayân kardan/

expression / ikspreshen / *n* / بیان / bayân/

extend / ikstend / *n* / توسعه دادن / tosee dâdan/

extension / ikstenshen / *n* / توسعه / tosee/

exterminate / ikstermineyt / *vt* / ریشه کن کردن / rishekan kardan/

external / iksternl / *adj* / بیرونی / biruni/

extinct / ikstinkt / *adj* / خاموش / khâmush/

extinction / ikstinkshen / *n* / نابودی / nâbudi/

extra / ekstrâ / *n* / اضافی / ezâfi/

extract / ekstrakt / *n* / عصاره / osareh/

extraordinary / ikstrordinerii / *adj* / استثنایی / estesnâyi/

extravagant / ikstravagent / *adj* / ولخرج / velkharj/

extreme / ikstriim / *adj* / نهایی / nahâii/

extremely / ikstriimlii / *adv* / فوق العاده / fogholâde/

extremity / ikstremitii / *n* / منتها درجه / montahâ daraje/

exultant / igzâltant / *adj* / خوشی کننده / khoshi konande/

eye / ây / *n* / چشم / cheshm/

eyeball / âybol / *n* / تخم چشم / tokme cheshm/

eyebrow / âybrow / *n* / ابرو / abru/

eyelash / âylash / *n* / مژگان / mozhgân/

eyelid / âylid / *n* / پلک چشم / pelke cheshm/

F

fable / feybel / *n* / قصه / ghesse/
face / feys / *n* / صورت / surat/
facilitate / fasiliteyt / *vt* / تسهیل کردن / tashil kardan/
facilities / fasilitiiz / *n* / تسهیلات / tahs-hilât/
facility / fasilitii / *n* / استعداد / esteedâd/
fact / fakt / *n* / واقعیت / vâgheiyyat/
factory / fakterii / *n* / کارخانه / kârkhâne/
fade / feyd / *vi* / پژمرده شدن / pazhmorde shodan/
fail / feyl / *vt* / رد شدن / radshodan/
failure / feylyur / *n* / آدم ناموفق / âdame nâmovaffagh/
fair / fer / *n* / منصف / monsef/
fairly / ferlii / *adv* / نسبتاً / nesbatan/
faith / feyth / *n* / اعتقاد / ooteghâd/
faithful / feylhiful / *adj* / باوفا / bâvafâ/
faithfully / feythfulii / *adv* / صادقانه / sâdeghâne/
fall / fol / *n* / سقوط / seghut/
fall / fol / *vi* / افتادن / oftâdan/
false / fols / *adj* / دروغی / durughi/
fame / feym / *n* / شهرت / shohrat/

familiar / familyâr / *adj* / آشنا / âshenâ/

family / familii / *n* / خانواده / khânevâde/

famous / feymes / *adj* / مشهور / mashhur/

fancy / fansii / *vt* / تصور کردن / tasavvor kardan/

fantastic / fantastik / *adj* / شگفت / shegeft/

far / fâr / *adj* / دور / dur/

far away / fârewey / *adj* / دوردست / durdast/

fare / fer / *n* / کرایه / kerâye/

farewell / ferwel / *intj* / خدا حافظ / khodâ hâfez/

farm / fârm / *n* / مزرعه / mazrae/

farmer / fârmer / *n* / مزرعه دار / mazraedâr/

farther / fârdher / *adv* / دورتر / durtar/

fascinating / fasineyting / *adj* / جالب / jâleb/

fascination / fasineyshen / *n* / جاذبه / jâzebe/

fashion / fashen / *n* / روش / ravesh/

fashionable / fashenebel / *adj* / مُد / mod/

fast / fast / *adj* / تند / tond/

fasten / fasen / *vt* / بستن / bastan/

fat / fat / *adj* / چاق / châgh/

fatal / feytal / *adj* / مهلک / mohlek/

father / fâdher / *n* / پدر / pedar/

fatigue / fâtiig / *n* / خستگی / khastegi/

fault / folt / *n* / عیب / eeyb/

favor / feyver / *n* / لطف / lotf/
favorite / feyverit / *adj* / محبوب / mahbub/
fear / fiyer / *n* / ترس / tars/
fearful / fiyerful / *adj* / هولناک / holnâk/
fearless / fiyerlis / *adj* / نترس / natars/
feast / fiist / *n* / ضیافت / ziyâfat/
feather / fedher / *n* / پر / par/
feature / fiicher / *n* / صورت / surat/
February / februwerii / *n* / فوریه / fevriye/
fee / fii / *n* / دستمزد / dastmozd/
feeble / fiibel / *adj* / ضعیف / zaiif/
feebly / fiiblii / *adv* / با ضعف / bâ zaaf/
feed / fiid / *vt* / تغذیه کردن / taghziye kardan/
feel / fiil / *vt* / حس کردن / hes kardan/
feeling / fiiling / *n* / حس / hes/
fellow / felo / *n* / مرد / mard/
female / fiimeyl / *adj* / ماده / mâde/
feminine / feminin / *adj* / زنانه / zanâne/
fertile / fertil / *adj* / حاصلخیز / hâselkhiz/
festival / festivâl / *n* / جشن / jashn/
fever / fiiver / *n* / تب / tab/
few / fyoo / *adj* / محدود / maadud/
fib / fib / *n* / چاخان / châkhân/

fiber / fâyber / *n* ليف / lif/

fiction / fikshen / *n* داستان / dâstân /

field / fiild / *n* مزرعه / mazrae/

fifteen / fiftiin / *adj* پانزده / pânzdah/

fifteenth / fiftiinth / *n, adj* پانزدهم / pânezdahom/

fifth / fifth / *n, adj* پنجمی / panjomi/

fiftieth / fiftiiyeth / *n, adj* پنجاهم / panjâhom/

fifty / fiftii / *n, adj* پنجاه / panjâh/

fight / fâyt / *n* جنگ / jang/

fight / fâyt / *vi* دعوا کردن / daavâ kardan/

fighter / fâyter / *n* جنگجو / jangju/

figure / figyer / *n* رقم / ragham/

fill / fil / *vt* پر کردن / por kardan/

film / film / *n* فیلم / film/

filter / filter / *n* صافی / sâfi/

final / fâynâl / *adj* نهایی / nehâyi/

find / fâynd / *vt* پیدا کردن / peydâ kardan/

fine / fâyn / *adj* خوب / khub/

fine / fâyn / *n* جریمه / jarime/

finger / finger / *n* انگشت / angosht/

finish / finish / *n* تمام کردن / tamâm kardan/

fire / fâyer / *n* آتش / âtash/

fire / fâyer / *vt* شلیک کردن / shellik kardan/

fireman / fâyermen / *n* / مامور آتش نشانی / mamure âtash neshani/

fireplace / fâyerpleys / *n* / شومینه / shomine/

firm / ferm / *adj* / محکم / mohkam/

firm / ferm / *n* / شرکت / sherkat/

firmly / fermlii / *adv* / محکم / mohkam/

first / ferst / *n, adj* / اولین / avvalin/

fish / fish / *n* / ماهی / mâhi/

fisherman / fishermen / *n* / صیاد / sayyâd/

fishing / fishing / *n* / ماهیگیری / mâhigiri/

fist / fist / *n* / مشت / mosht/

fit / fit / *adj* / مناسب / monâseb/

fit / fit / *vt* / تناسب داشتن / tanâsob dâshtan/

five / fâyv / *n, adj* / پنج / panj/

fix / fiks / *vt* / نصب کردن / nasb kardan/

flag / flag / *n* / پرچم / parcham/

flame / fluym / *n* / شعله / shoele/

flash / flash / *n* / درخشش / drakhshesh/

flashback / flashbak / *n* / فلاش بک / flâshbak/

flat / flat / *adj* / هموار / hamvâr/

flat / flat / *n* / آپارتمان / âpârtemân/

flavor / fleyver / *n* / طعم / taam/

flee / flii / *vt* / فرار کردن / farâr kardan/

flesh / flesh / *n* / گوشت / gusht/

flight / flâyt / *n* / پرواز / parvâz/

float / flot / *vi, vt* / شناورشدن / shenâvarshodan/

floor / flor / *n* / طبقه / tabaghe/

flow / flo / *vi* / جاری شدن / jâri shodan/

flower / flaower / *n* / گل / gol/

flowerbed / flaowerbed / *n* / باغچه / baghche/

flu / floo / *n* / آنفلوانزا / ânfulânzâ/

fluctuate / flukchooate / *vt* / نوسان کردن / navasân kardan/

fluctuation / flukchooashen / *n* / نوسان / navasân/

fly / flây / *n* / مگس / magas/

fly / flây / *vi* / پرواز کردن / parvâz kardan/

focus / fokes / *n* / کانون / kânun/

fog / fâg / *n* / مه / meh/

foggy / fâgi / *adj* / آلود مه / mehâlud/

fold / fold / *vt* / تا کردن / tâ kardan/

folder / folder / *n* / پوشه / pushe/

folk / fok / *n* / مردم / mardom/

follow / fâlo / *vt* / دنبال کردن / donbâl kardan/

following / fâlo-ing / *adj* / بعد / baad/

fond / fond / *adj* / شیفته / shifteh/

food / food / *n* / غذا / ghazâ/

fool / fool / *n* / آدم احمق / âdame ahmagh/

foot / fut / *n* / پا / pâ/

football / futbol / *n* فوتبال / futbâl/

footsteps / futsteps / *n* ردّ پا / radde pâ/

for / for / *conj* چون / chon/

for / for / *prep* برای / barâye/

for instance / forinstans / *n* مثلاً / masalan/

forbid / forbid / *vt* قدغن کردن / ghadaghan kardan/

force / fors / *n* زور / zur/

force / fors / *vt* مجبور کردن / majbur kardan/

forecast / forkast / *vt* پیشبینی / pishbini/

forefathers / forfâdherz / *n* اجداد / ajdâd/

foreign / fârin / *adj* خارجی / khâreji/

foreigner / fârner / *n* خارجی / khâreji/

forest / fârist / *n* جنگل / jangal/

forever / forever / *adv* همیشه / hamishe/

forget / forget / *vt* فراموش کردن / farâmush kardan/

forgive / forgiv / *vt* بخشیدن / bakhshidan/

fork / fork / *n* چنگال / changal/

form / form / *n* صورت / surat/

formal / formâl / *adj* رسمی / rasmi/

format / format / *n* شکل / sheki/

formation / formeyshen / *n* شکل گیری / shekl giri/

former / former / *adj* قبلی / ghabli/

formerly / formerlii / *adv* قبلاً / ghablan/

formidable / formidebel / *adj* / ترسناک / tarsnâk/

formula / formyula / *n* / فرمول / formul/

fort / fort / *n* / دژ / dezh/

fortieth / fortiyeth / *n, adj* / چهلم / chehelom/

fortnight / fortnâyt / *n* / دوهفته / dohafte/

fortunately / forchoonitlii / *adv* / خوشبختانه / khoshbakhtâne/

fortune / forchoon / *n* / بخت / bakht/

forty / fortii / *n, adj* / چهل / chehel/

forward(s) / forwârd(z) / *adv* / جلو / jelo/

fossil / fâsl / *n* / سنگواره / sangvâre/

foul / faol / *adj* / نا پاک / nâ pâk/

foundation / faondeyshen / *n* / بنیاد / bonyâd/

fountain / faontin / *n* / فواره / favvâre/

four / for / *n, adj* / چهار / châhâr/

fourteen / fortiin / *n, adj* / چهارده / châhârdah/

fourteenth / fortiinth / *n, adj* / چهاردهم / châhârdahom/

fourth / forth / *n, adj* / چهارم / châhârom/

fox / fâks / *n* / روباه / rubâh/

frame / freym / *n* / قاب / ghâb/

France / frans / *n* / فرانسه / farânse/

frantic / frantik / *adj* / هراسان / harâsân/

free / frii / *adj* / آزاد / âzâd/

freedom / friidem / *n* / آزادی / âzâdi/

freeze / friiz / *vi* / یخ بستن / yakh bastan/
French / french / *n, adj* / فرانسوی / farânsavi/
frenzy / frenzii / *n* / حالت جنون / hâlate jenun/
frequent / friikwent / *adj* / فراوان / farâvân/
frequent / friikwent / *adj* / همیشگی / hamishegi/
frequently / friikwentlii / *adv* / زیاد / ziyâd/
fresh / fresh / *adj* / تازه / tâze/
freshwater / freshwoter / *adj* / آب شیرین / âbe shirin/
Friday / frâydi / *n* / جمعه / jomee/
friend / frend / *n* / دوست / dust/
friendly / frendlii / *adj* / دوستانه / dustâne/
friendship / frendship / *n* / دوستی / dusti/
fright / frâyt / *n* / ترس / tars/
frog / frog / *n* / وزغ / vazagh/
from / frâm / *prep* / از / az/
front / frânt / *n* / جلو / jelo/
frontier / frântiiyer / *n* / مرز / marz/
frost / frâst / *n* / یخبندان / yakhbandan/
frosty / frâstii / *adj* / بسیار سرد / besiyâr sard/
fruit / froot / *n* / میوه / mive/
frying pan / frâying pan / *n* / ماهی تابه / mâhitâbe/
fuel / fyoo-el / *n* / سوخت / sukht/
fugitive / fyoojitiv / *n* / فراری / farâri/

full / ful / *n* / پر / par/

fully / fullii / *adv* / کاملاً / kâmelan/

fun / fân / *n* تفریح / tafrih/

fundamental / fândementl / *adj* اساسی / asâsi/

funny / fânii / *adj* خنده دار / khandedâr/

furious / fyuriiyes / *adj* عصبانی / asabâni/

furnished / fernisht / *adj* مبله / moble/

furniture / fernicher / *n* وسایل خانه / vasâyele khâne/

further / ferdher / *adv* دورتر / durtar/

furthest / ferdhist / *adv* دورترین / durtarin/

fuss / fâs / *n* هیاهو / hayâhu/

futile / fyootâyl / *adj* بی ثمر / bi samar/

future / fyoocher / *adj* آینده / âyande/

G

gain / geyn / *vt* / کسب کردن / kasb kardan/
gale / geyl / *n* / توفان / tufân/
gallery / galerii / *n* / نگارخانه / negârkhâne/
gallop / galop / *vi* / چهارنعل رفتن / châhârnaal raftan/
game / geym / *n* / بازی / bâzi/
gang / gang / *n* / باند / bând/
gangster / gangster / *n* / تبهکار / tabahkâr/
gap / gap / *n* / شکاف / shekaf/
garage / garaj / *n* / پارکینگ / pârking/
garage / garâzh / *n* / تعمیرگاه / taamirgâh/
garden / gârden / *n* / باغ / bâgh/
gardener / gârdner / *n* / باغبان / bâghbân/
gardening / gârdning / *n* / باغبانی / bâghbâni/
garlic / gârlik / *n* / سیر / sir/
gas / gas / *n* / بنزین / benzin/
gasoline / gasoliin / *n* / بنزین / benzin/
gate / geyt / *n* / دروازه / darvâze/
gather / gadher / *vi* / جمع شدن / jam shodan/
gay / gey / *adj* / شاد / shâd/

287

gear / giyer / *n* / دنده / dande/

general / jenrâl / *adj* / عمومی / umumi/

generally / jenrâlii / *adv* / معمولاً / mamulan/

generation / jenereyshen / *n* / تولید / tolid/

generator / jenereyter / *n* / مولد / movalled/

generous / jeneres / *adj* / سخاوتمند / sekhâvatmand/

genetics / jinetiks / *n* / علم وراثت / elme verâsat/

genius / jiinyes / *n* / نابغه / nâbeghe/

gentle / jentel / *adj* / مهربان / mehrebân/

gentleman / jentelmân / *n* / آقا / âghâ/

gently / jentlii / *adv* / به آرامی / beârâmi/

geography / jiiyâgrafii / *n* / جغرافیا / joghrâfiyâ/

German / jermân / *n, adj* / آلمان / âlmân/

Germany / jermanii / *n* / آلمانی / âlmâni/

gesture / jescher / *n* / ژست / zhest/

get / get / *vt* / گرفتن / gereftan/

ghost / gost / *n* / روح / ruh/

giant / jâyent / *n* / غول / ghul/

gift / gift / *n* / کادو / kâdo/

girl / gerl / *n* / دختر / dokhtar/

give / giv / *vt* / دادن / dâdan/

glad / glad / *adj* / خوشحال / khoshhâl/

glamorous / glameres / *adj* / دلربا / delrobâ/

gland / gland / *n* / غدّه / ghodde/

glass / glas / *n* / شیشه / shishe/

glasses / glasiz / *n* / عینك / eynak/

global / globl / *adj* / جهانی / jahâni/

glory / glorii / *n* / افتخار / eftekhâr/

glove / glâv / *n* / دستکش / dastkesh/

go / go / *vi* / رفتن / raftan/

goal / gol / *n* / هدف / hadaf/

God / gâd / *n* / خدا / khoda/

go-getter / go-geter / *n* / آدم جاه طلب / âdame jâhtalab/

gold / gold / *n* / طلا / talâ/

golden / golden / *adj* / طلایی / talâyi/

good / gud / *adj* / خوب / khub/

good-bye / gudbây / *intj* / خدا حافظ / khodâ hâfez/

goods / gudz / *n* / كالا / kâlâ/

goose / goos / *n* / غاز / ghâz/

govern / gâvern / *vt* / حکومت کردن / hukumat kardan/

government / gâvernment / *n* / دولت / dolat/

governor / gâverner / *n* / فرماندار / farmândâr/

grace / greys / *n* / زیبایی / zibâii/

gracious / greyshes / *adj* / مهربان / mehrabân/

grade / greyd / *n* / درجه / daraje/

gradual / grajuwal / *adj* / تدریجی / tadriji/

gradually / grajulii / *adv* / به تدریج / betadrij/

grammar / gramer / *n* / دستورزبان / dasturezabân/

grammar school / gramerskool / *n* / دبستان / dabestân/

grammatical / gramatikâl / *adj* / دستوری / dasturi/

grand / grand / *adj* / خوب / khub/

grandchildren / granchildren / *n* / نوه ها / navehâ/

grandfather / granfâdher / *n* / پدر بزرگ / pedar bozorg/

grandmother / granmâdher / *n* / مادر بزرگ / mâdar bozorg/

grape / greyp / *n* / انگور / angur/

grapefruit / greypfroot / *n* / گریپفر / giripfer/

graph / grâf / *n* / نمودار / nemudâr/

grasp / grasp / *vt* / محکم / mohkam/

grateful / greytful / *adj* / سپاسگزار / sepâsgozâr/

grave / greyv / *n* / گور / gur/

gravity / gravitii / *n* / جاذبه / jâzebe/

grease / griis / *n* / روغن / roghan/

great / greyt / *adj* / بزرگ / bozorg/

Greece / griis / *n* / یونان / yunân/

Greek / griik / *adj* / یونانی / yunâni/

green / griin / *adj* / سبز / sabz/

greenhouse / griinhaos / *n* / گلخانه / golkhâne/

greet / griit / *vt* / سلام کردن / salâm kardan/

greeting / griiting / *n* / سلام / salâm/

gray / grey / *adj* /خاکستری / khâkestari/

grill / gril / *n* /کباب پز / kabâbpaz/

grin / grin / *n* /پوزخند / poz khand/

grip / grip / *n* /گرفتن / gereftan/

grocer / groser / *n* /بقال / baghghâl/

ground / graond / *n* /زمین / zamin/

group / groop / *n* /گروه / guruh/

grow / gro / *vi* /رشد کردن / roshd kardan/

grown-up / gronâp / *adj* /بزرگ / bozorg/

guard / gârd / *n* /نگاهبان / negahbân/

guess / ges / *n* /حدس / hads/

guest / gest / *n* /مهمان / mehmân/

guide / gâyd / *n* /راهنما / râhnamâ/

guilt / gilt / *n* /گناه / gonâh/

guilty / giltii / *adj* /گناهکار / gonâhkâr/

guitar / gitâr / *n* /گیتار / gitâr/

gum / gâm / *n* /چسب / chasb/

gun / gân / *n* /سلاح / selâh/

gunpowder / gânpaoder / *n* /باروت / bârut/

guy / gây / *n* /مرد / mard/

H

habit / habit / *n* عادت / âdat/

hair / her / *n* مو / mu/

half / haf / *n* نصف / nesf/

hall / hâl / *n* سالن / sâlon/

ham / ham / *n* ژامبون / zhâmbon/

hammer / hamer / *n* چکش / chakkosh/

hand / hand / *n* دست / dast/

handful / handful / *n* معدودی / maadudi/

handicap / handiikap / *n* نقص / naghs/

handkerchief / hangkerchif / *n* دستمال / dastmâl/

handle / handel / *n* دسته / daste/

handsome / hansâm / *adj* قشنگ / ghashang/

hang / hang / *vt* آویختن / âvikhtan/

happen / hapen / *vi* اتفاق افتادن / ettefâgh oftâdan/

happening / hapening / *n* رویداد / ruydâd/

happiness / hapiinis / *n* خوشی / khoshi/

happy / hapii / *adj* خوش / khosh/

harbor / hârber / *n* بندرگاه / bandar/

hard / hârd / *adj* سخت / sakht/

hardly / hârdlii / *adv* / به سختی / be sakhti/

harm / hârm / *n* / اذیت / aziyat/

harmful / hârmful / *adj* / مضر / mozer/

harmless / hârmlis / *adj* / بی ضرر / bi zarar/

harshly / hârsli / *adv* / با بیرحمی / bâ birahmi/

haste / heyst / *n* / شتاب / shetâb/

hasten / heysen / *vi* / عجله کردن / ajale kardan/

hasty / heystii / *adj* / عجول / ajul/

hat / hat / *n* / کلاه / kolâh/

hate / heyt / *vt* / بیزار بودن / bizâr budan/

hateful / heytful / *adj* / زشت / zesht/

have / hav / *vt* / داشتن / dâshtan/

he / hii / *pron* / او / u/

head / hed / *n* / سر / sar/

headache / hedeyk / *n* / سردرد / sardard/

headlight / hedlâyt / *n* / چراغ / cherâgh/

headline / hodlâyn / *n* / عنوان / onvân/

heal / hiil / *vi, vt* / بهبود یافتن / behbud yâftan/

health / helth / *n* / سلامت / salâmat/

healthy / helthii / *adj* / سالم / sâlem/

heap / hiip / *n* / توده / tude/

hear / hiyer / *vt* / شنیدن / shenidan/

heart / hârt / *n* / قلب / ghalb/

heat / hiit / *n* / حرارت / harârat/

heating / hiiting / *n* / گرم کننده / garm konande/

heaven / heven / *n* / بهشت / behesht/

heavy / hevii / *adj* / سنگین / sangin/

height / hâyt / *n* / ارتفاع / ertefâ/

hell / hel / *n* / جهنم / jahannam/

hello / helo / *intj* / سلام / salâm/

help / help / *n* / کمک / komak/

help / help / *vt* / کمک کردن / komak kardan/

helpful / helpful / *adj* / مفید / mofid/

hemophilia / hiimefiilye / *n* / رقت خون / reghghate khun/

her / her / *pron* / او را / u râ/

here / hiyer / *adv* / دراینجا / darinjâ/

heritage / heritij / *n* / میراث / mirâs/

hero / hiiro / *n* / قهرمان / ghahramân/

herself / herself / *pron* / خودش را / khodashrâ/

hesitate / heziteyt / *vi* / تردید کردن / tardid kardan/

hesitation / heziteyshen / *n* / تردید / tardid/

heterogeneous / heterojiinyes / *adj* / مختلف / mokhtalef/

hey / hey / *intj* / !آهای / âhây/

hide / hâyd / *vt* / مخفی کردن / makhfi kardan/

high / hây / *adj* / بلند / boland/

highway / hâywey / *n* / شاهراه / shâhrâh/

hijack / hâyjak / *vt* / ربودن / rebudan/

hijacker / hâyjaker / *n* / هواپیما ربا / havâpeymârobâ/

hijacking / hâyjaking / *n* / هواپیما ربایی / havâpeymâ robâii/

hill / hil / *n* / تپه / tape/

him / him / *pron* / اورا / urâ/

himself / himself / *pron* / خودش را / khodoshrâ/

hippie / hipii / *n* / هیپی / hipi/

hippopotamus / hipopâtemes / *n* / اسب آبی / asbeâbi/

hire / hâyr / *vt* / کرایه کردن / kerâye kardan/

his / hiz / *pron* / مال او / mâle u/

historical / historikâl / *adj* / تاریخی / târikhi/

history / histrii / *n* / تاریخ / târikh/

hit / hit / *vt* / زدن / zadan/

hitchhiking / hich-hâyking / *n* / اتواستاپ / otostâp/

hobby / hâbii / *n* / سرگرمی / sargarmi/

hockey / hâkii / *n* / هاکی / hâki/

hold / hold / *n* / گیر / gir/

hold / hold / *vt* / نگاه داشتن / negâh dâshtan/

hole / hol / *n* / سوراخ / surâkh/

holiday / hâlidey / *n* / تعطیل / taatil/

holy / holii / *adj* مقدس / maghaddas/

home / hom / *n* خانه / khâne/

homemade / hommeyd / *adj* خانگی / kânegi/

homework / homwerk / *n* تکلیف / taklif/

honest / ânist / *adj* درست کار / dorost kâr/

honestly / ânıstlii / *adv* صادقانه / sâdeghâne/

honey / hânii / *n* عسل / asal/

honeymoon / hânimoon / *n* ماه عسل / mâhe asal/

honor / âner / *n* افتخار / eftekhâr/

hood / hud / *n* کاپوت / kâput/

hook / huk / *n* قلاب / ghollâb/

hooligan / hooligen / *n* لات / lât/

hooray / hoorey / *intj* هورا! / hura/

hopeful / hopful / *adj* امید / omid/

horizon / herâyzn / *n* افق / ofogh/

horrible / hâribel / *adj* وحشتناك / vahshatnâk/

horror / hârer / *n* وحشت / vahshat/

horse / hors / *n* اسب / asb/

hospital / hâspitâl / *n* بیمارستان / bimârestân/

hospitality / hâspitalitii / *n* مهمان نوازی / mehmân navâzi/

hostess / hostis / *n* مهماندار / mehmândâr/

hostile / hâstâyl / *adj* خصمانه / khasmâne/

hot / hât / *adj* / داغ / dâgh/

hotel / hotel / *n* / هتل / hotel/

hour / aor / *n* / ساعت / sâat/

house / haos / *n* / خانه / khâne/

housewife / haoswâyf / *n* / خانم خانه / khânome khâne/

how / hao / *adv* / چطور / chetor/

however / haoever / *adv* / هرچند / harchand/

howl / haol / *n* / زوزه / zuze/

huddle / hâdel / *vt* / چسبیدن / chasbidan/

huge / hyooj / *adj* / عظیم / azim/

human / hyoomen / *adj* / انسان / ensân/

humor / hyoomer / *n* / شوخی / shukhi/

humorist / hyoomerist / *n* / آدم شوخ طبع / âdame shukhtab/

humorous / hyoomeres / *adj* / بامزه / bâmaze/

hump / hâmp / *n* / کوهان / kuhân/

hundred / hândred / *n, adj* / صد / sad/

hundredth / handredth / *n, adj* / صدمین / sadomin/

hunger / hânger / *n* / گرسنگی / gorosnegi/

hungry / hângrii / *adj* / گرسنه / gorosne/

hunt / hânt / *vt* / شکار کردن / shekâr kardan/

hunter / hânter / *n* / شکارچی / shekârchi/

hurry / hârrii / *vi* / عجله کردن / ajale kardan/

hurt / hert / *vt* درد کردن / dard kardan/
husband / hâzbend / *n* شوهر / shohar/
hush / hâsh / *n* هیس! / his/
hut / hât / *n* کلبه / kolbe/
hybrid / hâybrid / *n* حیوان دورگه / heyvane dorage/
hydrogen / hâydrojen / *n* هیدروژن / hidrojen/
hymn / him / *n* سرود مزهبی / surude mazhabi/
hysteria / histeriiyâ / *n* هیستری / histeri/

I

I / ây / *pron* من / man/

ice / âys / *n* یخ / yakh/

ice cream / ayskriim / *n* بستنی / bastani/

idea / âydiyâ / *n* فکر / fekr/

ideal / âydiyel / *adj* دلخواه / delkhâh/

identical / âydentikâl / *adj* یکسان / yeksân/

identify / âydentifây / *vt* شناختن / shenâkhtan/

identity / âydentiti / *n* هویّت / hoviyyat/

idiom / idiem / *n* اصطلاح / estelâh/

idiot / idiyet / *n* احمق / ahmagh/

idiotic / idiyâtik / *adj* احمقانه / ahmaghâne/

if / if / *conj* اگر / agar/

ignorance / ignorens / *n* بی خبری / bi khâbari/

Ignorant / ignorent / *adj* ناآگاه / nâ âgâh/

ignore / ignor / *vt* اعتنا نکردن / eetenâ nakardan/

illegal / iliigl / *adj* غیر قانونی / gheyre ghânuni/

illness / ilnis / *n* بیماری / bimâri/

illustrate / ilâstreyt / *vt* روشن ساختن / roshan sâkhtan/

image / imij / *n* تصویر / tasvir/

imaginary / imajineri / *adj* خیالی / khiyâli/

299

imagination / imajineyshen / *n* تخیل / takhayyol/

imaginative / imajinetiv / *adj* تخیلی / takhayyoli/

imagine / imajin / *vt* تصور کردن / tasavvor kardan/

imitate / imiteyt / *vt* تقلید کردن / taghlid kardan/

imitation / imiteyshen / *n* تقلید / taghlid/

immediate / imiidiyet / *adj* فوری / fori/

immediately / imiidiyetlii / *adv* فوراً / foran/

immense / imens / *adj* عظیم / azim/

immigrant / imigrent / *n* مهاجر / mohâjer/

immigration / imigreyshen / *n* مهاجرت / mohâjerat/

immobile / imobâyl / *adj* بی حرکت / biharekat/

immobility / imobilitii / *n* بی حرکتی / biharekati/

immortal / imortâl / *adj* جاودانه / jâvedâne/

impatient / impeyshent / *adj* بی تاب / bitâb/

impatiently / impeyshentlii / *adv* بی صبرانه / bi sabrâne/

imperial / impiriyâl / *adj* سلطنتی / saltanati/

imperious / impiriyes / *adj* مغرور / maghrur/

impolite / impolâyt / *adj* بی‌ادب / biadab/

import / import / *vt* وارد کردن / vared kardan/

importance / importens / *n* اهمیت / ahammiyyat/

important / importent / *adj* مهم / mohem/

importation / importeyshen / *n* واردات / vâredât/

impose / impoz / *vt* تحميل كردن / tahmil kardan/

impossible / impâsibel / *adj* ناممكن / nâmomken/

impress / impres / *vt* اثرگذاشتن / asar gozâshtan/

impression / impreshen / *n* تأثير / taasir/

impressive / impresiv / *adj* باعظمت / bâazamat/

improve / improov / *vt* بهترکردن / behtar kardan/

improvement / improovment / *n* بهبود / behbud/

in / in / *adv* درخانه / dar khâne/

in / in / *prep* در / dar/

incapable / inkeypebei / *adj* ناتوان / nâtavân/

inch / inch / *n* اينچ / inch/

incident / insident / *n* حادثه / hâdese/

include / inklood / *vt* شامل بودن / shâmel budan/

inclusion / inkloozhen / *n* شمول / shemul/

inclusive / inkloosiv / *adj* شامل / shâmel/

income / inkâm / *n* درآمد / darâmad/

income tax / inkâmtaks / *n* ماليات بردرامد / mâliyât bardarâmad/

incompetent / inkâmpitent / *adj* نالايق / nâ lâyegh/

incorporate / inkorporeyt / *vt* ملحق كردن / molhagh kardan/

incorrect / inkârekt / *adj* غلط / ghalat/

increase / inkriis / *n* افزايش دادن / afzâyesh dâdan/

increase / inkriis / *vi* افزایش / afzâyesh/

indeed / indiid / *adv* راستی / râsti/

independence / indipendens / *n* استقلال / esteghlâl/

India / indiyâ / *n* هند / hend/

Indian / indiyen / *adj, n* هندی / hendi/

indicate / indikeyt / *vt* نشان دادن / neshân dâdan/

indication / indikeyshen / *n* نشان / neshân/

indigenous / indigines / *adj* بومی / bumi/

individual / indivijuwâl / *adj* فردی / fardi/

indoor / indor / *adj* خانگی / khânegi/

indulge / indâlj / *vt* لوس کردن / lus kardan/

industrial / indâstriyel / *adj* صنعتی / sanaati/

industry / indâstri / *n* صنعت / sanaat/

inefficient / inifishent / *adj* بی کفایت / bikefâyat/

inequality / inikwâlitii / *n* نابرابری / nâbarâbar/

infant / infent / *n* کودک / kudak/

infect / infekt / *vt* آلوده کردن / âlude kardan/

infection / infekshen / *n* عفونت / ofonat/

infectious / infekshes / *adj* مسری / mosri/

influence / influ-ens / *n* نفوذ / nefuz/

inform / inform / *vt* مطلع کردن / mottalee kardan/

information / informeyshen / *n* اطلاعات / ettelâât/

inhabitant / inhabitent / *n* ساكن / sâkene/

initiative / inishiyetiv / *n* ابتكار / ebtekâr/

inject / injekt / *vt* تزریق كردن / tazrigh kardna/

injection / injekshen / *n* تزریق / tazrigh/

injest / injest / *n* به شوخى / beshukhi/

injure / injer / *vt* مجروج كردن / majruh kardan/

injury / injerii / *n* آسیب / âsib/

injustice / injâstis / *n* بى عدالتى / bi adâleti/

ink / ink / *n* مركّب / morakkab/

inn / in / *n* مسافرخانه / mosâfer khâne/

innocent / inosent / *adj* بى گناه / bi gonâh/

inquire / inkwayr / *vi* پرسیدن / porsidan/

inquiry / inkwâyrii / *n* پرسش / porsesh/

inscription / inskripshen / *n* نوشته / neveshte/

inscrutable / inskrootebel / *adj* غیر قابل درک /
　gheyr ghâbele dark/

insect / insekt / *n* حشره / hashare/

Inside / insâyd / *adv* درون / darun/

insist / insist / *vi* اصراركردن / esrâr kardan/

insomnia / insâmnie / *n* بى خوابى / bi khâbi/

inspection / inspekshen / *n* معاینه / moâyene/

inspector / inspekter / *n* بازرس / bâzras/

install / instol / *vt* نصب كردن / nasb kardan/

installation / instoleyshen / *n* / نصب / nasb/
instance / instans / *n* / مثال / mesâl/
instead / insted / *adv* / درعوض / daravaz/
instinct / instink / *n* / غريزه / gharize/
institute / institoot / *n* / مؤسسه / moassese/
instruction / instrâkshen / *n* / آموزش / âmuzesh/
instructor / instâkter / *n* / معلم / moallem/
instrument / instrument / *n* / وسيله / vasile/
instruct / instrâkt / *vt* / ياد دادن / yâd dâdan/
insurance / inshurens / *n* / بيمه / bime/
insure / inshur / *vt* / بيمه كردن / bime kardan/
intellectual / intilekchuwâl / *adj* / عقلانى / aghlâni/
intelligence / intelijens / *n* / هوش / hush/
intelligent / intelijent / *adj* / باهوش / bâhush/
intend / intend / *vt* / خواستن / khâstan/
intense / intens / *adj* / شديد / shadid/
intensive / intensiv / *adj* / عميق / amigh/
intention / intenshen / *n* / قصد / ghasd/
interest / intrist / *n* / علاقه / alâghe/
interested / intristid / *adj* / علاقه مند / alâghemand/
interesting / intristing / *adj* / جالب / jâleb/
intermission / intermishen / *n* / فاصله / fâsele/

internal / intenl / *adj* / درونی / daruni/

international / internashnâl / *adj* / بین المللی / beynalmelati/

internet / internet / *n* / انترنت / internet/

interpret / interprit / *vt* / ترجمه کردن / tarjome kardan/

interpretation / interpriteyshen / *n* / تعبیر / taabir/

interrupt / interâpt / *vt* / قطع کردن / ghatee kardan/

interruption / interâpshen / *n* / وقفه / vaghfe/

interval / intervâl / *n* / فاصله / fâsele/

interview / interviyoo / *n* / مصاحبه / mosâhebe/

into / intoo / *prep* / تو / tu/

intolerable / intâlerebel / *adj* / غیر قابل تحمل /
gheyr ghâbele tahammul/

intrigue / intriig / *vi* / توطئه چیدن / totee chidan/

introduce / introdyoos / *vt* / معرفی کردن / moarrefi kardan/

introduction / introdâkshen / *n* / معرفی / moarrefi/

invade / inveyd / *vt* / تجاوز کردن / tajâvoz kardan/

invasion / Inveyzhen / *n* / حمله / hamle/

invent / invent / *vt* / اختراع کردن / ekhterââ kardan/

invention / invenshen / *n* / اختراع / ekhterâ/

inventive / inventiv / *adj* / خلاق / khallâgh/

invert / invert / *vt* / وارونه کردن / vârune kardan/

invest / invest / *vt* / سرمایه گذاری کردن /
sarmâyegozâri kardan/

investigate / investigeyt / *vt* / تحقیق کردن / tahghigh kardan/

investigation / investigeyshen / *n* / تحقیق / tahghigh/

investment / investment / *n* / سرمایه گذاری / sarmâye gozâri/

invisible / invizibel / *adj* / نامرئ / nâmarii/

invitation / inviteyshen / *n* / دعوت / daavat/

invite / invâyt / *vt* / دعوت کردن / daavat kardan/

involuntary / invâlenterii / *adj* / غیرارادی / gheyrerâdi/

involve / invâlv / *vt* / گرفتار کردن / gereftâr kardan/

Iran / irân / *n* / ایران / irân/

Iranian / ireynien / *adj, n* / ایرانی / irâni/

Ireland / âyerland / *n* / ایرلند / irland/

Irish / âyerish / *adj, n* / ایرلندی / irlandi/

iron / âyern / *n* / آهن / âhah/

ironic / âyrânik / *adj* / طنزآمیز / tanz âmiz/

is / iz / *vi* / است / ast/

Islam / izlâm / *n* / اسلام / eslâm/

Islamic / izlâmik / *adj* / اسلامی / eslâmi/

island / âyland / *n* / جزیره / jazire/

isolate / âysoleyt / *vt* / جدا کردن / jodâ kardan/

it / it / *pron* / آن / ân/

Italian / italiyen / *adj, n* / ایتالیایی / itâliyâyi/

Italy / italii / *n* ایتالیا / itâliyâ/

itself / itself / *pron* خودش را / khodashrâ/

J

jacket / jakit / *n* / كُت / kot/

jail / jeyl / *n* / زندان / zendân/

jam / jam / *n* / مربا / morabba/

Jamaica / jemeykâ / *n* / جامایکا / jâmâykâ/

January / janyuwerii / *n* / ژانویه / zhânviye/

Japan / japan / *n* / ژاپن / zhâpon/

Japanese / japaniiz / *adj, n* / ژاپنی / zhâponi/

jaw / jâw / *n* / آرواره / ârvâre/

jazz / jaz / *n* / جاز / jâz/

jealous / jeles / *adj* / حسود / hasud/

jealousy / jelesii / *n* / حسادت / hasâdat/

jeans / jiinz / *n* / شلوارجین / shalvârejin/

jest / jest / *n* / شوخی / shukhi/

jet / jet / *n* / فواره / favvâre/

jet lag / jet lag / *n* / درنگ زدگی / derang zadegi/

Jew / joo / *n* / یهودی / yahudi/

jewel / juwel / *n* / جواهر / javâher/

jewelry / juwelrii / *adj, n* / جواهرات / javâherât/

Jewish / joo-ish / *adj,n* / یهودی / yahudi/

job / jâb / n / کار / kâr/

join / joyn / vt / متصل کردن / mottasel kardan/

joint / joynt / n / مفصل / mafsal/

joke / jok / n / لطیفه / latife/

journal / jernâl / n / نشریه / nashriye/

journalist / jernâlist / n / روزنامه نگار / ruzhâme negâr/

journey / jerni / n / سفر / safar/

joy / joy / n / شادی / shâdi/

joyous / joyes / adj / شادمان / shâdemân/

joyously / joyeslii / adv / با شادمانی / bâ shâdemâni/

judge / jâj / n / قاضی / ghâzi/

judgment / jâjment / n / حکم / hokm/

juice / joos / n / آب (میوه) / âb (e mive)/

juicy / joosii / adj / آبدار / âbdâr/

July / joolây / n / ژونیه / zhuiye/

jump / jâmp / vi / پریدن / paridan/

jumper / jâmper / n / پلیور / poliver/

junction / jânkshen / n / اتصال / ettesâl/

June / joon / n / ژوئن / zhoan/

junior / jooniyer / adj / کوچک / kuchak/

just / jâst / adv / درست / dorost/

justice / jâstis / n / عدالت / adâlat/

justification / jâstifikeyshen / *n* توجیه / tojih/
justify / jâstifây / *vt* توجیه کردن / tojih kardan/
jut / jât / *vi* پیش رفتن / pish raftân/

K

karate / karâti / *n* کاراته / kârâte/
kebab / kebab / *n* کباب / kabâb/
keen / kiin / *adj* تیز / tiz/
keep / kiip / *vt, vi* نگه داشتن / negah dâshtan/
ketchup / kechâp / *n* سُس گوجه فرنگی / sose gojefarangi/
kettle / ketel / *n* کتری / ketri/
key / kii / *n* کلید / kelid/
khaki / kâki / *n* خاکی / khâki/
kick / kik / *n* لگد / lagad/
kid / kid / *n* بچه / bachche/
kidnap / kidnap / *vt* آدم دزدیدن / âdam dozdidan/
kidney / kidni / *n* کلیه / koliye/
kill / kil / *vt* کشتن / koshtan/
killer / kiler / *n* قاتل / ghâtel/
kilo / kiilo / *n* کیلو / kilo/
kilometer / kilemiiter / *n* کیلومتر / kilometr/
kind / kâynd / *adj* مهربان / mehrabân/
kind / kâynd / *n* نوع / no/
kindness / kâyndnis / *n* مهربانی / mehrabâni/

king / king / *n* / پادشاه / pâdeshâh/
kiosk / kiâsk / *n* / دکه / dakke/
kipper / kiper / *n* / ماهی دودی / mâhi dudi/
kiss / kis / *n* / بوسه / buse/
kitchen / kichin / *n* / آشپز خانه / âshpazi khane/
knee / nii / *n* / زانو / zânu/
kneel / niil / *vt* / زانو زدن / zânu zadan/
knife / nâyf / *n* / کارد / kârd/
knob / nâb / *n* / دستگیره / dastgire/
knock / nâk / *vt* / زدن / zadan/
knot / nât / *n* / گره / gereh/
know / no / *vt* / دانستن / dânestan/
knowledge / nâlij / *n* / دانش / dânesh/
Koran / keran / *n* / قرآن / ghorân/

L

labor / leyber / n / کار / kâr/
laborer / leyberer / n / کارگر / kârgar/
lack / lak / vt, vi, n / نداشتن / nadâshtan/
ladder / lader / n / نردبان / nardebân/
ladies / leydiiz / n / بانوان / bânovan/
lady / leydii / n / خانم / khânom/
lake / leyk / n / دریاچه / daryâche/
lamb / lam / n / بره / barre/
lamp / lamp / n / چراغ / cherâgh/
lamppost / lamp post / n / تیر چراغ / tire cherâgh/
land / land / n / زمین / zamin/
land / land / vi / فرود آمدن / furud âmadan/
landscape / landskeyp / n / منظره / manzaré/
lane / leyn / n / راه / râh/
language / langwij / n / زبان / zabân/
lantern / lantern / n / فانوس / fânus/
laptop / laptâp / n / کامپیوتر زانویی / kâmpiotere zânuyi/
large / lârj / adj / بزرگ / bozorg/
laser / leyzer / n / لیزر / leyzer/

last / last / *adj* آخر / âkhar/

last / last / *vi* ادامه / edâme/

late / leyt / *adj* دیروقت / dirvaght/

lately / leytlii / *adv* اخیراً / akhiran/

latest / leytist / *adj* آخرین / âkharin/

Latin / latin / *n* زبان لاتین / zabâne lâtin/

laugh / lâf / *vi* خندیدن / khandidan/

laughter / lâfter / *n* خنده / khande/

lavatory / lavatorii / *n* توالت / tuvâlet/

law / lâ / *n* قانون / ghânun/

lawful / lâfl / *adj* قانونی / ghânuni/

lawn / lân / *n* چمن / chaman/

lawyer / loyer / *n* وکیل / vakil/

lay / ley / *vt* قرار دادن / gharâr dâdan/

lazy / leyzi / *adj* تنبل / tanbal/

lead / led / *n* سرب / sorb/

lead / liid / *n* راهنمایی / râhtamâyi/

lead / liid / *vt* جلو رفتن / jelo raftan/

leader / liider / *n* رهبر / rahbar/

leaf / liif / *n* برگ / barg/

league / liig / *n* پیمان / peymân/

lean / liin / *vi* تکیه دادن به / tekiye dâdan be/

leap / liip / *vi* پریدن / paridan/

learn / lern / *vt* یادگرفتن / yâdgereftan/

learner / lerner / *n* کارآموز / kârâmuz/

least / liist / *adj* کمترین / kamtarin/

leather / ledher / *n* چرم / charm/

leave / liiv / *vt* رفتن / raftan/

left / left / *adj* چپ / chap/

leg / leg / *n* پا / pâ/

legal / liigl / *adj* قانونی / ghânuni/

leisure / lezher / *n* فراغت / farâghat/

leisurely / lezherlii / *adv* با تآنی / bâ taanni/

lemon / lemon / *n* لیموترش / limutorsh/

lemonade / lemoneyd / *n* لیموناد / limunâd/

lend / lend / *vt* قرض دادن / gharz dâdan/

length / length / *n* درازا / derâzâ/

lens / lenz / *n* عدسی / adasi/

leopard / leperd / *n* پلنگ / palang/

less / les / *adv* کمتر / kamtar/

let / let / *vt* اجازه دادن / ejâze dâdan/

letter / leter / *n* نامه / nâme/

letterbox / leterbâks / *n* صندوق پست / sandughe post/

level / level / *n* سطح / sath/

liberty / libertii / *n* / آزادی / âzâdi/

library / lâybrerii / *n* / کتابخانه / ketâbkhâne/

license / lâysens / *n* / پروانه / parvane/

lick / lik / *vi* / لیسیدن / lisidan/

lie / lây / *vi* / دراز کشیدن / derâz keshidan/

lie / lây / *vi* / دروغ گفتن / durugh goftan/

life / lâyf / *n* / حیات / hayât/

lifeboat / lâyfbot / *n* / قایق نجات / ghâyeghe nejât/

life jacket / lâyf jakit / *n* / جلیقهٔ نجات / jaligheye nejât/

lifeless / lâyflis / *adj* / بی جان / bi jân/

lifetime / lâyftâym / *n* / عمر / omr/

lift / lift / *vt* / بلند کردن / boland kardan/

light / lâyt / *adj* / سبک / sabok/

light / lâyt / *adj* / نور / nur/

light / lâyt / *vt* / روشن کردن / roshan sahodan/

lighter / lâyter / *n* / فندک / fandak/

lightning / lâytning / *n* / برق / bargh/

like / lâyk / *prep* / شبیه / shabih/

like / lâyk / *vt* / خواستن / khâstan/

likely / lâyklii / *adj* / محتمل / mohtamal/

liking / lâyking / *n* / علاقه / alâghe/

limit / limit / *n* / حدمرز / hadomarz/

limp / limp / *vi* لنگيدن / langidan/

line / lâyn / *n* خط / khat/

linguistic / lingwistik / *adj* زبانى / zabâni/

link / link / *n* حلقه زنجير / halgeye zanjir/

lion / lâyen / *n* شير / shir/

lip / lip / *n* لب / lab/

lipstick / lipstik / *n* ماتيک / mâtik/

liquid / likwid / *n* مايع / mâyee/

list / list / *n* فهرست / fehrest/

listen / lisen / *vi* گوش دادن / gush dâdan/

literature / litrecher / *n* ادبيات / adabiyât/

little / litel / *adj* کوچک / kuchak/

live / liv / *vi* زنده بودن / zende budan/

lively / lâyvlii / *adj* زنده / zende/

liver / liver / *n* کبد / kabad/

living / living / *n* زندگى / zendegi/

load / lod / *n* بار / bâr/

local / lokâl / *adj* محلى / mahalli/

locally / lokâli / *adv* موضعى / mozeii/

lock / lâk / *n* قفل / ghofl/

logic / lâjik / *n* منطق / mantegh/

logical / lâjikl / *adj* منطقى / manteghi/

lonely / lonli / *adj* / تنها / tanhâ/

long / lâng / *adj* / دراز / derâz/

longer / lânger / *adv* / بيشتر / bishtar/

look / luk / *n* / نگاه / negâh/

look / luk / *vi* / نگاه کردن / negâh kardan/

looks / luks / *n* / ظاهر / zâher/

loop / loop / *n* / حلقه / halghe/

loose / loos / *adj* / آزاد / âzâd/

Lord / lord / *n* / اشراف زاده / ashrâfzâde/

lose / looz / *vt* / گم کردن / gom kardan/

lot / lât / *n* / زياد / ziyâd/

loud / laod / *adj* / بلند / boland/

loudly / laodlii / *adv* / بلند / boland/

loudspeaker / laod spiiker / *n* / بلندگو / bolandgu/

lounge / laonj / *n* / سالن (استراحت) / sâlone esterâhat/

lovable / lâvebel / *adj* / دوست داشتنی / dust dâshtani/

love / lâv / *n* / عشق / eshgh/

love / lâv / *vt* / دوست داشتن / dust dâshtan/

lovely / lâvelii / *adj* / دوست داشتنی / dust dâshtani /

lover / lâver / *n* / عاشق / âshegh/

low / lo / *adj* / کوتاه / kutah/

loyal / loyâl / *adj* / وفادار / vafâdâr/

loyally / loyâlii / *adv* وفادارانه / vafâdârâne/

luck / lâk / *n* شانس / shâns/

lucky / lâkii / *adj* خوشبخت / khoshbakht/

luggage / lâgij / *n* چمدان / chamadân/

lunch / lânch / *n* ناهار / nâhâr/

luxury / lâksherii / *n* تجمل / tajammol/

lyric / liirik / *n* غزل / ghazal/

M

machine / meshiin / *n* / ماشین / mâshin/

mad / mad / *adj* / دیوانه / divâne/

madam / madem / *n* / خانم / khânom/

magazine / magaziin / *n* / مجله / majalle/

magic / majik / *n* / جادو / jâdu/

magician / majishen / *n* / جادوگر / jâdugar/

magnificent / magnifisent / *adj* / عالی / âli/

mail / meyl / *n* / پست / post/

mailbox / meylbâks / *n* / صندوق پست / sandughe post/

main / meyn / *adj* / عمده / omde/

mainly / meynli / *adv* / عمدتاً / omdatan/

maintain / meynteyn / *vt* / حفظ کردن / hefz kardan/

major / meyjer / *adj* / بزرگ / bozorg/

majority / majâritii / *n* / اکثریت / aksariyyat/

make / meyk / *n* / نوع / noe/

make / meyk / *vt* / ساختن / sâkhtan/

male / meyl / *adj* / نر / nar/

malicious / melishes / *adj* / مغرضانه / moghrezâne/

mammal / maml / *n* / پستاندار / pestândâr/

man / man / *n* / مرد / mard/

manage / manij / *vt* / اداره کردن / edâre kardan/

management / manijment / *n* / مدیریت / modiriyyat/

manager / manijer / *n* / مدیر / modir/

manifestation / manifesteyshen / *n* / ابراز / ebrâz/

mankind / mankâynd / *n* / نوع بشر / noee bashar/

manner / maner / *n* / طرز / tarz/

many / menii / *adj* / زیاد / ziyâd/

map / map / *n* / نقشه / nasghshe/

marathon / marathân / *n* / مسابقه دوی ماراتون /
mosâbegheye doe mârâton/

March / mârch / *n* / مارس / mârs/

margin / mârjin / *n* / حاشیه / hâshiye/

mark / mârk / *n* / نشان / neshân/

mark / mârk / *vt* / نمره دادن / nomre dâdan/

market / mârkit / *n* / بازار / bâzâr/

marmalade / mârmeleyd / *n* / مربای پرتقال /
morabbâye portaghâl/

marriage / marij / *n* / ازدواج / ezdevâj/

marry / marii / *vt* / ازدواج کردن / ezdevâch kardan/

martian / marshen / *adj* / اهل مریخ / ahle merrikh/

marvelous / mârveles / *adj* / حیرت انگیز / heyrat angiz/

mass / mas / *n* / توده / tude/

mass media / masmiidiya / *n* / رسانه های گروهی /
rasânehâye guruhi/

321

mass production / mas prodâkshen / *n* / تولید انبوه /
tolide anbuh/

mast / mâst / *n* / دکل / dakal/

master / mâster / *n* / آقا / âghâ/

match / mach / *n* / کبریت / kebrit/

match / mach / *n* / مسابقه / mosâbeghe/

matchbox / machbâks / *n* / (قوطی) کبریت / (ghutiye) kebrit/

material / matiriyel / *n* / ماده / mâdde/

mathematics / mathimatiks / *n* / ریاضیات / riyâziyât/

matter / mater / *n* / ماده / mâdde/

mattress / matris / *n* / تشک / toshak/

maximum / mâksimem / *n* / حداکثر / hadde aksar/

may / mey / *aux. v* / شاید / shâyad/

May / mey / *n* / مه / meh/

maybe / meybii / *adj* / شاید / shâyad/

me / mii / *pron* / مرا / marâ/

meal / miil / *n* / غذا / ghazâ/

mean / miin / *vt* / معنی دادن / maani dâdan/

meaning / miining / *n* / معنی / maani/

meaningful / miiningful / *adj* / با معنی / bâ maani/

meaningless / miiningles / *adj* / بی معنی / bi maani/

means / miinz / *n* / وسیله / vasile/

meanwhile / miinwâyl / *adv* / دراین فاصله / darin fâsele/

measure / mezher / *n* / مقیاس / meghyâs/

measure / mezher / *vt* / اندازه گرفتن / andâze gereftan/

measurement / mezherment / *n* / اندازه گیری / andâzegiri/

meat / miit / *n* / گوشت (قرمز) / gusht (e ghermez)/

mechanic / mikanik / *n* / مکانیک / mekânik/

mechanical / mikanikâl / *adj* / مکانیکی / mekâniki/

mechanism / mekanizim / *n* / مکانیسم / mekanism/

medal / medâl / *n* / نشان / neshân/

medical / medikâl / *adj* / پزشکی / pezeshki/

medicine / medsin / *n* / دارو / dâru/

meditate / mediteyt / *vt* / فکر کردن / fekr kardan/

meet / miit / *vt* / ملاقات کردن / molâghat kardan/

meeting / miiting / *n* / جلسه / jalase/

megalopolis / megalopolis / *n* / کلانشهر / kalânshahr/

melt / melt / *vt* / آب کردن / âb kardan/

member / member / *n* / عضو / ozv/

membership / membership / *n* / عضویت / ozviyyat/

memory / memorii / *n* / حافظه / hâfeze/

menace / menis / *n* / تهدید / tahdid/

mend / mend / *vt* / تعمیر کردن / taamir kardan/

mental / mentâl / *adj* / ذهنی / zehni/

mention / menshen / *vt* / ذکر کردن / zekr kardan/

menu / menyoo / *n* / صورت غذا / surat ghazâ/

merely / miyerlii / *adv* / فقط / faghat/

merit / merit / *vt* / ارزش داشتن / arzesh dâdan/

merry / merii / *adj* / شاد / shâd/

merry-go-round / merigoraond / *n* / چرخ وفلك / charkhofalak/

mess / mes / *n* / پاشیدگی / pâshidegi/

message / mesij / *n* / پیغام / peyghâm/

messenger / mesinjer / *n* / قاصد / ghâsed/

metal / metâl / *n* / فلز / felez/

meteor / miitiyor / *n* / شهاب / shahâb/

meter / miiter / *n* / متر / metr/

method / methed / *n* / روش / ravesh/

microphone / mâykrofon / *n* / میکروفن / mikrofon/

mid / mid / *adj* / نیمه / nime/

midday / middey / *n* / ظهر / zohr/

middle / midel / *adj, n* / وسط / vasat/

Middle Ages / mideleyjiz / *n* / قرون وسطی / ghurune vostâ/

midnight / midnâyt / *n* / شب نیمه / nimeshab/

midwife / midwâyf / *n* / ماما / mâ mâ/

mild / mâyld / *adj* / آرام / ârâm/

mile / mâyl / *n* / میل / meyl/

military / militerii / *adj* / نظامی / nezâmi/

milk / milk / *n* / شیر / shir/

mill / mil / *n* / کارخانه / karkhâne/

million / milyen / *n* / میلیون / milyon/

millionaire / milyener / *n* / میلیونر / milyoner/

mind / mâynd / *n* / ذهن / zehn/

mind / mâynd / *vt* / مواظب بودن / movâzeb budan/

mine / mâyn / *n* / معدن / maadan/

mine / mâyn / *pron* / مال من / mâle man/

miner / mâyner / *n* / معدنچی / madanchi/

miniature / minicher / *n* / مینیاتور / minyâtur/

minimum / minimem / *n* / حداقل / haddeaghal/

minister / minister / *n* / وزیر / vazir/

ministry / ministrii / *n* / وزارت / vezârat/

minor / mâyner / *adj* / جزئ / jozii/

minority / mâynâritii / *n* / اقلیت / aghaliyyat/

minute / minit / *n* / دقیقه / daghighe/

mirror / mirer / *n* / آیینه / âyine/

miserable / mizrebel / *adj* / بدبخت / badbakht/

Miss / mis / *n* / دوشیزه / dushize/

miss / mis / *vt* / ازدست دادن / azdast dâdan/

missile / misâyl / *n* / موشک / mushak/

mission / mishn / *n* / مأموریت/ mamuriyyat/

mist / mist / *n* / مه / meh/

mistake / misteyk / *n* / اشتباه / eshtebâh/

mistress / mistris / *n* / خانم معلم / khânome moallem/

mix / miks / *vt, vi* / مخلوط کردن / makhlut kardan/

mixture / mikscher / *n* مخلوط / makhlut/

moan / mon / *vt* ناله کردن / nâle kardan/

mobile / mobâyl / *adj* متحرک / motaharrek/

mobility / mobilitii / *n* تحرک / taharrok/

model / mâdel / *n* مدل / model/

modem / modem / *n* متصل کننده / mottasel konande/

modern / mâdern / *adj* جدید / jadid/

molder / molder / *vt* پوسیدن / pusidan/

mom / mâm / *n* مامان / mâmân /

moment / moment / *n* لحظه / lahze/

Monday / mândi / *n* دوشنبه / doshanbe/

money / mânii / *n* پول / pul/

monitor / mâniter / *n* اکران / ekrân/

monkey / mânkii / *n* میمون / meymun/

monster / mânster / *n* هیولا / hayulâ/

monument / mânyument / *n* بنای یادبود / benâye yâdbud/

mood / mood / *n* حال / hâl/

moon / moon / *n* ماه / mâh/

moral / morâl / *adj* اخلاقی / akhlâghi/

more / mor / *adj* بیشتر / bishtar/

morning / morning / *n* صبح / sobh/

mosque / mâsk / *n* مسجد / masjed/

most / most / *adj* بیشترین / bishtarin/

mostly / mostlii / *adv* / عمداً / omdatan/

motel / motel / *n* / مُتل / motel/

mother / mâdher / *n* / مادر / mâdor/

motion / moshn / *n* / جنبش / jonbesh/

motor / motor / *n* / موتور / motor/

motorbike / motorbâyk / *n* / موتورسیکلت / motorsikelet/

motorcycle / motorsâykel / *n* / موتورسیکلت / motorsiklet/

motorway / motorwey / *n* / اتوبان / otobân/

mountain / maontin / *n* / کوه / kuh/

mourning / morning / *n* / سوگواری / sogvâri/

mouse / maos / *n* / موش / mush/

moustache / mâstash / *n* / سبیل / sibil/

mouth / maoth / *n* / دهان / dahân/

mouthful / maothful / *n* / لقمه / loghme/

move / moov / *vt* / حرکت دادن / harakat dâdan /

movement / moovment / *n* / حرکت / harakat /

mover / moover / *n* / فعال / faaâl /

movie / moovii / *n* / سینما / sinamâ /

mow / mo / *vt* / چیدن / chidan /

Mr. / mister / *n* / آقای / aghâye /

Mrs. / misiz / *n* / خانم / khânom /

much / mâch / *adj* / زیاد / ziyâd /

mud / mâd / *n* / گل / gel /

multicolored / mâltikâlerd / *adj* رنگارنگ / rangârang /

multiply / mâltiplây / *vt* ضرب کردن / zarb kardan /

multitude / mâltitood / *n* جمعیت / jameyat /

municipality / myunisipaletii / *n* شهرداری / shahrdâri /

murder / merder / *n* قتل / ghatl /

murderer / merderer / *n* قاتل / ghâtel /

muscle / mâsel / *n* ماهیچه / mâhiche /

museum / myooziyem / *n* موزه / muze /

mushroom / mâshrum / *n* قارچ / ghârch /

music / myoozik / *n* موسیقی / museghi /

musician / myoozishen / *n* نوازنده / navâzande /

Muslim / mâzlem / *adj* مسلمان / mosalmân/

must / mâst / *aux, v* باید / bâyad /

mustard / mâsterd / *n* خردل / khardal /

mutton / mâten / *n* گوشت گوسفند / gushte gusefand /

myself / mâyself / *pron* خودم / khodam /

mystic / mistik / *n* اهل تصوف / ahle tasavvof /

mysterious / mistiriyes / *adj* مرموز / marmuz /

mystery / mistrii / *n* راز / râz /

myth / mith / *n* اسطوره / osture /

N

nail / neyl / *n* ناخن / nâkhon /

naïve / nây-iiv / *adj* ساده لوح / sâde loh /

naked / neykid / *adj* لخت / lokht /

name / neym / *n* اسم / esm /

narrate / nareyt / *vt* نقل کردن / naghl kardan /

narration / nareyshen / *n* نقل / naghl /

narrative / narativ / *n* داستان / dâstan /

narrator / nareyter / *n* قصه گو / ghessegu /

narrow / naro / *adj* باریک / bârik /

nasty / nâstii / *adj* بد / bad /

nation / neyshen / *n* ملت / mellat /

national / nashenâl / *adj* ملی / melli /

nationalism / nashenalizem / *n* ملی گرایی / melligarâyi /

nationalist / nashenalist / *adj* وطن پرست / vatanparast /

nationality / nashenalitii / *n* ملیت / melliyat /

natural / nachrâl / *adj* طبیعی / tabii /

naturally / nachrâlii / *adv* ذاتاً / zâtan /

nature / neycher / *n* طبیعت / tabiat /

navy / neyvii / *n* نیروی دریایی / niruye daryâyi /

near / niyer / *adj* / نزديك / nazdik /

nearly / niyerlii / *adv* / تقريباً / taghriban /

necessary / neseserii / *adj* / لازم / lâzem /

neck / nek / *n* / گردن / gardan /

need / niid / *n* / نياز / niyâz /

need / niid / *aux, v* / بايد / bâyad /

needle / nidl / *n* / سوزن / suzan /

negative / negetiv / *adj* / منفى / manfi /

neighbor / neyber / *n* / همسايه / hamsâye /

neighborhood / neyberhud / *n* / همسايگى / hamsâyegi /

neither / nâydher / *pron, adj* / هيچ كدام / hig kodâm /

nerve / nerv / *n* / عصب / asab /

nervous / nerves / *adj* / عصبى / asabi /

nest / nest / *n* / لانه / lâne /

neurology / nurâlejii / *n* / عصب شناسى / asab shenâsi /

neutral / nyootrâl / *adj* / بى طرف / bi taraf /

never / never / *adv* / هرگز / hargez /

new / nyoo / *adj* / جديد / jadid /

newly / nyoolii / *adv* / به تازگى / be tâzegi /

news / nyooz / *n* / خبر / khâbâr /

newspaper / nyoozpeyper / *n* / روزنامه / ruznâme /

next / nekst / *adj* / بعد / baad /

nice / nâys / *adj* / خوب / khub /

nicely / nâyslii / *adv* / با دقت / bâ deghghat /

night / nâyt / *n* / شب / shab /

nightclub / nâytklâb / *n* / کلوب شبانه / klube shabâne /

nightmare / nâytmer / *n* / کابوس / kâbus /

nine / nâyn / *adj* / نه / noh /

nineteen / nâyntiin / *adj* / نوزده / nuzdah /

nineteenth / nâyntiinth / *n* / نوزدهمی / nuzdahomi /

ninety / nâyntii / *adj* / نود / navad /

ninth / nâynth / *n* / نهم / nohom /

no / no / *adj* / نه / na /

noble / nobel / *adj* / اشرافی / ashrafi /

nobody / nobâdii / *pron* / هیچکس / hichkas /

noise / noyz / *n* / سروصدا / sarosedâ /

noisy / noyzii / *adj* / شلوغ / shulugh /

none / nân / *pron* / هیچیک / hichyek /

nonsense / nânsens / *n* / چرند / charand /

nope / nop / *intj* / نه / na /

normal / normâl / *adj* / طبیعی / tabii /

normally / normâlii / *adv* / معمولاً / mamulan /

north / north / *n* / شمال / shomâl /

northern / nordhern / *adj* / شمالی / shomâli /

nose / noz / *n* / بینی / bini /

not / nât / *adv* / نه / na /

note / not / *n* / یادداشت / yaddâsht /

note / not / *vt* / توجه کردن / tavvajjoh kardan /

notebook / notbuk / *n* / دفتر یادداشت / daftare yâddâsht /

notepaper / notpeyper / *n* / کاغذ نامه / kâghaznâme /

nothing / nâthing / *n* / هیچ چیز / hich chiz /

notice / notis / *n* / آگهی / âgahi /

noun / nâun / *n* / اسم / esm /

novel / nâvel / *n* / داستان بلند / dâstâne boland /

November / november / *n* / نوامبر / novâmbr /

now / nao / *adv* / حالا / hâlâ /

nowadays / nao edeyz / *adv* / امروزه / emruze /

nowhere / nower / *adv* / هیچ جا / hichjâ /

nuclear / nyookliyer / *adj* / هسته ای / hasteii /

number / nâmber / *n* / عدد / adad /

numerous / nyoomeres / *adj* / زیاد / ziyâd /

nurse / ners / *n* / پرستار / parastâr /

nut / nât / *n* / میوه مغزدار / miveye maghzdâr /

nylon / nâylân / *n* / نایلون / nâylon /

nylons / nâylânz / *n* / جوراب نایلون / jurâbe naylon /

O

obey / obey / *vt* اطاعت کردن / etâat kardan /

object / âbjekt / *n* شیء / shey /

object / âbjekt / *vi* اعتراض کردن / eeterâz kardan /

objection / âbjekshen / *n* اعتراض / eeterâz /

objective / âbjectiv / *adj* واقعی / vâgheii /

obligation / âbligeyshen / *n* وظیفه / vazife /

oblige / âblâyj / *vt* مجبور کردن / majbur kardan /

observation / âbzerveyshen / *n* مشاهده / moshâhede /

observe / âbzerv / *vt* مشاهده کردن / moshâhede kardan /

observer / âbzerver / *n* مشاهده کننده /
moshâhede konande /

obstacle / âbstakel / *n* مانع / mânee /

obtain / âbteyn / *vt* به دست آوردن / be dast avardan /

obvious / âbviyes / *adj* آشکار / âshekâr /

obviously / âbviyeslii / *adv* ظاهراً / zâheran /

occasion / âkeyzhen / *n* فرصت / forsat /

occasionally / âkeyzhenâlii / *adv* گاه به گاه / gâh be gâh /

occupation / âkyupeyshen / *n* سکونت / sekunat /

occupy / akyupây / *vt* اشتغال کردن / eshteghâl kardan/

occur / âker / *vi* / اتفاق افتادن / ettefagh oftâdan /

ocean / oshen / *n* / اقیانوس / oghyânus /

o'clock / oklâk / *adv* / ساعت / sâat /

October / âktober / *n* / اکتبر / oktobr /

of / âv / *prep* / از / az /

off / âf / *adv* / دور / dur /

offensive / âfensiv / *adj* / آزارنده / âzârande /

offer / âfer / *vt* / پیشنهاد کردن / bishnahâd kardan /

office / âfis / *n* / دفتر / daftar /

officer / âfiser / *n* / افسر / afsar /

official / âfishâl / *adj* / رسمی / rasmi /

often / âfen / *adv* / اغلب / aghlab /

oil / oyl / *n* / روغن / roghan /

oil tanker / oyl tanker / *n* / نفتکش / naftkesh /

okay / okey / *adv* / باشه / bâshe /

old / old / *adj* / پیر / pir /

old-fashioned / oldfashend / *adj* / ازمدافتاده / azmodoftâde /

omelette / âmlit / *n* / املت / omlet /

on / ân / *adv* / روی / ruye /

once / wâns / *adv* / یکبار / yekbâr /

one / wân / *n* / عدد یك / adade yek /

oneself / wânself / *pron* / خود / khod /

onion / ânyen / *n* / پیاز / piyâz /

only / onlii / *adj* / تنها / tanhâ /
open / open / *adj* / باز / bâz /
open-air / open er / *adj* / روباز / rubâz /
openly / openlii / *adv* / آشکارا / âshekârâ /
opera / âperâ / *n* / اپرا / operâ /
operate / âpereyt / *vt* / به کار انداختن / bekâr andakhtan /
operation / âpereyshen / *n* / طرز کار / tarze kâr /
operator / âpereyter / *n* / گرداننده / gardânande /
opinion / opinyen / *n* / نظر / nazar /
opportunity / âportyoonitii / *n* / فرصت / forsat /
oppose / opoz / *vt* / مخالفت کردن / mokhâlefat kardan /
opposite / âpozit / *adj* / مخالف / mokhâlef /
opposition / âpozishen / *n* / مخالفت / mokhâlefat /
optimism / âptimizem / *n* / خوشبینی / khoshbini /
optimist / âptimist / *n* / نیک بین / nikbin /
optimistic / âptimistik / *adj* / خوشبینانه / khoshbinâne /
option / âpshn / *n* / اختیار / ekhtyâr /
or / or / *conj* / یا / yâ /
oral / orâl / *adj* / شفاهی / shefâhi /
orange / ârinj / *n, adj* / پرتقال / portaghâl /
orbit / orbit / *n* / مدار / madâr /
order / order / *n* / ترتیب / tartib /
order / order / *vt* / دستور دادن / dastur dâdan /

ordinary / ordinerii / *adj* / معمولی / maamuli /

organ / organ / *n* / اندام / andâm /

organic / organik / *adj* / آلی / âli /

organism / organizem / *n* / موجود زنده / mojude zende /

organization / organâyzeyshen / *n* / سازمان / sâzemân /

organize / organâyz / *vtn* / سازمان دادن / sâzemân dâdan /

organizer / organâyzer / *n* / گرداننده / gardânande /

origin / ârijin / *n* / منشا / manshaa /

original / orijinâl / *adj* / نخستین / nokhostin /

originally / orijinâlii / *adv* / دراصل / darasl /

ornament / ornament / *n* / تزیین / tazyin /

other / âdher / *adj* / دیگر / digar /

ought / ât / *v* / باید / bâyad /

ounce / aons / *n* / اونس / ons /

ours / aorz / *pron* / مال ما / mâle mâ /

ourselves / aorselvz / *pron* / خودمانرا / khodemânrâ /

oust / aost / *vt* / بر کنارکردن / bar kenâr kardan /

out / aot / *adv* / بیرون / birun /

outback / aotbak / *n* / جای پرت / jâye part /

outdoor / aotdor / *adj* / بیرونی / biruni /

outer / aoter / *adj* / بیرونی / biruni /

outing / aoting / *n* / سفر تفریحی / safare tafrihi /

outrun / aotrân / *vt* / تندتر / tondtar /

outside / aotsâyd / *adv* / بيرون / birun /

oval / ovl / *adj* / بيضى / beyzi /

over / over / *adv* / بالاى / bâlaye /

overcome / overkâm / *vt* / پيروز شدن / piruz shodan /

overcrowded / overkraodid / *adj* / پر جمعيت / por jamiyat /

overtake / overteyk / *vt* / گرفتن / gereftan /

overwork / overwerk / *vt* / زياد كار كردن / ziyâd kâr kardan /

owe / o / *vt* / بدهكار بودن / bedehkâr budan /

own / on / *adj* / خود / khod /

own / on / *vt* / صاحب بودن / sâheb budan /

owner / oner / *n* / مالك / mâlek /

ox / âks / *n* / گاو / gâv /

oxygen / âksijen / *n* / اكسيژن / oksizhen /

P

pace / peys / *n* / قدم / ghadam /

pack / pak / *vt* / بستن / bastan/

packing / paking / *n* / بسته بندی / bastebandi/

page / peyj / *n* / صفحه / safhe/

pain / peyn / *n* / درد / dard/

painful / peynful / *adj* / دردناك / dardnâk/

painfully / peynfulii / *adv* / به طور دردناکی / be tore dardnâki/

paint / peynt / *n* / رنگ / rang/

painter / peynter / *n* / نقاش / naghghâsh/

painting / peynting / *n* / نقاشی / naghghâshi/

pair / per / *n* / جفت / joft/

pajamas / pejâmâz / *n* / پیژامه / pizhâme/

pal / pal / *n* / رفیق / rafigh/

pale / peyl / *adj* / رنگ پریده / rang paride/

panic / panik / *n* / وحشت / vahshat/

panorama / panorâmâ / *n* / منظره / manzare/

paper / peyper / *n* / كاغذ / kâghaz/

paradise / paredâys / *n* / بهشت / behesht/

paragraph / paragrâf / *n* / بند / band/
parcel / pârsel / *n* / بسته / baste/
pardon / pârden / *n* / عفو / afv/
parent / perent / *n* / مادر پدر / mâdar pedar/
park / pârk / *n* / پارک / pârk/
parliament / pârliment / *n* / مجلس شورا / majlese shurâ/
part / pârt / *n* / قسمت / ghesmat/
partial / pârshâl / *adj* / جزئ / jozii/
partially / pârshâli / *adv* / به طور جزئی / be tore jozii/
particular / pârtikyuler / *adj* / خاص / khâs/
particularly / pârtikyulerli / *adv* / مخصوصا / makhsusan/
partly / pârtlii / *adv* / تاحدی / tahaddi/
partner / pârtner / *n* / شریک / sharik/
party / pârti / *n* / حزب / hezb/
pass / pas / *n* / گذر / gozar/
pass / pas / *vi* / گذشتن / gozâshtan/
passage / pasij / *n* / راهرو / rahro/
passenger / pasinjer / *n* / مسافر / mosâfer/
passion / pashen / *n* / عشق / eshgh/
passionate / pashenit / *adj* / احساساتی / ehsâsâti/
passport / pasport / *n* / گذرنامه / gozarnâme/
password / paswed / *n* / اسم عبور / esme ubur/
past / past / *n* / گذشته / gozashte/

paste / peyst / *n* خمیر / khamir/

paste / peyst / *vt* چسباندن / chasbândan/

pastime / pastâym / *n* سرگرمی / sargarmi/

pastry / peystri / *n* شیرینی / shirini/

path / path / *n* راه / râh/

patience / peyshens / *n* صبر / sabr/

patient / peyshent / *adj* صبور / sabur/

patient / peyshent / *n* بیمار / bimâr/

patiently / peyshentl, *adv* صبورانه / saburâne/

patriot / patriyât / *n* وطن پرست / vatanparast/

patriotic / patriyâtik / *adj* وطن پرست / vatanparast/

patrol / patrol / *n* گشت / gasht/

pattern / patern / *n* الگو / olgu/

pause / poz / *n* مکث / maks/

pave / peyv / *vt* فرش کردن / farsh kardan/

pavement / peyvment / *n* پیاده رو / piyâdero/

pay / pey / *vt* پرداخت کردن / pardâkht kardan/

payment / peyment / *n* پرداخت / pardâkht/

pea / pii / *n* نخود / nokhod/

peace / piis / *n* صلح / solh/

peach / piich / *n* هلو / hulu/

pear / per / *n* گلابی / golâbi/

peculiar / pikyooliyer / *adj* خاص / khâs/

pedal / pedel / *n* پدال / pedâl/

pedestrian / pidestriyen / *n* / عابر پیاده / âbere piyâde/
pen / pen / *n* / قلم / ghalam/
penalty / penâlti / *n* / جریمه / jarime/
pencil / pensil / *n* / مداد / medâd/
pension / penshen / *n* / مستمری / mostamari/
people / piipel / *n* / مردم / mardom/
pepper / peper / *n* / فلفل / felfel/
per / per / *prep* / هر / har/
percent / persent / *adj* / درصد / darsad/
percentage / persentij / *n* / درصد / darsad/
perfect / perfikt / *adj* / کامل / kâmel/
perfectly / perfektli / *adv* / کاملاً / kâmelan/
perform / perform / *vt* / انجام دادن / anjâm dadan/
performance / performens / *n* / اجرا / ejrâ/
perfume / perfyoom / *n* / عطر / atr/
perhaps / perhaps / *adv* / شاید / shâyad/
period / piriyed / *n* / دوره / doro/
periodical / piriyâdikâl / *adj* / دوره ای / dorehâye/
permanence / permanens / *n* / ثبات / sobet/
permanent / permanent / *adj* / ثابت / sâbet/
permission / permishen / *n* / اجازه / ejâze/
permit / permit / *vi* / اجازه دادن / ejâze dâdan/
pernicious / pernishes / *adj* / مضر / mozer/

341

perpetual / perpechuwâl / *adj* / ابدی / abadi/

perpetually / perpechuwâli *adv* / همیشگی / hamishegi/

Persia / pershe / *n* / ایران / irân/

Persian / perzhn / *adj* / ایرانی / irâni/

persist / pesist / *vi* / پافشاری کردن / pâfeshâri kardan/

person / persen / *n* / شخص / shakhs/

personal / persenâl / *adj* / شخصی / shakhsi/

personality / persenalitii / *n* / شخصیت / shakshsiyyat/

personally / personâlii / *adv* / شخصاً / shakhsan/

perspiration / perspireyshen / *n* / عرق / aragh/

pessimism / pesimizem / *n* / بدبینی / bad bini/

pessimist / pesimist / *n* / آدم بدبین / âdame badbin/

pessimistic / pesimistik / *adj* / بدبینانه / badbinâne/

pet / pet / *n* / جانور خانگی / jânevare khânegi/

petition / pitishen / *n* / تقاضا / taghâzâ/

petrol / petrol / *n* / بنزین / benzin/

pharmacist / fârmâsist / *n* / داروساز / dârusâz/

pharmacy / fâmesi / *n* / داروخانه / dârukhâne/

phenomenon / finâminen / *n* / پدیده / padide/

philosopher / filâsofer / *n* / فیلسوف / filsuf/

philosophical / filosâfikâl / *adj* / فلسفی / falsafi/

philosophy / filâsofi / *n* / فلسفه / falsafe/

phone / fon / *n* / تلفن / telefon/

phonetics / fenetiks / *n* آواشناسی / âvâshenâsi/

photograph / fotogrâf / *n* عكس / aks/

photographer / fotâgrafer / *n* عكاس / akkâs/

phrase / freiz / *n* عبارت / ebârat/

physician / fizishen / *n* پزشك / pezeshk/

physicist / fizisist / *n* فيزيكدان / fizikdân/

physics / fiziks / *n* فيزيك / fizik/

physiology / fiziyâloji / *n* فيزيولوژى / fiziyoloji/

piano / piyano / *n* پيانو / piyâno/

pick / pik / *vt* انتخاب كردن / entekhâb kardan/

pickpocket / pikpâkit / *n* جيب بُر / jibbor/

picnic / piknik / *n* پيكنيك / piknik/

picture / pikcher / *n* عكس / aks/

pie / pây / *n* پاى / pây/

piece / piis / *n* تكه / tekke/

pierce / piyers / *vt* سوراخ كردن / surâkh kardan/

pig / pig / *n* خوك / khuk/

pigeon / pijin / *n* كبوتر / kabutar/

pile / pâyl / *n* دسته / daste/

pilgrim / pilgrim / *n* زائر / zâeer/

pill / pil / *n* قرص / ghors/

pillar / piler / *n* ستون / sutun/

pillow / pilo / *n* بالش / bâlesh/

pilot / pâylet / *n* خلبان / khalabân/

pin / pin / *n* سنجاق / sanjâgh/

PIN / pin / رمز شخصی / ramze shakhsi/

pineapple / pâynapel / *n* آناناس / ânânâs/

pink / pink / *adj* صورتی / surati/

pint / pâynt / *n* پاینت / pâynt/

pioneer / pâyoniyer / *n* پیشگام / pishgâm/

pipe / pâyp / *n* لوله / lule/

pipeline / pâyp-lâyn / *n* خط لوله / khatte lule/

pipette / pipet / *n* پیپت / pipet/

pistol / pistel / *n* تپانچه / tapânche/

pity / piti / *n* رحم / rahm/

place / pleys / *n* جا / jâ/

plain / pleyn / *n* جلگه / jolge/

plan / plan / *n* نقشه / naghshe/

plane / pleyn / *n* هواپیما / havâpeyma/

planet / planit / *n* سیّاره / sayyâre/

plant / plant / *n* گیاه / giyâh/

plant / plant / *vt* کاشتن / kâshtan/

plantation / planteyshen / *n* کشتزار / keshtzâr/

plastic / plastik / *adj* پلاستیک / pelâstik/

plate / pleyt / *n* بشقاب / boshghâb/

platform / platform / *n* سکّو / sakku/

play / pley / *n* / بازی / bâzi/

play / pley / *vt* / بازی کردن / bâzi kardan/

player / pleyer / *n* / بازیکن / bâzi kon/

playground / pleygraound / *n* / تفریحگاه / tafrihgâh/

plaza / plâzâ / *n* / میدان / meydân/

plead / pliid / *vt* / دفاع کردن / defââ kardan/

pleasant / plezent / *adj* / دلپذیر / delpazir/

please / pliiz / *intj* / لطفا / lotfan/

please / pliiz / *vt* / راضی کردن / râzi kardan/

pleasing / pliizing / *adj* / خوشایند / khoshâyand/

pleasure / plezher / *n* / خوشی / khoshi/

plenty / plenti / *n* / وفور / vefur/

plot / plât / *n* / توطنه / totee/

plum / plâm / *n* / گوجه / goje/

plural / pluerel / *n* / جمع / jam/

plus / plâs / *conj.* / بعلاوه / baalâve/

p.m. (post meridiem) / piiem / *n* / بعداز ظهر / baad az zohr/

pocket / pâkit / *n* / جیب / jib/

poem / po-im / *n* / شعر / sheer/

poet / po-it / *n* / شاعر / shâeer/

poetry / po-itrii / *n* / شعر / sheer/

point / poynt / *n* / نقطه / noghte/

point / poynt / *vt* / اشاره کردن / eshâre kardan/

poison / poyzen / *n* / سم / sam/

poisonous / poyzenes / *adj* / سمّی / sammi/

pole / pol / *n* / تیر / tir/

pole / pol / *n* / قطب / ghotb/

police / poliis / *n* / پلیس / polis/

police station / poliissteyshen / *n* / کلانتری / kalântari/

polite / polâyt / *adj* / مؤدب / moaddab/

political / pâlitikâl / *adj* / سیاسی / siyâsi/

politics / pâlitiks / *n* / سیاست / siyâsat/

poll / pol / *vt* / رای دادن / ray dâdan/

pollute / poloot / *vt* / آلوده کردن / âlude kardan/

polluter / polooter / *n* / آلوده کننده / âlude konande/

pollution / polooshen / *n* / آلودگی / âludegi/

pool / pool / *n* / استخر / estakhr/

poor / pu-er / *adj* / فقیر / faghir/

popular / pâpyuler / *adj* / محبوب / mahbub/

population / pâpyuleyshen / *n* / جمعیت / jamiiyat/

porch / porch / *n* / ایوان / eyvân/

pork / pork / *n* / گوشت خوک / gushte khuk/

port / port / *n* / بندر / bandar/

porter / porter / *n* / باربر / bârbar/

position / pozishen / *n* / وضع / vaz/

possession / pozeshen / *n* / مالکیت / mâlekiyyat/

possibility / pâsibiliti / *n* امکان / emkân/

possible / pâsibel / *adj* ممکن / momken/

possibly / pâsiblii / *adv* شاید / shâyad/

post / post / *n* پست / post/

post office / post âfis / *n* پستخانه / postkhâne/

postage / postij / *n* هزینه پست / hazineye post/

postcard / postkârd / *n* کارت پستال / kartpostâl/

poster / poster / *n* پوستر / poster/

pot / pât / *n* ظرف / zarf/

potato / poteyto / *n* سیب زمینی / sibzamini/

pound / paond / *n* پوند / pond/

pour / por / *vi* ریختن / rikhtan/

power / pawer / *n* نیرو / niru/

powerful / pawerful / *adj* قوی / ghavi/

practical / praktikâl / *adj* عملی / amali/

practically / praktikli / *adv* عملاً / amalan/

practice / praktis / *n* عمل / amal/

praise / preyz / *vt* تحسین کردن / tahsin kardan/

pray / prey / *vt* دعا کردن / doâ kardan/

prayer / preyer / *n* دعا / doa/

precedent / president / *n* سابقه / sâbeghe/

precious / preshes / *adj* قیمتی / gheymati/

precise / prisâys / *adj* دقیق / daghigh/

347

precisely / prisâysli / _adv_ درست / dorost/

precision / prisizhen / _n_ دقت / deghghat/

predict / pridikt / _vt_ پیش بینی کردن / bishbini kardan/

prediction / pridikshen / _n_ پیش بینی / bishbini/

prefer / prifer / _vt_ ترجیح دادن / tarjih dâdan/

preferably / prefebli / _adv_ ترجیحاً / tarjihan/

preference / preferens / _n_ رجحان / rejhân/

pregnant / pregnent / _adj_ آبستن / âbestan/

prejudice / prejudis / _n_ پیشداوری / pishdâvari/

preparation / prepareyshen / _n_ آمادگی / âmâdegi/

prepare / priper / _vt_ آماده کردن / âmâde kardan/

preposition / prepezishn / _n_ حرف اضافه / harfe ezâfe/

prescription / priskripshen / _n_ نسخه / noskhe/

present / prezent / _adj_ حاضر / hâzer/

present / prezent / _n_ هدیه / hadiye/

present / prizent / _vt_ ارائه کردن / erâee kardan/

president / prezident / _n_ رئیس جمهور / raisjemhur/

press / pres / _vt_ فشار دادن / feshâr dâdan/

presume / prizyoom / _vt_ فرض کردن / farz kardan/

pretend / pritend / _vi_ تظاهر کردن / tazâhor kardan/

pretension / pritenshen / _n_ ادعا / eddeâ/

pretentious / pritenshes / _adj_ متظاهر / motazâher/

pretty / pritii / _adv_ نسبتاً / nesbatan/

pretty / pritii / *adj* / قشنگ / ghashang/

prevent / privent / *vt* / جلوگیری کردن / jelogiri kardan/

price / prâys / *n* / قیمت / ghaymat/

priceless / prâyslis / *adj* / ارزشمند / arzeshmand/

pride / prâyd / *n* / افتخار / eftekhâr/

priest / priist / *n* / کشیش / keshish/

primary / prâymeri / *adj* / نخستین / nokhostin/

prime minister / prâymminister / *n* / نخست وزیر / nokhost vazir/

prince / prins / *n* / شاهپور / shahpur/

principal / prinsipâl / *adj* / عمده / omde/

principal / prinsipâl / *n* / رئیس / rais/

print / print / *vt* / چاپ کردن / châp kardan/

prison / prizen / *n* / زندان / zendân/

private / prâyvit / *adj* / شخصی / shakhsi/

privilege / privilij / *n* / امتیاز / emtiyâz/

prize / prâyz / *n* / جایزه / jâyeze/

probable / prâbebl / *adj* / احتمالی / ehtemâli/

probably / prâbeblii / *adv* / احتمالاً / ehtemâlan/

problem / prâblem / *n* / مسئله / masale/

proceed / prosiid / *vi* / پیش رفتن / pishraftan/

process / prâses / *n* / فرآیند / farâyand/

proclaim / prokleym / *vt* / اعلام کردن / eelâm kardan/

proclamation / prâklameyshen / *n* / اعلان / eelân/

produce / prodyoos / *vt* نشان دادن / neshân dâdan/

product / prâdâkt / *n* محصول / mahsul/

production / prodâkshen / *n* تولید / tolid/

productive / prodâktiv / *adj* حاصل خیز / hasel khiz/

profession / profeshen / *n* حرفه / herfe/

professional / profeshenâl / *adj* حرفه ای / herfeii/

profit / prâfit / *n* سود / sud/

program / program / *n* برنامه / barnâme/

progress / progres / *n* پیشرفت / pishraft/

progressively / progresivlii / *adv* بطور پیشرونده /
betore pishravande/

prohibit / prohibit / *vt* منع کردن / manee kardan/

prohibition / prohibishn / *n* منع / manee/

project / prâjekt / *n* طرح / tarh/

project / projekt / *vt* برنامه ریزی کردن /
barnâmerizi kardan/

projective / protektiv / *adj* تصویری / tasviri/

promise / prâmis / *n* قول / ghol/

promise / prâmis / *vi* قول دادن / ghol dâdan/

pronounce / pronaons / *vt* تلفظ کردن / talaffoz kardan/

pronunciation / pronânsiyeshen / *n* تلفظ / talaffoz/

proof / proof / *n* دلیل / dalil/

prop / prâp / *n* تکیه گاه / tekiyegâh/

proper / prâper / *adj* مناسب / monâseb/

property / prâperti / n دارایی / dârâyi/

prophecy / prâfisi / n پیشگویی / pishguyi/

proposal / prepozl / n پیشنهاد / pishnehâd/

propose / propoz / vt پیشنهاد کردن / pishnehâd kardan/

proposition / prâpozishen / n موضوع / mozu/

prosper / prâsper / vi موفق شدن / movaffagh shodan/

prosperity / prâsperiti / n سعادت / saâdat/

prosperous / prâspres / adj موفق / movaffagh/

protect / protekt / vt محافظت کردن / mohâfezat kardan/

protection / protekshen / n محافظت / mohâfezat/

protest / protest / n اعتراض / eeterâz/

Protestant / prâtistent / n, adj پروتستان / protestân/

proud / praod / adj سرفراز / sarfarâz/

prove / proov / vt ثابت کردن / sâbet kardan/

proverb / prâverb / n ضرب المثل / zarbol masal/

provide / provâyd / vt تأمین کردن / tamin kardan/

provisional / provishenâl / adj موقت / movaghghat/

provocation / prâvokeyshen / n تحریک / tahrik/

provoke / provok / vt تحریک کردن / tahrik kardan/

psychology / sâykâlejii / n روان شناسی / ravânshenâsi/

pub / pâb / n بار / bâr/

public / pâblik / n مردم / mardom/

publication / pâblikeyshen / n انتشار / enteshâr/

publicity / pâblisiti / *n* / شهرت / shohrat/
pudding / puding / *n* / پودینگ / puding/
pull / pul / *vt* / کشیدن / keshidan/
pullover / pulover / *n* / پلوور / plover/
punish / pânish / *vt* / تنبیه کردن / tanbih kardan/
punishment / pânishment / *n* / تنبیه / tanbih/
pupil / pyoopil / *n* / شاگرد / shâgerd/
purchase / perchis / *n* / خرید / kharid/
pure / pyur / *adj* / خالص / khâles/
purity / pyuriti / *n* / خلوص / khulus/
purple / perpel / *n* / ارغوانی / arghavâni/
purpose / perpes / *n* / منظور / manzur/
purse / pers / *n* / کیف پول / kife pul/
pursuit / persyoot / *n* / تعقیب / taaghib/
push / push / *vt* / هُل دادن / hol dâdan/
put / put / *vt* / گذاشتن / gozâshtan/
pyjamas / pejâmâz / *n* / پیژامه / pijâme/

Q

quality / kwâliti / *n* / كيفيت / keyfiyat/
quantity / kwântiti / *n* / كميّت / kamiyyat/
quarrel / kwârel / *n* / دعوا / daavâ/
quarter / kworter / *n* / يك چهارم / yek châhârom/
queen / kwiin / *n* / ملكه / malake/
queer / kwiyer / *adj* / عجيب / ajib/
question / kweschen / *n* / پرسش / porsesh/
questionnaire / kweschener / *n* / پرسشنامه / porsechnâme/
queue / kyoo / *n, vi* / صف / saf/
quick / kwik / *adj* / تند / tond/
quickly / kwiklii / *adv* / تند / tond/
quiet / kwâyet / *adj* / ساكت / sâket/
quietly / kwâyetlii / *adv* / به آرامی / be ârâmi/
quite / kwâyt / *adv* / كاملاً / kâmelan/
quit / kwit / *vt* / ترك كردن / tark kardan/
quiz / kwiz / *n* / آزمون كوتاه / âzmune kutâh/

R

rabbit / rabit / *n* / خرگوش / khargush/

race / reys / *n* / مسابقه / mosâbeghe/

race / reys / *n* / نژاد / nazhâd/

racial / reyshâl / *adj* / نژادی / nazhâdi/

racket / rakit / *n* / راکت / râket/

radar / reydâr / *n* / رادار / râdâr/

radiator / reydiyeyter / *n* / رادیاتور / râdiyâtor/

radio / reydiyo / *n* / رادیو / râdio/

rag / rag / *n* / کهنه / kohne/

rage / reyj / *n* / خشم / khashm/

raid / reyd / *n* / حمله / hamle/

rail / reyl / *n* / ریل / reyl/

railway / reylwey / *n* / راه آهن / râhâhan/

rain / reyn / *n* / باران / bârân/

raincoat / reynkot / *n* / بارانی / bârani/

rainy / reynii / *adj* / بارانی / bârani/

raise / reyz / *vt* / بلند کردن / boland kardan/

range / reynj / *n* / رشته / reshte/

range / reynj / *vt* / ردیف کردن / radif kardan/

354

rank / rank / *n* رديف / radif/

rapid / rapid / *adj* تُند / tond/

rapidly / rapidlii / *adv* تند / tond/

rare / rer / *adj* نادر / nâder/

rarely / rerlii / *adv* به ندرت / be nodrat/

rat / rat / *n* موش / mush/

rate / reyt / *n* نرخ / nerkh/

rather / râdher / *adv* ترجیح دادن / tarjih dâdan/

ration / rashn / *n* جیره / jire/

raw / râ / *adj* خام / khâm/

ray / rey / *n* پرتو / partov/

razor / reyzer / *n* تیغ / tigh/

reach / riich / *vt* رسیدن / residan/

react / riakt / *vi* اثر گذاشتن / asar gozâshtan/

reaction / riakshen / *n* واکنش / vâkonesh/

read / riid / *vt* خواندن / khândan/

reader / riider / *n* خواننده / khânande/

reading / riiding / *n* خواندن / khândan/

ready / redii / *adj* حاضر / hâzer/

real / riyel / *adj* واقعی / vâgheii/

realize / riyalâyz / *vt* پی بردن / peybordan/

really / riyelii / *adv* واقعًا / vâghean/

rear / riyer / *n* عقب / aghab/

reason / riizen / n دلیل / dalil/

reasonable / riizenebel / adj منطقی / manteghi/

reassure / riieshor / vt اطمینان دادن / etminân kardan/

rebel / rebel / n شورشی / shureshi/

rebellion / ribelyen / n شورش / shuresh/

rebuild / riibild / vt از نو ساختن / az no sâkhtan/

recall / rikâl / vt احضار کردن / ehzâr kardan/

receipt / risiit / n دریافت / daryâft/

receive / risiiv / vt دریافت کردن / daryâft kardan/

recent / riisent / adj اخیر / akhir/

recently / riisentlii / adv اخیراً / akhiran/

reception / risepshen / n پذیرش / paziresh/

recession / riseshen / n رکود / rekud/

recipient / risipiyent / n گیرنده / girende/

recognize / rekonâyz / vt شناختن / shenâkhtan/

recommend / rekâmend / vt توصیه کردن / tosiye kardan/

recommendation / rekâmendeyshen / n توصیه / tosiye/

reconstruction / riikânstrâkshen / n بازسازی / bâzsâzi/

record / rekord / n یادداشت / yâddâsht/

record / rikord / vt ضبط کردن / zabt kardan/

recover / rikâver / vt بهبود یافتن / behbud yâftan/

recreation / riikriyeyshen / n بازآفرینی / bâzâfarini/

rectangle / rektangel / n مستطیل / mostatil/

red / red / *n* /قرمز/ ghermez/

reduce / ridyoos / *vt* /کم کردن/ kam kardan/

reduction / ridâkshen / *n* /کاهش/ kâhesh/

refer / rifer / *vt* /اشاره کردن به/ eshâre kardan be/

reference / referens / *n* /مرجع/ marjaa/

refine / rifâyn / *vt* /تصفیه کردن/ tasfiye kardan/

refinement / rifâynment / *n* /پالایش/ pâlâyesh/

reflect / riflekt / *vt* /منعکس کردن/ monaakes kardan/

reflection / riflekshen / *n* /انعکاس/ eneekâs/

reform / rifârm / *n* /اصلاح/ eslâh/

refugee / refyojii / *n* /پناهنده/ panâhande/

refusal / rifyoozâl / *n* /خودداری/ khoddari/

refuse / rifyooz / *vt* /جواب رد دادن/ javâbe rad dâdan/

regard / rigârd / *n* /توجه/ tavajjoh/

region / riijen / *n* /منطقه/ mantaghe/

register / rejister / *n* /ثبت/ sabt/

regrettable / rigretebel / *adj* /تآسف آور/ taassof âvar/

regular / regyuler / *adj* /مرتب/ morattab/

regularly / regyulârlii / *adv* /مرتباً/ morattaban/

regulation / regyuleyshen / *n* /تنظیم/ tanzim/

reign / reyn / *n* /سلطنت/ saltanat/

reject / rijekt / *vt* /رد کردن/ rad kardan/

relation / rileyshn / *n* /نسبت/ nesbat/

relationship / rileyshenship / *n* رابطه / râbete/

relative / reletiv / *adj* مربوط / marbut/

relatively / reletivlii / *adv* نسبتاً / nesbatan/

relax / rilaks / *vt* شل کردن / shol kardan/

relief / riliif / *n* تسکین / taskin/

relieve / riliiv / *vt* آسوده کردن / âsude kardan/

religion / rilijen / *n* دین / din/

religious / rilijes / *adj* دینی / dini/

remain / rimeyn / *vi* ماندن / mândan/

remains / rimeynz / *n* باقی / bâghi/

remark / rimârk / *n* اظهار نظر / ezhâr nazar/

remark / rimârk / *vt* اظهار داشتن / ezhâr dâshtan/

remarkable / rimârkebel / *adj* چشمگیر / cheshmgir/

remedy / remidi / *n* درمان / darmân/

remember / rimember / *vt* به یاد آوردن / beyâd âvardan/

remind / rimâynd / *vt* یادآوری کردن / yâdâvari kardan/

remove / rimoov / *vt* برداشتن / bardâshtan/

rent / rent / *n* اجاره / ejâre/

repair / riper / *vt* تعمیر کردن / taamir kardan/

repeat / ripiit / *vt* تکرار کردن / tekrâr kardan/

repetition / repitishen / *n* تکرار / tekrâr/

replace / ripleys / *vt* جایگزین کردن / jâygozin kardan/

report / riport / *vt* گزارش دادن / gozâresh dâdan/

reporter / riporter / *n* خبرنگار / khabarnegâr/

represent / reprizent / *vt* نشان دادن / neshân dâdan/

reproach / riproch / *vt* سرزنش کردن / sarzanesh kardan/

reproduce / riiprodyoos / *vt* تولید مثل کردن /
tolide mesl kardan/

reproduction / riiprodâkshen / *n* تولید مثل / tolide mesl/

reptile / reptâyl / *n* خزنده / khazande/

republic / ripâblik / *n* جمهوری / jemhuri/

repulsive / ripâlsiv / *adj* نفرت انگیز / nefrat angiz/

reputation / repyuteyshen / *n* شهرت / shohrat/

repute / ripyoot / *n* شهرت / shohrat/

request / rikwest / *n* خواهش / khâhesh/

require / rikwâyr / *vt* خواستن / khâstan/

requisition / rekwizition / *n* تقاضا / taghâzâ/

rescue / reskyoo / *vt* نجات دادن / nejât dâdan/

research / riiserch / *n* تحقیق / tahghigh/

resemblance / rizemblens / *n* شباهت / shebâhat/

resemble / rizembel / *vt* شبیه بودن / shabih budan/

reservation / rezerveyshen / *n* نگهداری / negahdâri/

reserve / rizerv / *vt* ذخیره کردن / zakhire kardan/

resign / rizâyn / *vt* استعفا کردن / esteefâ kardan/

resignation / rizigneyshen / *n* استعفا / esteefâ/

resist / rizist / *vt* مقاومت کردن / moghavemat kardan/

resistance / rizistens / *n* مقاومت / moghavemat/

resources / risorsiz / n منابع / manâbee/

respect / rispekt / n احترام / ehterâm/

respectable / rispektebel / adj محترم / mohtaram/

respond / rispând / vi پاسخ گفتن / pasokh koftan/

response / rispâns / n پاسخ / pasokh/

responsibility / rispânsibilitii / n مسؤلیّت / masuuliyyet/

responsible / rispânsibel / adj مسنول / masuul/

rest / rest / n استراحت / esterâhat/

restaurant / restrânt / n رستوران / resturân/

restless / restlis / adj بی قرار / bigharâr/

restrict / ristrikt / vt محدود کردن / mahdud kardan/

restriction / ristrikshen / n محدودیت / mahdudiyyat/

result / rizâlt / n نتیجه / hatije/

result / rizâlt / vi ناشی شدن از / nâshi shodan az/

resume / rizyoom / vt از سر گرفتن / az sargereftan/

retreat / ritriit / vi عقب نشینی کردن / aghabneshini kardan/

return / ritern / n برگشت / bargasht/

reveal / riviil / vt نشان دادن / neshân dâdan/

revenge / rivenj / n انتقام / enteghâm/

reverse / rivers / adj معکوس / maakus/

review / rivyu / n مرور / murur/

revolt / rivolt / vi شورش کردن / shuresh kardan/

revolution / revolooshen / n تحول / tahavvol/

revolver / rivâlver / *n* / تپانچه / tapânche/

revue / rivyoo / *n* / نمایش / nemâyesh/

rhythm / ridhem / *n* / ریتم / ritm/

ribbon / riben / *n* / نوار / navâr/

rice / râys / *n* / برنج / berenj/

rich / rich / *adj* / ثروتمند / servatmand/

rid / rid / *vt* / نجات دادن / nejât dâdan/

ride / râyd / *vi* / سوار شدن / savâr shodan/

ridiculous / ridikyules / *n* / خنده دار / khandedâr/

riding / râyding / *n* / سوارکاری / savârkâri/

rifle / râyfel / *n* / تفنگ / tofang/

right / râyt / *adj* / درست / dorost/

right / râyt / *adv* / مستقیم / mostaghim/

rigid / rijid / *adj* / سفت / seft/

ring / ring / *n* / حلقه / halge/

ripe / râyp / *adj* / رسیده / reside/

rise / râyz / *n* / افزایش / afzâyesh/

rise / râyz / *vi* / طلوع کردن / teluu kardan/

risk / risk / *n* / خطر / khatar/

rival / râyvâl / *n* / رقیب / raghib/

river / river / *n* / رود / rud/

road / rod / *n* / جاده / jâdde/

roar / ror / *n* / غرش / ghorresh/

roast / rost / *vt* کباب کردن / kabâb kardan/

rob / râb / *vt* دستبرد زدن / dastbord zadan/

robber / râber / *n* دزد / dozd/

rock / râk / *n* سنگ / sang/

rock / râk / *vt* تکان دادن / tekân dâdan/

rocket / râkit / *n* موشك / mushak/

rod / râd / *n* میل / meyl/

role / rol / *n* نقش / naghsh/

roll / rol / *n* توپ / tup/

roll / rol / *vi* غلتیدن / ghaltidan/

romantic / romantik / *adj* عاشقانه / âsheghâne/

roof / roof / *n* سقف / saghf/

room / room / *n* اتاق / otâgh/

root / root / *n* ریشه / rishe/

rope / rop / *n* طناب / tanâb/

rose / roz / *n* گل سرخ / gole sorkh/

rough / râf / *adj* ناهموار / nâhamvâr/

round / raond / *adj* گرد / gerd/

route / root / *n* راه / râh/

routine / rootiin / *n* امور روزمره / emure ruzmerre/

row / ro / *n* ردیف / radif/

royal / royâl / *adj* سلطنتی / saltanati/

rubber / ruber / *n* کائوچو / kauchu/

rug / râg / *n* / قالیچه / ghâliche/
rugby / râgbii / *n* / راگبی / râgbi/
ruin / roo-in / *n* / خرابی / kharâbi/
rule / rool / *n* / قاعده / ghâede/
ruler / rooler / *n* / حاکم / hâkem/
rumor / roomer / *n* / شایعه / shâyee/
run / rân / *n* / دو / do/
runner / râner / *n* / دونده / davande/
rush / râsh / *vi* / عجله کردن / ajale kardan/
rush hour / râshaor / *n* / شلوغی / sholughi/

S

sack / sak / *n* / کیسه / kise/
sad / sad / *adj* / غمگین / ghamgin/
sadly / sadli / *adv* / با اندوه / bâ anduh/
safe / seyf / *adj* / سالم / sâlem/
safely / seyflii / *adv* / بسلامت / besalâmat/
safety / seyftii / *n* / ایمنی / imeni/
safety pin / seyftii pin / *n* / سنجاق قفلی / sanjâghe ghofli/
sail / seyl / *n* / بادبان / bâdbân/
sailor / seyler / *n* / ملوان / malavân/
sake / seyk / *n* / خاطر / khâter/
salad / salad / *n* / سالاد / sâlâd/
salary / salerii / *n* / حقوق / hughugh/
sale / seyl / *n* / فروش / furush/
saloon / saloon / *n* / سالن / sâlon/
salt / sâlt / *n* / نمک / namak/
same / seym / *adj* / همان / haman/
sand / sand / *n* / ماسه / mâse/
sandy / sandii / *adj* / شنی / sheni/
sapphire / safâyr / *n* / یاقوت کبود / yâghute kabud/

satellite / satelâyt / *n* / ماهواره / mâhvâre/

satisfaction / satisfakshen / *n* / خشنودی / khoshnudi/

satisfactory / satisfakterii / *adj* / رضایت بخش / rezâyet bakhsh/

satisfy / satisfây / *vt* / ارضا کردن / erzâ kardan/

Saturday / saterdi / *n* / شنبه / shanbe/

saucer / soser / *n* / نعلبکی / naalbaki/

sausage / sâsij / *n* / سوسیس / sosis/

savage / savij / *adj* / وحشی / vahshi/

savagely / savijlii / *adv* / وحشیانه / vahshiyâne/

save / seyv / *vt* / نجات دادن / nejat dâdan/

saving / seyving / *n* / پس انداز / pasandâz/

say / sey / *vt* / گفتن / goftan/

scan / skan / *vt* / تقطیع کردن / taghtii kardan/

scarce / skers / *adj* / کمیاب / kamyâb/

scare / sker / *vt* / ترساندن / tarsândan/

scarf / skârf / *n* / روسری / rusari/

scatter / skater / *vt* / پخش / pakhsh/

scene / siin / *n* / صحنه / sahne/

schedule / skejul / *n* / برنامه / barnâme/

school / skool / *n* / مدرسه / madrase/

science / sâyens / *n* / علم / elm/

scientific / sâyentifik / *adj* / علمی / elmi/

scientist / sâyentist / *n* / دانشمند / dâneshman/

sci-fi / sâyfây / *adj* / داستان علمی‌تخیلی /
dâstane elmitakhayyali/

scissors / sizerz / *n* / قیچی / gheychi/

scooter / skooter / *n* / روروک / ro rovak/

score / skor / *n* / امتیاز / emtiyâz/

scorpion / skorpiyen / *n* / عقرب / agharab/

scout / skaot / *n* / دیده ور / didevar/

scream / skriim / *vi* / جیغ زدن / jigh zadan/

screen / skriin / *n* / پرده / parde/

sculpture / skâlpcher / *n* / مجسمه سازی / mojassame sâzi/

sea / sii / *n* / دریا / daryâ/

seasick / siisik / *n* / دریازده / daryâzade/

seaside / siisâyd / *n* / کناردریا / kanâredaryâ/

season / siizen / *n* / فصل / fasl/

seasonal / sizenl / *adj* / موسمی / mosemi/

seat / siit / *n* / صندلی / sandali/

second / sekend / *n* / دوم / dovvom/

secondary / sekendrii / *adj* / ثانوی / sânavi/

secret / siikrit / *n* / راز / râz/

secretary / sekreterii / *n* / منشی / monshi/

secretly / siikritlii / *adv* / محرمانه / mahramâne/

security / sikyuritii / *n* / امنیت / amniyyat/

sedative / sedativ / *n* / مسکن / mosakken/

see / sii / *vi* / دیدن / didan/

seed / siid / *n* / دانه / dâne/

seek / siik / *vt* / جستجو کردن / jostejv kardan/

seem / siim / *vi* / به نظر رسیدن / benazar residan/

segregation / segrigeyshen / *n* / جدایی / jodâii/

seize / siiz / *vt* / مصادره کردن / mosâdere kardan/

seldom / seldem / *adv* / به ندرت / be nodrat/

selection / silekshen / *n* / انتخاب / entekhâb/

self / self / *n* / خود / khod/

selfish / selfish / *adj* / خودخواه / khodkhâh/

self-service / self-servis / *adj* / سلف سرویس / selfservis/

sell / sel / *vt* / فروختن / frukhtan/

send / send / *vt* / فرستادن / frestâdan/

senior / siiniyer / *n* / بزرگتر / bozorghtar/

sensation / senseyshen / *n* / احساس / ehsâs/

sense / sens / *n* / حس / hes/

sentence / sentens / *n* / جمله / jomle/

separate / seprit / *adj* / جدا / jodâ/

separately / sepritlii / *adv* / جداگانه / jodâgâne/

September / september / *n* / سپتامبر / septâmbr/

sergeant / sârjent / *n* / گروهبان / guruhbân/

series / siriiz / *n* / سری / seri/

serious / siriyes / *adj* / جدّی / jeddi/

seriously / siriyeslii / *adv* / سخت / sakht/

servant / servent / *n* / خدمتکار / khedmatkâr/

serve / serv / *vt* / خدمت کردن / khedmat kardan/

service / servis / *n* / خدمت / khedmat/

servitude / servityood / *n* / بردگی / bardegi/

session / seshen / *n* / واگذاری / vâgozâri/

set / set / *adj* / ثابت / sâbet/

set / set / *vt* / غروب کردن / ghurub kardan/

settle / setel / *vt* / ساکن شدن / sâken shodan/

settlement / setelment / *n* / پرداخت / pardâkht/

settler / setler / *n* / مهاجر / mohâjer/

seven / seven / *adj* / هفت / haft/

seventeen / seventiin / *adj* / هفده / hefdah/

seventeenth / seventiinth / *adj* / هفدهمین / hefdahomin/

seventh / seventh / *adj* / هفتمین / haftomin/

seventy / seventii / *adj* / هفتاد / haftâd/

several / severâl / *adj* / چند / chand/

severe / siviyer / *adj* / جدی / jeddi/

severely / siviyerlii / *adv* / شدیداً / shahidan/

sew / so / *vt* / دوختن / dukhtan/

sewing machine / so-ing mashiin / *n* / چرخ خیاطی / charkhe khayyati/

sex / seks / *n* / جنس / jens/

sexual / sekshuwâl / *adj* / جنسی / jensi/

shade / sheyd / *n* / سایه / sâye/

shake / sheyk / *vt* جنباندن / jonbândan /

shame / sheym / *n* خجالت / khejâlat /

shape / sheyp / *n* شکل / shekl /

share / sher / *n* سهم / sahm /

shark / shârk / *n* کوسه / kuse /

sharp / shârp / *adj* تیز / tiz /

shave / sheyv / *vt* ریش زدن / rish zadan /

she / shii / *pron* او / u /

sheep / shiip / *n* گوسفند / gusefand /

sheet / shiit / *n* برگ / barg /

shell / shel / *n* پوست / pust /

shelter / shelter / *n* پناه / panâh /

shepherd / sheperd / *n* چوپان / chupân /

sheriff / sherif / *n* کلانتر / kalântar /

shine / shâyn / *vi* درخشیدن / derakhshidan /

ship / ship / *n* کشتی / kashti /

shirt / shert / *n* پیراهن / pirâhan /

shiver / shiver / *vi* لرزیدن / larzidan /

shock / shâk / *n* تکان / tekân /

shocking / shâking / *adj* تکان دهنده / tekân dahande /

shoe / shoo / *n* کفش / kafsh /

shoot / shoot / *vt, vi* شلیک کردن / shellik kardan /

shop / shâp / *n* مغازه / maghâze /

shopkeeper / shâpkiiper / *n* مغازه دار / maghâzedâr/

shore / shor / *n* ساحل / sâhel/

short / short / *adj* کوتاه / kutâh/

shot / shât / *n* شلیك / shellik/

should / shud / *aux, v* باید / bâyad/

shoulder / sholder / *n* شانه / shâne/

shout / shaot / *n* فریاد / faryâd/

show / sho / *n* نمایش / nemâyesh/

show / sho / *vt* نشان دادن / neshân dâdan/

shower / shao-er / *n* دوش / dush/

shrink / shrink / *vi* کوچک شدن / kuchak shodan/

shut / shât / *vt* بستن / bastan/

shy / shây / *adj* خجالتی / khejâlati/

sick / sik / *adj* بیمار / bimâr/

side / sâyd / *n* طرف / taraf/

sidewalk / sâydwok / *n* پیاه رو / piyâdero/

sieve / siv / *n* الک / alak/

sight / sâyt / *n* بینایی / binâyi/

sightless / sâytlis / *adj* کور / kur/

sign / sâyn / *n* علامت / alâmat/

signal / signâl / *n* علامت / alâmat/

signature / signicher / *n* امضا / emzâ/

silence / sâylens / *n* سکوت / sekut/

silent / sâylent / *adj* ساکت / sâket/

silently / sâylentlii / *adv* آهسته / âheste/

silk / silk / *n* ابریشم / abrisham/

silly / silii / *adj* احمق / ahmagh/

silver / silver / *n* نقره / noghre/

similar / similâr / *adj* همانند / hamânand/

simple / simpel / *adj* ساده / sâde/

since / sins / *adv* از هنگامی که / az hengâmi ke/

sincere / sinsiyer / *adj* اصیل / asil/

sincerely / sinsiyerlii / *adv* صادقانه / sâdeghâne/

sing / sing / *vi* خواندن / khândan/

singer / singer / *n* خواننده / khânande/

single / singel / *adj* تک / tak/

sir / sur / *n* آقا / âghâ/

sister / sister / *n* خواهر / khâhar/

sit / sit / *vi* نشستن / neshastan/

site / sâyt / *n* محل / mahal/

situation / sichuweyshen / *n* وضعیّت / vaziyyat/

six / siks / *adj* شش / shesh/

sixteen / sikstiin / *adj* شانزده / shânzdah/

sixteenth / sikstiinth / *n* شانزدهمی / shânzdahomi/

sixth / siksth / *n* ششمین / yeksheshomin/

sixty / sikstii / *adj* شصت / shast/

size / sâyz / *n* / اندازه / andâze/

skeleton / skeliten / *n* / اسکلت / eskelet/

ski / skii / *n* / اسکی / eski/

skill / skil / *n* / مهارت / mahârat/

skin / skin / *n* / پوست / pust/

skirt / skert / *n* / دامن / dâman/

skull / skâl / *n* / جمجمه / jomjome/

sky / skây / *n* / آسمان / âsemân/

slap / slap / *vt* / سیلی زدن / sili zadan/

slash / slash / *n* / چاک / châk/

slave / sleyv / *n* / برده / barde/

slavery / sleyverii / *n* / بردگی / bardegi/

sleep / sliip / *n* / خواب / khâb/

sleeping bag / sliiping bag / *n* / کیسه خواب / kiseye khâb/

sleepy / sliipii / *adj* / خواب آلود / khâbâlud/

sleeve / sliiv / *n* / آستین / âstin/

slice / slâys / *n* / برش / boresh/

slide / slâyd / *vi* / لغزیدن / laghzidan/

slight / slâyt / *adj* / جزئی / jozii/

slim / slim / *adj* / باریک / bârik/

slip / slip / *n* / لغزش / laghzesh/

slip / slip / *vi* / لغزیدن / laghzidan/

slow / slo / *adj* / آهسته / âheste/

slow / slo / *adv* / یواش / yavâsh/

slowly / slolii / *adv* / آهسته / âheste/

small / smâl / *adj* / کوچک / kuchek/

smart / smârt / *adj* / زرنگ / zerang/

smell / smel / *n* / بویایی / buyâyi/

smelly / smelii / *adj* / بدبو / badbu/

smile / smâyl / *n* / لبخند / labkhand/

smoke / smok / *n* / دود / dud/

smooth / smoodh / *adj* / صاف / sâf/

snack / snak / *n* / غذای سبک / ghazâye sabok/

snake / sneyk / *n* / مار / mâr/

snobbish / snâbish / *adj* / متکبر / motakabber/

snore / snor / *n* / خرناس / khornâs/

snow / sno / *n* / برف / barf/

snowball / snobâl / *n* / گلوله برف / gululeye barf/

snowman / snoman / *n* / آدم برفی / âdam barfi/

so / so / *adv* / زیاد / ziyad/

soap / sop / *n* / صابون / sâbun/

social / soshâl / *adj* / اجتماعی / ejtemâii/

socialist / soshâlist / *n* / سوسیالیست / sasiyalist/

society / sosâyetii / *n* / جامعه / jâmee/

sock / sâk / *n* / جوراب / jurab/

soft / sâft / *adj* / نرم / narm/

softly / sâftlii / *adv* با ملایمت / bâ molâyemat/

soil / soyl / *n* خاك / khâk/

solar / solâr / *adj* خورشیدی / khorshidi/

soldier / soljer / *n* سرباز / sarbâz/

solid / sâlid / *adj* جامد / jâmed/

solidarity / sâlidaritii / *n* اتحاد / ettehâd/

solitary / sâliterii / *adj* تنها / tanhâ/

solution / solooshen / *n* راه حل / râhehal/

solve / sâlv / *vt* حل کردن / hal kardan/

some / sâm / *adj* قدری / ghadri/

somebody / sâmbâdii / *pron* کسی / kasi/

somehow / sâmhao / *adv* یکجوری / yekjuri/

someone / sâmwân / *pron* کسی / kasi/

something / sâmthing / *pron* چیزی / chizi/

sometimes / sâmtâymz / *adv* زمانی / zamâni/

somewhat / sâmwât / *adv* تاحدی / tahaddi/

somewhere / sâmwer / *adv* جایی / jâyii/

son / sân / *n* پسر / pesar/

song / sâng / *n* آواز / âvâz/

soon / soon / *adv* به زودی / be zudi/

sorrow / sâro / *adv* تاسف / taassof /

sorry / sârii / *adj* متاسف / matoossef/

sorry / sârii / *intj* ببخشید / bebakhshid/

sort / sort / *n* جور / jur/

soul / sol / *n* روح / ruh/

sound / saond / *n* صوت / sot/

sound / saond / *vt* به نظر / be nazar/

soup / soop / *n* سوپ / sup/

source / sors / *n* منبع / manbaa/

south / saoth / *n* جنوب / junub/

southeast / saothiist / *n* جنوب شوقی / jonubeshargh/

southern / sâdhern / *adj* جنوبی / jonub/

souvenir / sooveniyer / *n* یادگاری / yâdegâri/

sow / so / *vt* کاشتن / kâshtan/

space / speys / *n* فضا / fazâ/

spacious / speyshes / *adj* جادار / jâdâr/

spare / sper / *adj* اضافی / ezâfi/

speak / spiik / *vt* حرف زدن / harf zadan/

special / speshâl / *adj* مخصوص / makhsus/

specialist / speshâlist / *n* متخصص / motakhasses/

specialize / speshâlâyz / *vi* متخصص شدن / motakhasses shodan/

specially / speshâlii / *adv* مخصوصاً / makhsusan/

spectator / spekteyter / *n* تماشاچی / tamâshâchi/

speech / spiich / *n* گفتار / goftâr/

speed / spiid / *n* سرعت / soraat/

speedometer / spiidâmiter / *n* / کیلومتر شمار / kilometr shomâr/

spell / spel / *vt, vi* / هجی کردن / hojji kardan/

spelling / speling / *n* / هجی / hojji/

spend / spend / *vt* / خرج کردن / kharj kardan/

spirit / spiirit / *n* / روح / ruh/

spiritual / spiirichowâl / *adj* / روحی / ruhi/

spite / spâyt / *n* / کینه / kine/

splendid / splendid / *adj* / باشکوه / bâ shokun/

sponge / spânj / *n* / اسفنج / esfanj/

spoon / spoon / *n* / قاشق / ghâshogh/

sport / sport / *n* / ورزش / varzesh/

spot / spât / *n* / خال / khâl/

spread / spred / *vt* / پهن کردن / pahn kardan/

spring / spring / *n* / بهار / bahâr/

spy / spây / *n* / جاسوس / jâsus/

square / skwer / *adj* / مربع / morabbaa/

square / skwer / *n* / میدان / meydân/

squirrel / skwirel / *n* / سنجاب / sanjâb/

stab / stab / *vt, vi* / چاقو زدن / châghu zadan/

stable / steybel / *adj* / استوار / ostovâr/

stable / steybel / *n* / اصطبل / establ/

stadium / steydiyem / *n* / ورزشگاه / varzeshgâh/

stage / steyj / *n* / صحنه / sahne/

stairs / sterz / *n* پلكان /pellekân/

stamp / stamp / *n* تمبر /tamr/

stand / stand / *vi* ايستادن /istâdan/

standard / standerd / *adj* رايج /rayej/

star / stâr / *n* ستاره /stâre/

start / stârt / *n* شروع /suhuru/

start / stârt / *vi* شروع كردن / shuruu kardan/

state / steyt / *n* وضع /vazee/

statement / steytment / *n* اظهار / ezhâr/

station / steyshen / *n* ايستگاه /istgâh/

statistics / statistiks / *n* آمار / âmâr/

statue / stachoo / *n* مجسمه / mojassame/

stay / stey / *vi* ماندن /mândan/

steady / stedii / *adj* محكم /mohkam/

steak / steyk / *n* اِستيك / esteyk/

steal / stiil / *vt* دزديدن / dozdidan/

steam / stiim / *n* بخار /bokhâr/

steam / stiim / *vt* بخار كردن / bokhâr kardan/

steel / stiil / *n* فولاد /fulâd/

steer / stiyer / *vt* هدايت كردن / hedâyat kardan/

steering / stiyering / *n* هدايت / hedâyat/

steering wheel / stiyering wiil / *n* فرمان / farmân/

step / step / *n* قدم / ghadam/

steward / styuwerd / *n* / مهماندار /mehmândâr/

stewardess / styuwerdis / *n* / مهماندار زن /
mehmândâre zan/

stick / stik / *n* / تکه چوب /tekke chub/

still / stil / *adv* / هنوز /hanuz/

sting / sting / *n* / نیش /nish/

stir / ster / *vt* / تکان دادن /tekân dâdan/

stock / stâk / *n* / موجودی /mojudi/

stocking / stâking / *n* / جوراب ساقه بلند زنانه /
jurâbe sâghebolande zanâne/

stomach / stâmak / *n* / معده /meede/

stone / ston / *n* / سنگ /sang/

stony / stonii / *adj* / سنگی /sangi/

stop / stâp / *n* / ایست /ist/

stop / stâp / *vt* / متوقف کردن /motavaghghef kardan/

store / stor / *n* / ذخیره /zakhire/

storm / storm / *n* / توفان /tufan/

story / storii / *n* / داستان /dâstân/

stove / stov / *n* / اجاق /ojâgh/

straight / streyt / *adj* / راست /râst/

strange / streynj / *adj* / عجیب /ajib/

stranger / streynjer / *n* / غریبه /gharibe/

strategy / stratijii / *n* / رزم آرایی /razm ârâyi/

straw / strâ / *n* / کاه /kâh/

strawberry / strâwberii / *n* / توت فرنگی / tutfarangi/

stray / strey / *vi* / منحرف شدن / monharef shodan/

stream / striim / *n* / جویبار / juybâr/

street / striit / *n* / خیابان / khiyâbân/

strength / strength / *n* / قدرت / ghodrat/

stretch / strech / *n* / کشیدن / keshidan/

strict / strikt / *adj* / سختگیر / sakhtgir/

strictly / striktlii / *adv* / اکیداً / akidan/

strike / strâyk / *n* / اعتصاب / eetesâb/

strike / strâyk / *vt* / زدن / zadan/

string / string / *n* / نخ / nakh/

stripe / strip / *n* / نوار / navâr/

strong / strâng / *n* / قوی / ghavi/

structure / strâkcher / *n* / ساخت / sâkht/

struggle / strâgel / *vi* / تقلا کردن / taghallâ kardan/

student / stoodent / *n* / دانش آموز / dâneshâmuz/

studio / stoodiyo / *n* / استودیو / estodiyo/

study / stâdii / *n* / مطالعه / motâlee/

stuff / stâf / *n* / مادّه / mâdde/

stupid / styoopid / *adj* / گیج / gij/

style / stâyl / *n* / مد / mod/

subject / sâbjikt / *n* / موضوع / mozuu/

submit / sâbmit / *vt* / اطاعت کردن / etâat kardan/

suburb / sâberb / *n* / حومه / home/

suburban / sâberben / *adj* / حومه / home/

subway / sâbwey / *n* / مترو / metro/

succeed / sâksiid / *vi* / موفق شدن / movaffagh shodan/

success / sâkses / *n* / موفقیت / movaffaghiyat/

successful / sâksesful / *adj* / موفق / movaffagh/

successfully / sâksesfulii / *adv* / با موفقیت /
bâ movaffaghiyyat/

successively / sâksesivlii / *adv* / به طور متوالی /
be tore motavâli/

such / sâch / *adj* / چنین / chenin/

sudden / sâden / *adj* / ناگهانی / nâgahâni/

suddenly / sâdenlii / *adv* / ناگهان / nâgahân/

suffer / sâfer / *vi* / (درد) داشتن / (dard) dâshtan/

suffice / sâfâys / *vt* / کفایت کردن / kefâyet kardan/

sufficient / sâfishent / *adj* / کافی / kâfi/

sugar / shuger / *n* / شکر / shakar/

suggest / sâjest / *vt* / پیشنهاد کردن / pishnehâd kardan/

suggestion / sâjeschen / *n* / پیشنهاد / pishnahâd/

suit(cloth) / soot / *n* / دست لباس / dastlebâs/

suit / soot / *n* / مناسب بودن / monâseb budan/

suitable / sootebel / *adj* / مناسب / monâseb/

sum / sâm / *n* / مبلغ / mablagh/

summer / sâmer / *n* / تابستان / tâbestan/

sun / sân / *n* / خورشید / khorshid/

Sunday / sândi / *n* / یکشنبه / yekshanbe/

sunglasses / sânglasiz / *n* عینک آفتابی / eynake âftabi/

sunny / sânii / *adj* / آفتابی / âftabi/

sunrise / sânrâyz / *n* طلوع / teluu/

sunset / sânset / *n* غروب / ghurub/

sunshine / sânshâyn / *n* آفتاب / âftab/

superficial / sooperfishâl / *adj* سطحی / sathi/

superior / soopiiriyer / *adj* برتر / bartar/

supermarket / soopermârkit / *n* فروشگاه بزرگ /
  furusgâhe bozorg/

supersonic / soopersânik / *adj* فراصوتی / farâsoti/

supper / sâper / *n* شام / shâm/

supply / sâplây / *vt* تآمین کردن / taamin kardan/

support / sâport / *vt* حمایت کردن / hemâyat kardan/

supporter / sâporter / *n* حامی / hâmi/

suppose / sâpoz / *vt* فرض کردن / farz kardan/

suppress / sâpres / *vt* سرکوب کردن / sarkub kardan/

suppression / sâpreshen / *n* سرکوب / sarkub/

sure / shur / *adj* مطمئن / motmaen/

surely / shurlii / *adv* قطعا / ghataan/

surface / serfis / *n* سطح / sath/

surgeon / serjen / *n* جرّاح / jarrâh/

surgery / serjerii / *n* جرّاحی / jarrâhi/

surname / serneym / *n* / نام خانوادگی / nâme khânevâdegi/

surprise / serprâyz / *n* / تعجّب / taajjob/

surrender / sârender / *vt* / تسلیم شدن / taslim shodan/

surround / sâraond / *vt* / احاطه کردن / ehâte kardan/

survival / servâyvel / *n* / بقاء / baghâ/

survivor / servâyver / *n* / با زمانده / bâzmânde/

swear / swer / *vt* / قسم خوردن / ghasam khordan/

sweater / sweter / *n* / ژاکت / zhâket/

sweep / swiip / *vt* / جارو کردن / jâru kardan/

sweet / swiit / *adj* / شیرین / shirin/

swift / swift / *adj* / چابك / châbok/

swiftly / swiftlii / *adv* / به سرعت / besoraat/

swim / swim / *vi* / شنا کردن / shenâ kardan/

swimmer / swimer / *n* / شناگر / shenâgar/

swimming pool / swiming pool / *n* / استخر / estakhr/

swing / swing / *vi* / تاب خوردن / tâb khordan/

sword / sord / *n* / شمشیر / shamshir/

syllable / silâbel / *n* / هجا / hejâ/

symbol / simbel / *n* / نماد / nemâd/

sympathy / simpathii / *n* / همدردی / hamdardi/

synagogue / sinâgâg / *n* / کنیسه / kanise/

system / sistem / *n* / نظام / nezâm/

T

table / teybel / *n* / ميز / miz/
tablet / tablit / *n* / قرص / ghors/
tackle / takel / *n* / ابزار / abzâr/
tail / teyl / *n* / دُم / dom/
tailor / teyler / *n* / خياط / khayyat/
take / teyk / *vt* / گرفتن / gereftan/
talent / talent / *n* / استعداد / esteedâd/
talk / tok / *n* / صحبت / sohbat/
talk / tok / *vt* / صحبت کردن / sohbat kardan/
tall / tol / *adj* / بلند / boland/
tame / teym / *adj* / رام / râm/
tap / tap / *n* / شیر / shir/
tape / teyp / *n* / نوار / navâr/
target / târgit / *n* / هدف / hadaf/
task / tâsk / *n* / کار / kâr/
taste / teyst / *n* / چشایی / cheshâyi/
tasteless / teystlis / *adj* / بی مزه / bi maze/
tax / taks / *n* / مالیات / mâliyât/
tea / tii / *n* / چای / chay/

teach / tiich / *vt* / یاد دادن / yâd dâdan/

teacher / tiicher / *n* / معلم / moallem/

team / tiim / *n* / گروه / guruh/

tear / tiyer / *n* / اشك / ashk/

tear / ter / *vt* / پاره کردن / pâre kardan/

technique / tekniik / *n* / مهارت / mahârat/

technologically / teknolâjiklii / *adv* / از نظر فنی / aznazare fanni/

technology / teknâloji / *n* / فن شناسی / fanshenâsi/

teenage / tiineyj / *adj* / نوجوانی / nojavâni/

teenager / tiineyjer / *n* / نوجوان / nojavân/

teens / tiinz / *n* / دورهٔ نو جوانی / doreye nojavâni/

telegram / teligram / *n* / تلگرام / telgerâm/

telegraph / teligrâf / *n* / تلگراف / telgerâf/

telepathic / telipathik / *adj* / ارتباط دل بدل / ertebât del bedel/

telephone / telifon / *n* / تلفن / telefon/

television / telivizhen / *n* / تلویزیون / televiziyon/

tell / tel / *vt* / گفتن / goftan/

teller / teler / *n* / صندوقدار / sandughdâr/

temper / temper / *n* / خُلق / kholgh/

temperature / temprecher / *n* / دما / damâ/

temple / templ / *n* / معبد / maabad/

ten / ten / *adj, n* / ده / dah/

tend / tend / *vi* / متمایل بودن / motamâyel budan/
tennis / tenis / *n* / تنیس / tenis/
tense / tens / *adj* / عصبی / asabi/
tense / tens / *n* / زمان / zamân/
tension / tenshen / *n* / كشش / keshesh/
tent / tent / *n* / چادر / châdor/
tenth / tenth / *n* / یك دهم / yekdahom/
term / term / *n* / دوره / dore/
terminal / terminâl / *n* / ترمینال / terminâl/
terms / termz / *n* / شرایط / sharâyet/
terrible / teribel / *adj* / وحشتناك / vahshatnâk/
terribly / teriblii / *adv* / بطور مخوف / betor makhof/
terrific / terifik / *adj* / فوق العاده / fogholâde/
terrify / terifây / *vt* / ترساندن / tarsândan/
terrifying / terifâying / *adj* / وحشتناك / vahshatnâk/
territory / teritorii / *n* / قلمرو / ghalamro/
terror / terer / *n* / وحشت / vahshat/
test / test / *n* / آزمون / âzmun/
text / tekst / *n* / متن / matn/
textile / tekstâyl / *n* / نساجی / nassâji/
than / dhan / *conj* / از / az/
thanks / thanks / *n* / متشکرم / motashakkeram/
that / dhat / *adj* / آن / ân/

theater / thiiyater / *n* / تئاتر / teâtr/

their / dher / *adj* / آنها / ânhâ/

theirs / dherz / *pron* / مال آنها / mâle ânhâ/

them / dhem / *pron* / آنهارا / ânhârâ/

themselves / dhemselvz / *pron* / خودشان را / khodeshân râ/

then / dhen / *conj, adv* / بعد / baad/

theory / tiirii / *n* / نظریه / nazariye/

therapeutic / terepyutik / *adj* / درمانی / darmâni/

therapy / terepii / *n* / درمان / darmân/

there / dher / *adv* / آنجا / ânjâ/

therefore / dherfor / *adv* / بنابراین / banâbarin/

they / dhey / *pron* / آنها / ânhâ/

thick / thik / *adj* / كلفت / koloft/

thief / thiif / *n* / دزد / dozd/

thin / thin / *adj* / لاغر / lâghar/

thing / thing / *n* / چیز / chiz/

think / think / *vi* / فكر كردن / fekr kardan/

third / therd / *adj* / سوم / sevvom/

thirst / therst / *n* / تشنگی / teshnegi/

thirsty / therstii / *adj* / تشنه / teshne/

thirteen / thertiin / *adj* / سیزده / sizdah/

thirteenth / thertiinth / *adj* / سیزدهمین / sizdahomin/

thirtieth / thertiyeth / *n* / سی ام / siyom/

thirty / thertii / *adj* / سی / si/

this / dhis / *pron* / این / in/

thought / thot / *n* / فکر / fekr/

thoughtful / thotful / *adj* / متفکر / motafakker/

thoughtfully / thotfulii / *adv* / با ملاحظه / bâ molâheze/

thousand / thaozend / *adj* / هزار / hezâr/

threaten / threten / *vt* / تهدید کردن / tahdid kardan/

three / thrii / *n, adj* / سه / se/

throat / throt / *n* / گلو / galu/

through / throo / *adv* / تو / tu/

throw / thro / *vt* / انداختن / andâkhtan/

thumb / thâm / *n* / شَسَت / shast/

thunder / thânder / *n* / رعد / raad/

thunderstorm / thânderstorm / *n* / رعد و برق / raadobargh/

Thursday / therzdi / *n* / پنجشنبه / panjshanbe/

thus / dhâs / *adv* / بدین ترتیب / bedin tartib/

ticket / tikit / *n* / بلیت / belit/

tide / tâyd / *n* / جزر و مد / jazromad/

tidy / tâydii / *adj* / مرتب / morattab/

tie / tây / *n* / کراوات / krâvât/

tie / tây / *vt* / بستن / bastan/

tiger / tâyger / *n* / ببر / babr/

tight / tâyt / *adj* / محکم / mohkam/

till / til / *conj* / تا /tâ/

time / tâym / *n* / زمان /zamân/

tip / tip / *n* / انعام /anââm/

tire / tâyer / *n* / تایر /tâyer/

tired / tâyerd / *adj* / خسته /khaste/

tiring / tâyering / *adj* / خسته کننده /khaste konande/

tissue / tishoo / *n* / بافته /bâfte/

titanic / tâytanik / *adj* / بسیارکلان /besiyâr kalân/

title / tâytel / *n* / عنوان /onvân/

to / too / *prep* / تا /tâ/

tobacco / tobako / *n* / توتون /tutun/

today / toodey / *adv* / امروز /emruz/

together / toogedher / *adv* / باهم /bâham/

toil / toyl / *n* / زحمت /zahmat/

toilet / toylit / *n* / توالت /tuvâlet/

tolerance / tâlerens / *n* / تحمل /tahammol/

tolerate / tâlereyt / *vt* / تحمل کردن /tahammol kardan/

tomato / tomeyto / *n* / گوجه فرنگی /gojefarangi/

tomorrow / toomâro / *adv* / فردا /fardâ/

ton / tân / *n* / تُن /ton/

tone / ton / *n* / آهنگ /âhang/

tongue / tâng / *n* / زبان /zabân/

tonight / toonâyt / *adv* / امشب /emshab/

too / too / *adv* / نيز / niz/

tool / tool / *n* / ابزار / abzâr/

tooth / tooth / *n* / دندان / dandân/

toothache / tootheyk / *n* / دندان درد / dandân dard/

toothbrush / toothbrâsh / *n* / مسواك / mesvâk/

toothpaste / toothpeyst / *n* / خمير دندان / khamir dandân/

top / tâp / *n* / نوك / nuk/

topic / tâpik / *n* / موضوع / mozu/

torch / torch / *n* / مشعل / mashal/

torment / torment / *vt* / عذاب دادن / azâb dâdan/

torture / torcher / *n* / شكنجه / shekanje/

total / totâl / *adj* / كامل / kâmel/

totally / totâlii / *adv* / كاملاً / kâmelan/

touch / tâch / *n* / لامسه / lâmese/

touch / tâch / *vt* / لمس كردن / lams kardan/

tough / tâf / *adj* / سفت / seft/

tour / tur / *n* / تور / tur/

tourist / turist / *n* / جهانگرد / jahângard/

toward(s) / tuword(z) / *prep* / به طرف / betarafe/

towel / tao-el / *n* / حوله / hole/

tower / tao-er / *n* / برج / borj/

town / taon / *n* / شهر / shahr/

toy / toy / *n* / اسباب بازى / asbâbbâzi/

track / trak / *n* / ردّ / rad/

trade / treyd / *vi* / تجارت کردن / tejârat kardan/

trader / treyder / *n* / بازرگان / bâzargân/

tradition / tradishen / *n* / سنّت / sonnat/

traditional / tradishenâl / *adj* / سنّتی / sonnati/

traffic / trafik / *n* / ترافیک / terafik/

trail / treyl / *n* / ردّ / rad/

trailer / treyler / *n* / تریلر / treyler/

train / treyn / *n* / قطار / ghatâr/

training / treyning / *n* / تربیت / tarbiyat/

tram / tram / *n* / تراموای / tramvâi/

transfer / transfer / *n* / انتقال / enteghâl/

transfer / transfer / *vt* / انتقال دادن / enteghâl dâdan/

translate / transleyt / *vt* / ترجمه کردن / tarjome kardan/

translation / transleyshen / *n* / ترجمه / tarjome/

transport / transport / *n* / حمل / haml/

transportation / transporteyshen / *n* / ترابری / tarâbari/

trap / trap / *n* / دام / dâm/

trapper / traper / *n* / صیاد / sayyad/

travel / travel / *n* / سفر / safar/

travel / travel / *vt* / سفر کردن / safar kardan/

traveler / travler / *n* / مسافر / mosâfer/

tray / trey / *n* / سینی / sini/

treason / triizen / n خیانت / khiyânat/

treasure / trezher / n گنج / ganj/

treat / triit / vt معالجه کردن / moâleje kardan/

treaty / triitii / n پیمان / peyman/

tree / trii / n درخت / derakht/

tremble / trembel / vt لرزیدن / larzidan/

trial / trâyâl / n محاکمه /mohâkeme/

triangle / trâyangel / n مثلث / mosallas/

trick / trik / n کلک / kalak/

trip / trip / n مسافرت / mosâferat/

triumph / trâyumf / n پیروزی / piruzi/

trophy / trofii / n جایزه / jâyeze/

trouble / trâbel / n زحمت / zahmat/

trousers / traozerz / n شلوار / shalvâr/

truck / trâk / n کامیون / kâmyon/

true / troo / adj راست / râst/

trunk / trânk / n تنه / tane/

trust / trâst / vt اعتماد کردن / eetemâd kardan/

truth / trooth / n حقیقت / haghighat/

try / trây / vt سعی کردن / saay kardan/

tube / tyoob / n لوله / lule/

Tuesday / tyoozdi / n سه شنبه / seshanbe/

tune / tyoon / n آهنگ / âhang/

tunnel / tânel / *n* تونل / tunel/

Turk / terk / *n* ترک / tork/

turkey / terkii / *n* بوقلمون / bughalamun/

Turkey / terkii / *n* ترکیه / torkiye/

Turkish / terkish / *n* ترکی / torki/

turn / tern / *n* پیچ / pich/

turn / tern / *vt* گشتن / gashtan/

twelfth / twelfth / *adj* دوازدهم / davâzdahom/

twelve / twelv / *adj* دوازده / davâzdah/

twentieth / twentiyeth / *adj* بیستم / bistom/

twenty / twentii / *adj* بیست / bist/

twice / twâys / *adv* دوبار / dobâr/

twin / twin / *n* دوقلو / dogholu/

two / too / *n, adj* دو / do/

type / tâyp / *vt* تایپ کردن / tayp kardan/

typewriter / tâyprâyter / *n* ماشین تحریر / mâshine tahrir/

typical / tipikâl / *adj* نمونه / nemune/

typist / tâypist / *n* ماشین نویس / mâshin nevis/

U

ugly / âglii / *adj* / زشت / zesht/
umbrella / âmbrelâ / *n* / چتر / chatr/
unable / âneybel / *adj* / ناتوان / nâtavân/
unbelievable / ânbiliivebel / *adj* / باور نکردنی /
bâvar nakardani/
uncle / ânkel / *n* / دایی / dâyi/
uncomfortable / ânkâmfterbel / *adj* / ناراحت / nârâhat/
under / ânder / *prep* / زیر / zir/
underdog / ânderdâg / *n* / بازنده / bâzande/
underground / ândergraound / *adj* / زیر زمینی / zirzamini/
understand / ânderstand / *vt* / فهمیدن / fahmidan/
understanding / ânderstanding / *n* / درک / dark/
underwater / ânderwoter / *adj* / زیرآبی / zirâbi/
underwear / ânderwer / *n* / زیر لباس / lebâse zir/
undisputed / ândispyootid / *adj* / مسلّم / mosallam/
unearthly / ânerthlii / *adj* / خارق العاده / khâregholâdde/
unemployed / ânimployd / *adj* / بیکار / bikâr/
unemployment / ânimployment / *n* / بیکاری / bikâri/
unexpected / ânikspektid / *adj* / غیر منتظره /
gheyr montazere/

unfair / ânfer / *adj* / غیر منصفانه / gheyr monsefâne/

unforgettable / ânforgetebel / *adj* / به یاد ماندنی / be yâd mândani/

unfortunate / ânforchunit / *adj* / بدشانس / badshâns/

unfortunately / ânforchunitlii / *adv* / متآسفانه / motassefâne/

unhappy / ânhapii / *adj* / غصه دار / ghosse dâr/

unhealthy / ânhelthii / *adj* / ناسالم / nâsâlâm/

unidentified / ânâydentifâyd / *adj* / ناشناس / nâshenâs/

uniform / yooniform / *n* / لباس فرم / lebâse form/

union / yoonyen / *n* / اتحاد / ettehad/

unite / yoonâyt / *vi* / متحد شدن / mottahed shodan/

united / yoonâytid / *adj* / متحد / mottahed/

United Nations / yunâytid neyshenz / *n* / سازمان ملل متحد / sâzemâne melale mottahed/

United States / yoonâytid steyts / *n* / متحده ایالات / ayâlâte motahede/

unity / yoonitii / *n* / وحدت / vahdat/

universe / yoonivers / *n* / جهان / jahân/

university / yooniversitii / *n* / دانشگاه / dâneshgâh/

unknown / ânnon / *adj* / ناشناخته / nâshenâkhte/

unless / ânles / *conj* / مگر این که / magarinke/

unlimited / ânlimitid / *adj* / نا محدود / nâ mahdud/

unlucky / ânlâkii / *adj* / بدشانس / bad shâns/

unnecessary / ânneseserii / *adj* / غیر ضروری /
gheyre zaruri/

unpleasant / ânplezent / *adj* / ناخوشایند / nâ khoshâyand/

unreal / ânriyel / *adj* / تخیّلی / ta khauyoil/

until / ântil / *prep* / تا / tâ/

unusual / ânyoozhuwâl / *adj* / غیرعادی / gheyreâdi/

unwilling / ânwiling / *adj* / بی میل / bimeyl/

up / âp / *adv* / بالا / bâlâ/

upon / âpân / *prep* / روی / ruye/

upper / âper / *adj* / بالایی / bâlâyi/

upset / âpset / *vt* / برگرداندن / bargardândan/

upstairs / âpsterz / *adv* / طبقه بالا / tabaghey‌e bâlâ/

uptown / âptaon / *adj* / بالای شهر / bâlâye shahr/

urban / urben / *adj* / شهری / shahri/

urgent / urjent / *adj* / فوری / fori/

urologist / yurolojist / *n* / کلیه شناس / koliye shenâs/

us / âs / *pron* / مارا / mârâ/

use / yoos / *n* / استفاده / estefade/

use / yooz / *vt* / به کار بردن / bekâr bordan/

useful / yoosful / *adj* / مفید / mofid/

user / yoozer / *n* / مصرف کننده / masraf konande/

usual / yoozhuwâl / *adj* / عادی / âdi/

usually / yoozhuwâlii / *adv* / معمولاً / mamulan/

utilize / yootilâyz / *vt* / به کار بردن / bekâr bordan/

V

vacant / veykent / *adj* / خالی / khâli/
vacation / vakeyshen / *n* / تعطیلات / taatilât/
vaccine / vaksiin / *n* / مایه / mâye/
vacuum / vakyoom / *n* / خلأ / khalaa/
valid / valid / *adj* / معتبر / motabar/
valley / valii / *n* / درّه / darre/
valuable / valyubel / *adj* / ارزنده / arzande/
value / valyoo / *n* / ارزش / arzesh/
van / van / *n* / وانت / vânet/
vanilla / vânilâ / *n* / وانیل / vânil/
vanish / vanish / *vi* / ناپدید شدن / nâpadid shodan/
variation / veriyeyshen / *n* / تنوع / tanavvoo/
variety / varâyetii / *n* / تنوع / tanavvoo/
various / veriyes / *adj* / گوناگون / gunâgun/
vary / verii / *vi* / تغییر کردن / taghiir kardan/
vase / vâz / *n* / گلدان / goldân/
vast / vast / *adj* / کلان / kalân/
vegetable / vejitabel / *n* / گیاه / giyâh/
vehement / viyement / *adj* / پرشور / porshur/

vehemently / viyementlii / *adv* / تند / tond/

vehicle / viyikel / *n* / وسیله نقلیه / vasileye naghliye/

vein / vein / *n* / سیاهرگ / siyâhrag/

vein / veyn / *n* / رگ / rag/

velvet / velvit / *n* / مخمل / makhmal/

venerate / venereyt / *vt* / احترام کردن / ehterâm kardan/

vertical / vertikâl / *adj* / قائم / ghâem/

very / verii / *adv* / خیلی / kheyli/

veteran / veteren / *adj, n* / کهنه کار / kohne kâr/

victim / viktim / *n* / قربانی / ghorbâni/

victory / viktrii / *n* / پیروزی / piruzi/

video / video / *n* / ویدئو / video/

view / vyoo / *n* / دید / did/

village / vilij / *n* / ده / deh/

villager / vilijer / *n* / روستایی / rustâyi/

violence / vâyolens / *n* / خشونت / khushunat/

violent / vâyolent / *adj* / خشن / khashen/

violet / vâyolit / *n* / بنفشه / banafshe/

violin / vâyelin / *n* / ویلن / viyolen/

virgin / verjin / *adj* / باکره / bâkere/

virtually / verchuwâlii / *adv* / تقریباً / taghriban/

virtue / verchoo / *n* / حسن / hosn/

virus / vâyres / *n* / ویروس / virus/

visa / viizâ / *n* / رواديد / ravadid/

visible / vizibel / *adj* / قابل رؤيت / ghâbele royat/

visit / vizit / *vt* / ديدن / didan/

visitor / viziter / *n* / بازديد كننده / bâzdid konande/

visual / vizhooel / *adj* / بصرى / basari/

vital / vâytl / *n* / حياتى / hayâti/

vitamin / vâytemin / *n* / ويتامين / vitâmin/

vivid / vivid / *adj* / روشن / roshan/

vocabulary / vokabyulerii / *n* / واژگان / vâzhgân/

voice / voys / *n* / صدا / sedâ/

volt / volt / *n* / ولت / volt/

volume / vâlyum / *n* / جلد / jeld/

volunteer / vâlentiyer / *n* / داوطلب / dâvtalab/

vote / vot / *n* / رأى / ray/

voyage / voyij / *n* / سفر دريايى / safare daryâyi/

voyager / voyejer / *n* / مسافر دريا / mosâfere deryâ/

W

wagon / wagen / *n* / گاری / gâri/

wait / weyt / *vi* / صبرکردن / sabr kardan/

waiter / weyter / *n* / پیشخدمت / pishkhedmat/

waiting room / weyting-rum / *n* / اتاق انتظار / otaghe entezâr/

waitress / weytris / *n* / پیشخدمت زن / pishkhedmate zan/

wake / weyk / *vi* / بیدارشدن / bidâr shodan/

walk / wok / *vi* / قدم زدن / ghadam zadan/

wall / wol / *n* / دیوار / divâr/

wallet / wâlit / *n* / کیف بغلی / kife baghali/

want / wânt / *vt* / خواستن / khâstan/

war / wor / *n* / جنگ / jang/

warm / worm / *adj* / گرم / garm/

warn / worn / *vt* / هشدار دادن / hoshdâr dâdan/

warning / worning / *n* / اخطار / ekhtâr/

warship / worship / *n* / رزم ناو / razmnâv/

wash / wâsh / *vt* / شستن / shostan/

washer / wâsher / *n* / ماشن لباسشویی / mâshine lebâs-shuii/

waste / weyst / *n* / اتلاف / etlâf/

waste / weyst / *vt* تلف کردن / talaf kardan/

wastepaper basket / weyst peyper baskit / سطل (کاغذ باطله) *n* / satle (kaghaz bâtele)/

watch / wâch / *n* ساعت / sâat/

watch / wâch / *vi* تماشا / tamâshâ/

watchful / wâchful / *adj* گوش به زنگ / gush be zang/

water / wâter / *n* آب / âb/

wave / weyv / *n* موج / moj/

wave / weyv / *vi* جنبیدن / jonbidan/

wax / waks / *n* موم / mum/

way / wey / *n* راه / râh/

we / wii / *pron* ما / mâ/

weak / wiik / *adj* ضعیف / zaiif/

wealth / welth / *n* ثروت / servat/

weapon / wepen / *n* سلاح / selâh/

wear / wer / *vt* پوشیدن / pushidan/

wearily / wiyerilii / *adv* باخستگی / bâkhastegi/

weary / wiyerii / *adj* خسته / khaste/

weather / wedher / *n* هوا / havâ/

weave / wiiv / *vt* بافتن / bâftan/

wedding / weding / *n* عروسی / arusi/

Wednesday / wenzdi / *n* چهارشنبه / châhârshanbe/

week / wiik / *n* هفته / hafte/

weekday / wiikdey / *n* روز هفته / ruz hafte/

weekend / wiikend / *n* تعطیلات آخر هفته / taatilâte âkharehafte/

weekly / wiiklii / *adj* هفتگی / haftegi/

weep / wiip / *vi* گریه کردن / gerye kardan/

weigh / wey / *vt* وزن کردن / vazn kardan/

weight / weyt / *n* وزن / vazn/

welcome / welkâm / *n* خوش آمد / khoshâmad/

weld / weld / *vt* جوش دادن / jush dâdan/

well / wel / *adj* خوب / khub/

west / west / *n* غرب / gharb/

western / western / *adj* غربی / gharbi/

wet / wet / *adj* خیس / khis/

whale / weyl / *n* بال / bâl/

what / wât / *adj* چه / che/

wheel / wiil / *n* فرمان / farmân/

when / wen / *adv* چه وقت / che vaght/

whenever / wenever / *adv* هروقت / harvaght/

where / wer / *adv* کجا / kojâ/

wherever / werever / *adv* هرجاکه / harjâke/

whether / wedher / *conj* آیا / âyâ/

which / wich / *adj* کدام / kodam/

while / wâyl / *conj* موقعی که / mogheii ke/

whisky / wiskii / *n* ویسکی / viski/

whisper / wisper / *vi* نجوا کردن / najvâ kardan/

whistle / wisel / *n* سوت / sut/

white / wâyt / *adj* سفید / sefid/

who / hoo / *pron* کی / ki/

whole / hol / *adj* همه / hame/

whom / hoom / *pron* چه کسی / che kasi/

whose / hooz / *pron* مال کی / mâle ki/

why / wây / *adv* چرا / cherâ/

wide / wâyd / *adj* پهن / pahn/

width / width / *n* پهنا / pahnâ/

wife / wâyf / *n* خانم / khânom/

wild / wâyld / *adj* وحشی / vahshi/

wildness / wâyldnis / *n* وحشیگری / vahshigari/

will / will / *n* اراده / erâde/

willing / wiling / *adj* راغب / râgheb/

win / win / *vt* بردن / bordan/

wind / wind / *n* باد / bâd/

window / windo / *n* پنجره / panjare/

windy / windii / *adj* توفانی / tufâni/

wine / wâyn / *n* شراب / sharâb/

wing / wing / *n* بال / bâl/

winner / winer / *n* برنده / barande/

winter / winter / *n* زمستان / zemestân/

wipe / wâyp / *vt* پاک کردن / pâk kardan/

wire / wâyer / *n* سیم / sim/

wireless / wâyerlis / *adj* بی سیم / bisim/

wisdom / wizdem / *n* عقل / aghl/

wise / wâyz / *adj* خردمند / kheradmand/

wish / wish / *vt* آرزو کردن / ârezu kardan/

with / widh / *prep* با / bâ/

within / widhin / *prep* در / dar/

without / widhaot / *prep* بدون / bedune/

witness / witnis / *n* شاهد / shâhed/

wolf / wulf / *n* گرگ / gorg/

woman / wuman / *n* زن / zan/

wonder / wânder / *n* شگفتی / shegefti/

wonderful / wânderful / *adj* عالی / âli/

wood / wud / *n* چوب / chub/

wool / wul / *n* پشم / pashm/

woolen / wulen / *adj* پشمی / pashmi/

word / werd / *n* کلمه / kalame/

work / werk / *n* کار / kâr/

work / werk / *vi* کار کردن / kâr kardan/

worker / werker / *n* کارگر / kârgar/

workman / werkman / *n* کارگر / kârgar/

world / werld / *n* دنیا / donya/

worldwide / werldwâyd / *adj* جهانی / jahâni/

worry / wârii / *vt* ناراحت کردن / nârâhat kardan/

worship / wership / *vt* پرستیدن / parastidan/

worst / werst / *adj* بدترین / badtarin/

worth / werth / *n* ارزش / arzesh/

worthy / werdhii / *adj* سزاوار / sazâvâr/

wound / woond / *n* زخم / zakhm/

wounded / woondid / *adj* زخمی / zakhmi/

wrap / rap / *vt* پیچیدن / pichidan/

wrist / rist / *n* مچ / moch/

write / râyt / *vt* نوشتن / neveshtan/

writer / râyter / *n* نویسنده / nevisande/

writing / râyting / *n* نوشته / neveshte/

wrong / râng / *adj* اشتباه / eshtebâh/

X

xenophile / zenefayl / *n* بیگانه پرست / bigâneparast/
xerox / ziirâks / *n* زیراکس / zirâks/
Xerxes / zerksiiz / *n* خشایارشا / khashâyârshâ/
X-mas / krismas / *n* کریسمس / kirismas/
X-ray / eksrey / *n* اشعه ایکس / ashaeye iks/

Y

yard / yârd / *n* / حیاط / hayât/
yeah / ye / *adv* / آره / âre/
year / yiir / *n* / سال / sâl/
yellow / yelo / *adj* / زرد / zard/
yes / yes / *adv* / بله / bale/
yesterday / yesterdi / *adv* / دیروز / diruz/
yet / yet / *adv* / هنوز / hanuz/
yoga / yoge / *n* / یوگا / yugâ/
yogurt / yogert / *n* / ماست / mâst/
you / yoo / *pron* / شما / shoma/
young / yâng / *adj* / جوان / javân/
yours / yorz / *pron* / مال تو / mâle to/
yourself / yorself / *pron* / خودت را / khodat râ/
yourselves / yorselvz / *pron* / خودتان را / khodetân râ/
youth / yooth / *n* / جوانی / javani/
youthful / yoothful / *adj* / جوان / javân/

Z

zany / zeynii / *adj* دلقک / dalghak/
zeal / ziil / *n* شور / shur/
zebra / ziibrâ / *n* گوراسب / gureasb/
zero / ziiro / *n* صفر / sefr/
zest / zest / *n* مزه / maze/
zigzag / zigzag / *adj* جناغی / jenâghi/
zinc / zink / *n* روی / roy/
zip code / zip kod / *n* کدپستی / kode posti/
zonal / zonl / *adj* منطقه ای / mantagheyi/
zone / zon / *n* منطقه / mantaghe/
zoo / zoo / *n* باغ وحش / bâghvahsh/
zoology / zoâlejii / *n* جانورشناسی / jânevar shenâsi/
Zoroaster / zoroaster / *n* زرتشت / zartosht/
Zoroastrian / zoroastriien / *n, adj* زرتشتی / zartoshti/

GEOGRAPHICAL INDEX

MOUNTAINS

RIVERS

PROVINCES AND CENTERS

اردبیل/Ardabil-
Ardabil/اردبیل

بوشهر/Bushehr-
Bushehr/بوشهر

Chaharmahal-o-Bakhtiyari/چهارمحال و بختیاری-
Shahr-e-Kord/شهرکرد

East Azarbayjan/آذربایجان شرقی-
Tabriz/تبریز

اصفهان/Esfehan-
Esfehan/اصفهان

فارس/Fars-
Shiraz/شیراز

گیلان/Gilan-
Rasht/رشت

همدان/Hamadan-
Hamadan/همدان

Hormozgan/هرمزگان-
Banda-e-Abbas/بندرعباس

Ilam/ایلام-
Ilam/ایلام

lorestan/لرستان-
Khoramabad/خرم آباد

Kerman/کرمان-
Kerman/کرمان

Kermanshah/کرمانشاه-
Kermanshah/کرمانشاه

Khorasan/خراسان-
Mashhad/مشهد

Khuzestan/خوزستان-
Ahvaz/اهواز

Kohgiluye-o-Bayrahmat/کهگیلویه و بویراحمد-
Yasuj/یاسوج

کردستان/Kordestan-
سنندج/Sanandaj

مرکزی/Markazi-
اراک/Arak

مازندران/Mazandaran-
ساری/Sari

سمنان/Semnan-
سمنان/Semnan

سیستان و بلوچستان/Sistan-o-Baluchestan-
زاهدان/Zahedan

تهران/Tehran-
تهران/Tehran

آذربایجان غربی/West Azarbayjan-
ارومیه/Urumieh

یزد/Yazd-
یزد/Yazd

زنجان/Zanjan-
زنجان/Zanjan

NEIGHBORS AND THEIR CAPITALS

افغانستان/Afghanistan-
کابل/Kabul

ارمنستان/Armenia-
ایروان/Yerevan

آذربایجان/Azarbayjan-
باکو/Baku

عراق/Iraq-
بغداد/Baghdad

پاکستان/Pakistan-
اسلام آباد/Islamabad

ترکیه/Turkey-
آنکارا/Ankara

ترکمنستان/Turkmenistan-
عشق آباد/Ashghabat

Also available from Hippocrene Books . . .

Farsi (Persian) Dictionary & Phrasebook
In addition to a pronunciation guide and transliteration system of the Farsi alphabet, included are a resourceful two-way dictionary containing more than 4,000 entries, an informative grammar section, and a collection of travel-oriented phrases. Observations related to travel and culture are also interspersed throughout the phrasebook.

4,000 entries · ISBN 0-7818-1073-6 · $14.95pb

English-Farsi (Persian) Standard Dictionary
40,000 entries · ISBN 0-7818-0056-0 · $24.95pb

Beginner's Persian with 2 Audio CDs
Iranian Persian (Farsi)
Mohammad Mehdi Khorrami

Perfect for both independent and classroom learners, this guide introduces the critical skills students need to speak, read, and write Persian with confidence.

- 10 lessons with dialogues, vocabulary, grammar and exercises.

- Audio CD accompaniments for each dialogue.

- Guide to reading and writing the Persian script.

- Persian-English and English-Persian glossaries.

ISBN 978-0-7818-1274-0 · $29.95pb

Dari-English/English-Dari Practical Dictionary,
Second Edition
Carleton Bulkin

The only two-way dictionary of its size available, the *Dari Practical Dictionary* provides an indispensable resource for travelers, businesspeople, and government relief personnel.

- Updated terminology to reflect recent linguistic developments.
- Contains both Perso-Arabic script and Romanization for English speakers
- Loaded with important cultural, military, health and political terminology
- Over 30,000 total entries

ISBN 978-0-7818-1284-9 · $24.95pb

Beginner's Dari with Audio CD
Shaista Wahab

This book introduces the Dari language in an easy-to-follow, step-by-step format. The first part teaches how to read, write, and pronounce each of the 32 letters of the Dari alphabet. Subsequent sections cover basic grammar, syntax, and vocabulary. Each chapter contains exercises that help reinforce the material presented in the lesson. The audio CD allows the reader to hear and practice correct pronunciation of the language.

ISBN 0-7818-1139-2 · $25.00pb

Dari Dictionary & Phrasebook
5000 entries · ISBN 0-7818-0971-1 · $14.95pb

Tajik-English/English-Tajik
Dictionary & Phrasebook
1,400 entries · ISBN 978- 0-7818-0662-X · $11.95pb

Tajik-English/English-Tajik Practical Dictionary
ISBN 978-0-7818-1233-X · $22.95pb

Arabic-English/English-Arabic
Dictionary & Phrasebook
4,500 entries · ISBN 0-7818-0973-8 · $14.95pb

Arabic-English/English-Arabic
Practical Dictionary
18,000 entries · ISBN 0-7818-1045-0 · $27.50pb

Mastering Arabic 1 with 2 Audio CDs, Third Edition
ISBN 978-0-7818-1338-9 · $40.00pb

Mastering Arabic 2 with 2 Audio CDs
ISBN 978-0-7818-1254-2 · $35.00pb

Beginner's Iraqi Arabic with 2 Audio CDs
ISBN 0-7818-1098-1 · $29.95pb

English-Arabic/Arabic-English
Modern Military Dictionary
11,000 entries · ISBN 0-7818-0243-1 · $16.95pb

Azerbaijani-English/English-Azerbaijani
Concise Dictionary
8,000 entries · ISBN 0-7818-0244-X · $14.95pb

Azerbaijani-English/English-Azerbaijani
Dictionary & Phrasebook
4,000 entries · ISBN 0-7818-0684-4 · $16.95pb

Kurdish (Sorani)-English/English-Kurdish (Sorani)
Dictionary & Phrasebook
4,000 entries · ISBN 978-0-7818-1245-0 · $14.95pb

Pashto-English/English-Pashto
Dictionary & Phrasebook
5,000 entries · ISBN 0-7818-0972-X · $14.95pb

Urdu-English/English-Urdu
Dictionary & Phrasebook (*Romanized*)
3,000 entries · ISBN 0-7818-0970-3 · $14.95pb

Urdu-English/English-Urdu Practical Dictionary
22,000 entries · ISBN 978-0-7818-1340-2
· $24.95pb

Uzbek-English/English-Uzbek
Dictionary & Phrasebook
3,000 entries · ISBN 978- 0-7818-0959-X · $13.95pb

Uzbek-English/English-Uzbek Concise Dictionary
7,500 entries · ISBN 0-7818-0165-6 · $15.95pb

Prices subject to change without prior notice. **To
purchase Hippocrene Books** contact your local
bookstore or visit www.hippocrenebooks.com.